Middle Way Philosophy
The Path of Objectivity

By Robert M. Ellis
with a foreword by Iain McGilchrist

Volume 1 of a 4-volume series on Middle Way Philosophy

First edition copyright © Robert M. Ellis 2012
This second edition copyright © Robert M Ellis 2015

Published by Lulu, Raleigh, N. Carolina

ISBN 978-1-4716-3265-5 (paperback)
     978-1-4716-3276-1 (e-book)

Cover picture: *Am Wasserfall* by Anton Romako
(this picture is in the public domain)

The Middle Way Philosophy series:
1. The Path of Objectivity
2. The Integration of Desire
3. The Integration of Meaning
4. The Integration of Belief

Other books by Robert M. Ellis, all available from www.lulu.com :
Migglism: A Beginner's Guide to Middle Way Philosophy
A Theory of Moral Objectivity
A New Buddhist Ethics
The Trouble with Buddhism
Truth on the Edge
Theme and Variations (fiction)
North Cape (poetry)

Foreword

The "Middle Way" Ellis argues for so cogently is far from being a simple compromise between existing polarities, but a departure at right angles to typical thinking in the modern Western world, which looks to me like the path to ancient wisdom.

The perception that objectivity is neither an absolute, nor any the less real for that, is central. Ellis argues for an approach that is incremental and continuously responsive to what is given, rather than abstract and absolute. This is the difference, as he notes, between the pragmatic, provisional, nuanced, never fixed position of the right hemisphere in the face of the absolutism towards which the left hemisphere always tends.

The need for certainty must inevitably lead to illusion, whether in philosophy or in the business of living, and here too Ellis makes clear – as far as I am aware for the first time – the connections between the cognitive distortions known to psychology and the fallacies identified in the process of philosophy.

This is an important, original work, that should get the widest possible hearing.

Iain McGilchrist

Iain McGilchrist is the author of 'The Master and his Emissary', fellow of All Soul's College Oxford and a former psychiatrist.

Acknowledgements

I would like to express gratitude to Anthony Martin, Iain McGilchrist and Viryanaya Ellis for reading and commenting on this book before publication.

This book also builds on previous work, in relation to which I would like to also renew my thanks to the following for their thoughtful and critical support: Michael Hammond, Vernon Pratt, David Bastow, Dhivan Thomas Jones, David Chapman, and Mike Price.

Robert M. Ellis

Middle Way Philosophy Series: Contents of this volume

FOREWORD	3
CONTENTS OF THIS VOLUME	5
CONTENTS OF THE REMAINING VOLUMES	8
INTRODUCTION	18
1. THE AVOIDANCE OF METAPHYSICS	**25**
A. SCEPTICAL ARGUMENTS	26
B. THE FAILURE OF PHILOSOPHICAL ARGUMENTS AGAINST SCEPTICISM	33
C. PROVISIONALITY	42
D. INCREMENTALITY	49
E. DISTINGUISHING NEGATIVE METAPHYSICS FROM AGNOSTICISM	54
F. AGAINST *A PRIORI* ARGUMENTS FOR METAPHYSICS	59
G. AGAINST REVELATORY METAPHYSICS	67
H. SCEPTICAL SLIPPAGE AND MODERN FORMS OF NEGATIVE METAPHYSICS	78
I. AGAINST THE FACT-VALUE DISTINCTION	85
J. METAPHYSICAL ASSUMPTIONS ABOUT THE SELF	92
2. THE APPEAL TO EXPERIENCE	**97**
A. EXPERIENCE AND ITS ADEQUACY	98
B. EXPERIENCE AND MEANING	104
C. THEORY IN RELATION TO EXPERIENCE	111
D. THE PHENOMENOLOGICAL USE OF TERMS	115
E. THE LIMITATIONS OF EMPIRICISM	118
3. THE MIDDLE WAY	**123**
A. BUDDHIST INSPIRATION WITHOUT BUDDHIST JUSTIFICATION	124

B. THE LIMITATIONS OF TRADITIONAL BUDDHIST PRESENTATIONS OF THE MIDDLE WAY 129

C. THE MIDDLE WAY IN CHRISTIANITY AND ISLAM 137

D. DEFINING THE POLES AVOIDED BY THE MIDDLE WAY 140

E. PRAGMATISM AND THE FEEDBACK LOOP 144

F. NO FINAL GOALS 149

G. DUALISM AND NON-DUALISM 154

H. THE MIDDLE WAY AND THE BRAIN 158

I. THE MIDDLE WAY AS MORAL GOOD 165

J. THE MIDDLE WAY AS INTEGRATION 171

K. DIALECTIC AND HOMEOSTASIS 175

L. DISTINGUISHING THE MIDDLE WAY FROM METAPHYSICS 179

4. ASPECTS OF OBJECTIVITY **184**

A. THE INCREMENTAL NATURE OF OBJECTIVITY 185

B. THE DISPOSITIONAL NATURE OF OBJECTIVITY 189

C. SCIENTIFIC OR FACTUAL OBJECTIVITY 192

D. MORAL OBJECTIVITY 198

E. COMPASSION 201

F. AESTHETIC OBJECTIVITY 206

G. OBJECTIVITY, ADAPTIVITY AND EVOLUTION 211

5. JUSTIFICATION **218**

A. REJECTION OF POSITIVE FOUNDATIONALISM 219

B. COHERENTISM 222

C. AGNOSTIC FOUNDATIONALISM 226

D. AGNOSTIC FOUNDATIONALISM IN RELATION TO FALSIFIABILITY 229

6. INTEGRATION **233**

A. EGO-IDENTIFICATION 234

B. THE PSYCHE 240

	C.	CONFLICT MODELS AND INTEGRATION MODELS	245
	D.	INTEGRATION IN RELATION TO OBJECTIVITY	249
	E.	INTEGRATION IN RELATION TO JUSTIFICATION	252
	F.	GROUP INTEGRATION	254
	G.	THE THREE TYPES OF INTEGRATION	258
7.		**ETHICS**	**261**
	A.	RESOLVING RELATIVISM	262
	B.	RESPONSIBILITY	267
	C.	NORMATIVITY	273
	D.	DISPOSITIONAL OBJECTIVITY AND VIRTUE	278
	E.	VIRTUES AND PRACTICES	282
	F.	DEONTOLOGICAL ETHICS AND AGNOSTIC FOUNDATIONALISM	286
	G.	MORAL AUTHORITY	294
	H.	CALCULATING CONSEQUENCES	300
	I.	PROVISIONALLY DERIVED RULES	311
	J.	RATIONALITY AND EMOTION	315

BIBLIOGRAPHY 319

BRIEF GLOSSARY 324

Contents of the remaining volumes

Volume 2: The Integration of Desire

INTRODUCTION	**14**
1. CONFLICTS OF DESIRE	**20**
A. EXPERIENCE OF CONFLICTING DESIRES	22
B. UNCONSCIOUS CONFLICT	35
C. CORPOREAL CONFLICT	44
D. BRAIN CONFLICT	52
E. GROUP CONFLICT	59
F. POLITICAL CONFLICT	66
G. VIOLENCE	73
2. INTEGRATION OF THE EGO	**78**
A. NON-FULFILMENT OF UNINTEGRATED DESIRES	79
B. THE PROCESS OF INTEGRATING DESIRES	87
C. FULFILMENT OF INTEGRATED DESIRES	95
D. ENDS AND MEANS	99
E. DESIRES AND VALUES	105
3. EGOISTIC IDEOLOGY	**108**
A. ALIENATION AND METAPHYSICS	109
B. MORAL FAILURES OF RELIGION	113
C. NATURAL LAW AND NATURALISM	118
D. HEDONISM	123
E. MARXISM AND FASCISM	126

F.	SUBJECTIVISM	133
G.	THE SPIRIT OF CAPITALISM	138

4. THE PRACTICE OF INTEGRATING DESIRE 144

A.	THE FOUR EXERTIONS	145
B.	THE STATE OF THE BRAIN	152
C.	THE IMPACT OF THE ENVIRONMENT	158
D.	EFFECT OF RELATIONSHIPS	163
E.	RECREATION	167
F.	MEDITATION	171

5. INTEGRATIVE ACHIEVEMENT 176

A.	RELIANCE OF INTEGRATION OF DESIRE ON OTHER INTEGRATIONS	177
B.	THE IRRELEVANCE OF TOTAL INTEGRATION	181
C.	TEMPORARY FORMS OF INTEGRATION	185
D.	ASYMMETRICAL INTEGRATION	190

6. INTEGRATION OF GOVERNMENT 195

A.	GOVERNMENT AND THE JUSTIFICATION OF POWER	197
B.	INTEGRATING GROUPS IN SOCIETY	208
C.	DEMOCRACY AND THE INTEGRATION OF THE INDIVIDUAL	214
D.	INTEGRATING PEOPLE WITH GOVERNMENT	218
E.	INTEGRATING GOVERNMENT	223
F.	INTEGRATION BETWEEN GOVERNMENTS	227

7. CASE STUDIES 231

A.	AUTOBIOGRAPHICAL	233
B.	SANGHARAKSHITA	243
C.	MARGARET THATCHER	252
D.	THE OTTOMAN EMPIRE	260
E.	NORTHERN IRELAND	267

8. CONCLUSION 273

Contents

BIBLIOGRAPHY 276

Volume 3: The Integration of Meaning

INTRODUCTION 15
1. **OUR EXPERIENCE OF MEANING**... 22
    A. THE COGNITIVE AND EMOTIONAL SPHERES OF MEANING 23
    B. MEANING AND COMMUNICATION 29
    C. LANGUAGE AND OTHER SYMBOLS 36
    D. THE PHYSICAL BASIS OF MEANING 41
    E. METAPHORICAL EXTENSION 49
    F. REPRESENTATION AND THE TWO HEMISPHERES 55
    G. THE PRACTICAL IMPORTANCE OF SEMANTICS 61
    H. THE ROLE OF LOGIC 64
    I. SUBLIMITY, CREATIVITY, AND HERON'S BEARD 68
2. **FRAGMENTATION OF MEANING** 76
    A. COGNITIVE MODELS AND DEFEASIBILITY CONTEXTS 78
    B. COGNITIVE AND EMOTIONAL FRAGMENTATION 86
    C. LINGUISTIC FRAGMENTATION 91
    D. CULTURAL FRAGMENTATION 96
    E. ARCHETYPAL FRAGMENTATION 102
    F. FRAGMENTATION AS A CONDITION FOR CONFLICT 108
3. **FRAGMENTING PHILOSOPHIES** 113
    A. LINGUISTIC IDEALISM 115
    B. REPRESENTATIONALISM AND RELIGION 122
    C. REPRESENTATIONALISM AND PHILOSOPHY 133
    D. REPRESENTATIONALISM AND POLITICS 143

	E.	EXPRESSIVISM 150
4.		**THE ARCHETYPES** **155**
	A.	THE ROLE OF ARCHETYPES IN MEANING 156
	B.	THE HERO 159
	C.	THE SHADOW 163
	D.	THE ANIMA/ ANIMUS 167
	E.	THE GOD ARCHETYPE 171
5.		**THE PROCESS OF INTEGRATING MEANING** **178**
	A.	THE DIALECTIC OF MEANING-INTEGRATION 179
	B.	THE PROLIFERATION OF SYMBOLS 183
	C.	CLARIFICATION 188
	D.	THE USES OF AMBIGUITY 195
	E.	INTEGRATING MEANING IN RELATION TO BELIEF 202
	F.	INTEGRATING MEANING IN RELATION TO DESIRE 206
	G.	THE MEANING OF THE MIDDLE WAY 209
6.		**THE PRACTICE OF INTEGRATING MEANING** **211**
	A.	INTEGRATING LANGUAGE 212
	B.	INTEGRATING CULTURE 220
	C.	MUSIC 225
	D.	THE VISUAL ARTS 230
	E.	POETRY 236
	F.	STORY AND LITERATURE 241
	G.	RITUAL AND THEATRE 247
	H.	FILM 252
	I.	INTEGRATING MEANING IN MEDITATION 257
	J.	FOCUSING 263
7.		**INTEGRATIVE ACHIEVEMENT IN MEANING** **266**
	A.	TEMPORARY FORMS OF MEANING-INTEGRATION 267

	B.	ASYMMETRICAL MEANING-INTEGRATION	272
	C.	THE LIMITS OF MEANING-INTEGRATION	274
8.		**POLITICAL FORMS OF MEANING-INTEGRATION**	277
	A.	LYING POLITICIANS	279
	B.	POLITICAL RITUAL	282
	C.	GOVERNMENT SUPPORT FOR THE ARTS	287
	D.	GOVERNMENT AND MEANINGFUL EDUCATION	292
CONCLUSION		296
BIBLIOGRAPHY		299

Volume 4: The Integration of Belief

INTRODUCTION		16
1.		**OUR EXPERIENCE OF BELIEF**	24
	A.	JUDGEMENT AND BELIEF	25
	B.	IMPLICIT BELIEF AND COGNITIVE MODELS	33
	C.	EXPLICIT BELIEF	37
	D.	FAITH AND TRUST	44
	E.	CONFIDENCE AND DOUBT	48
	F.	IDEOLOGY	55
2.		**THE PROVISIONALITY OF BELIEFS**	61
	A.	COMPLEXITY AND UNPREDICTABILITY	63
	B.	OPTIONALITY	67
	C.	ANTIFRAGILITY	74
	D.	ADAPTIVENESS	79
	E.	ANALYSIS AND SYNTHESIS	85
	F.	FAST AND SLOW THINKING	94

G.	INCREMENTALITY	99
H.	SUPPRESSION	105
I.	BALANCE AND INTEGRATION	111
3.	**DOGMATISM**	**114**
A.	METAPHYSICS AS A BLOCKAGE TO INTEGRATION	115
B.	THE FRAGILITY OF DOGMA	120
C.	COGNITIVE BIASES AND FALLACIES	124
D.	THE POSITIVE FEEDBACK CYCLE	132
E.	ABSOLUTISING SOURCES	141
	Personal and textual authority	*142*
	Group authority	*147*
	Circularity	*152*
F.	ABSOLUTISING THE SUBJECT	156
	Idealism	*157*
	The Self	*164*
	Agency	*169*
	Total Responsibility Fallacy	*173*
	Zero Responsibility Fallacy	*177*
	Projecting the self/ other dichotomy	*179*
	Projecting the act/ omission dichotomy	*184*
G.	ABSOLUTISING THE OBJECT	188
	Realism	*189*
	Rationalism	*194*
	Supervenience	*198*
	Cause	*203*
	Person	*211*
H.	ABSOLUTISING VALUES	218
	Moral Naturalism	*220*
	Relativism	*227*
	Value of self	*231*
	Value of desire	*234*
	Legalism	*240*
I.	LIMITING ATTENTION IN SPACE	246

	Coherentism *248*
	Limited attention *249*
	Limited identification *250*
	Limited availability of meaning *253*
	Limitation of evidence *258*
J.	ABSOLUTISING TIME *265*
	Absolutising the past *270*
	Absolutising the present over the past *273*
	Absolutising the present over the future *280*
	Absolutising the future *288*
K.	LIMITING ATTENTION IN TIME *296*
	Direct limitation of attention *297*
	Probability errors *301*
	Other statistical errors *311*
L.	LIMITING MEANING *316*
	Anchoring and framing *318*
	Dichotomies *324*
	Ambiguity *328*
	Definition *334*
	Metaphor *340*
	Expressivism *346*
M.	DOGMATISM AND COMPASSION *352*
N.	DOGMATISM AND EVIL.. *359*

4. DUALISTIC BELIEFS **365**

A.	METAPHYSICAL FIELD BELIEFS *367*
B.	MORAL ABSOLUTISM AND RELATIVISM *373*
C.	FREEWILL AND DETERMINISM *381*
	The meanings of 'freewill' and 'determinism' *381*
	Metaphysical freewill and the experience of choice *382*
	Determinism and the experience of causality *385*
	Compatibilism *390*
	Incrementalising conditioning *393*
	Incrementalising integration *395*
D.	REAL AND IDEAL *399*

	Rationalist idealism *400*
	Absolute idealism and dialectical materialism *404*
	Realism and naturalism *411*
	Interdependence *416*
E.	MIND AND BODY 421
	Mind-body dualism *422*
	Materialism of the brain *430*
	Behaviourism and functionalism *433*
F.	THEISM AND ATHEISM 440
	Theism *440*
	Atheism *449*
	Agnosticism *453*
G.	COSMIC JUSTICE 459
H.	POLITICAL IDEOLOGIES 465
	Haidt's six value foundations *465*
	Political ideologies in general *469*
	Socialism and Marxism *474*
	Liberalism *478*
	Conservatism *484*
	Nationalism *491*
	Political Islam *495*
	Green Ideology *499*
	Feminism *503*
I.	ECONOMIC DOCTRINES 508
	Rational choice theory *509*
	Perfect Information *511*
	The fact-value distinction and cosmic justice *512*
	Growth model *515*
	Profit maximisation *520*
J.	ARTISTIC DUALISMS 524
	Representation and abstraction *526*
	Form and formlessness *528*
	Sentimentality *531*

5. THE PRACTICE OF INTEGRATING BELIEF 533

| A. | WISDOM .... 535 |

B.	THE ROLE OF PHILOSOPHY	544
C.	CRITICAL THINKING	554
D.	SCIENTIFIC PRACTICE	561
E.	AUTOBIOGRAPHY	568
F.	HISTORICAL STUDY	573
G.	RELIGIOUS STUDIES	579
H.	EDUCATION	584
6.	**INTEGRATIVE ACHIEVEMENT IN BELIEF**	**590**
A.	TEMPORARY INTEGRATION OF BELIEF	591
B.	ASYMMETRICAL INTEGRATION OF BELIEF	595
C.	MEMORY AND IDENTITY	600
D.	OPTIMISING THEORY	605
E.	THE LIMITS OF BELIEF-INTEGRATION	608
7.	**POLITICAL INTEGRATION OF BELIEF**	**612**
A.	POLITICAL COMPETITION AND CRITICAL DIALOGUE	613
B.	PARTIES AND IDEOLOGIES	617
C.	IDEOLOGICAL CONSENSUS	621
D.	OBJECTIVITY AND FALSE NEUTRALITY	625
E.	POLITICAL EDUCATION	630
8.	**CONCLUSION**	**634**
A.	OVERVIEW OF THE SERIES	635
B.	THE MIDDLE WAY MEDITATION PRACTICE	645
C.	THE MIDDLE WAY SOCIETY	649

APPENDIX: TABLE OF RELATIONSHIPS BETWEEN TYPES OF METAPHYSICS, COGNITIVE BIASES AND FALLACIES 651

BIBLIOGRAPHY 655

GLOSSARY OF MIDDLE WAY PHILOSOPHY TERMS 678

Middle Way Philosophy 1: The Path of Objectivity

GLOSSARY OF COGNITIVE BIASES, FALLACIES AND METAPHYSICAL BELIEFS... 689

Introduction

- The headteacher of a church school is giving a boring address in a school assembly. He is talking about morality and God again. Most of his teenage audience are not in the least interested in what he feels obliged to say.
- A teenager is 'sod-casting' on a bus. The loud music coming from his mobile phone is annoying several other passengers, but they don't feel entitled to complain. His taste in music is different from theirs, but what right have they to impose silence on him?
- A scientist is giving a public lecture on evolution when she is heckled from a section of the audience. Evolution is just a theory, they say. Why isn't 'creation science' given equal billing alongside evolution?

What these examples have in common is that they are all indications of the failure of our models of objectivity. In ethics, when we are not limply relativist, we often flee to the opposite extreme of moral panic, dogmatically asserting grounds of ethics that many people feel to be dead, and others keep a fragile grasp on. If music is a personal matter, there seems to be no escape from relativism of taste. If science is shown to be merely a matter of theory, rather than of truth, no one theory seems better than any other. We might as well believe that the sun goes round the earth.

My thesis in this book is that many people in the modern world are confused about objectivity, and that the reason for this is that we have an unhelpful model of it. This confusion affects science, ethics, politics, the arts, in fact nearly every area of life. We tend to think of objectivity as absolute, but when we gain a critical perspective on that absolute objectivity we realise that it is a sham, a childish illusion. How can we believe that there is one right theory when there are many competing

Middle Way Philosophy 1: The Path of Objectivity

theories, all available to us on Wikipedia? How can we believe that there is one right culture when there are many cultures, all with equal rights under the constitution? The conservatives continue to insist that the old certainties are right, while the more open-minded end up with the confusions of relativism, where every view is as good as every other view. Since no group can prove they are right, philosophical discussion decays into mere analysis of the implications of these competing positions.

I will be arguing in this book that there *is* an alternative way of understanding objectivity, if we are willing to question the basic assumptions that underpin this confusion. We do not have to understand objectivity as an absolute view, ike the view God would have if he exists. Instead objectivity can be seen as personal and incremental – that is, something we ourselves can have, in our judgements and in our habitual attitudes, as a matter of degree.

If we base our understanding of objectivity on our experience rather than on dogmatic philosophical dualism, we find that experience is not, after all, merely relative. Different people's experiences vary in adequacy, and my own experience varies in adequacy at different times, according to the extent of the conditions I am taking into account. We usually improve the adequacy of our experience over our lifetime, from baby to mature person, and some groups have developed ways of relating that help them to pool their experience more adequately than others – compare a group of scientists with a group of quarrelsome thugs. If our experience is more adequate, so is our objectivity greater.

Our cultural traditions also suffer from over-specialisation, which has particularly separated facts from values and the objectivity of science from that of wise individuals. When philosophers theorise and analyse but never synthes se, it seems that the broad view we need to understand objectivity in general is closed to them. If anyone ever had the responsibility to clarify our confusion about objectivity it is philosophers, but it seems that they have largely failed in this task. One reason for this is that an understanding of objectivity must combine all the aspects of philosophy: epistemology, critical metaphysics, ethics, aesthetics and indeed all the other associated branches. Philosophy also needs to be considered in relation to psychology and to spiritual and political practice, not artificially separated from them. The theory I shall offer here is synthetic and inter-disciplinary, because the answers I can offer in different areas are mutually dependent.

I have called this theory Middle Way Philosophy, a name which reveals some original inspirations from the Buddhist tradition. When I first started working on this theory, fourteen years ago now, I took some initial insights from my own experience of Buddhist theory and practice and tried to apply them in an entirely Western way, arguing from first premises in a Western philosophical context. The initial result of this was my Ph.D. thesis, *A Buddhist Theory of Moral Objectivity*[1]. All the main features of the theory were developed in this thesis, but I have continued to refine it in the ten years since it was completed in 2001.

Since 2008 I have ceased to describe the theory as 'Buddhist' and have begun to see that label primarily as a distraction that tends to raise unhelpful expectations. I thus prefer to describe it as a *Middle Way* theory which begins with the idea that greater objectivity is found by avoiding both positive and negative types of metaphysical claim - 'eternalism' and 'nihilism' as they are described in the Buddhist tradition. I just happen to have first discovered this in the Buddha's teachings, even though it is available in other places too. Pragmatically, such an approach cannot create any guaranteed truths, but it can help us to avoid what are quite clearly delusions.

---

[1] Ellis (2001)

Middle Way Philosophy 1: The Path of Objectivity

In 2011 I also discovered a quite different way of approaching Middle Way Philosophy, inspired by reading Iain McGilchrist's fascinating and important book *The Master and his Emissary*[2]. I then realised that everything I had been saying from a philosophical point of view could alternatively be understood in terms of the relationships between our left and right brain hemispheres. This provided further insights that I have tried to incorporate into this book, for which I am extremely grateful to McGilchrist.

In my book *Truth on the Edge*[3], I tried to introduce Middle Way Philosophy more briefly and accessibly than in my Ph.D. thesis, starting with the idea that we are never justified in making claims about truth, but should nevertheless give the concept a regulatory role on the edge of our experience. We seek truth, but are aware in principle that we will never find it because of the basic conditions of our experience: finiteness, physicality, and the grounding of meaning and belief in our physical drives and practical purposes. Unlike the relativists, I do not let those conditions deny objectivity: rather it is through recognising them fully that we gain greater objectivity.

However, *Truth on the Edge* aimed merely to inspire interest rather than providing full argument. I have been referring those interested back to my thesis for fuller support, yet with increasing awareness of its limitations for that purpose. The thesis now seems rather inaccessibly written in many places, and it is also now out of date in the way it represents my thinking, with many points having become more refined or better explained from a different angle over a decade of discussion and re-presentation. I have been realising that a new full academic explanation of Middle Way Philosophy was needed.

---

[2] McGilchrist (2009)
[3] Ellis (2011c)

Introduction

However, this left me initially with a dilemma about the length and scope of a new academic book. To be anything other than comprehensive would be to offer a less balanced and less convincing account of Middle Way Philosophy, which works *because* it is comprehensive where other theories, in my view, address only a limited range of conditions. However, I also had to consider the difficulties of my readers, and the possibly off-putting prospect for them of another lengthy treatise. Eventually I hit upon the best solution: to plan out a linked series of books but issue them one at a time. This turned into a plan for five volumes, of which this is the first.

The overwhelming emphasis in this volume is philosophical. It aims to deal with all the major issues in Middle Way epistemology and ethics, with a full explanation of my critical approach to metaphysics. There will also be some explanation of the nature of the relationship with the Buddhist Middle Way, and a basic explanation of the integrative psychology which informs the approach. In doing this I have aimed to address the likely concerns of Western philosophers and others, and to balance clarity and comprehensiveness with readability.

The next three volumes of the four will be concerned with different levels of integration, which will give them more of a psychological emphasis. However, I will also need to deal with philosophical issues concerning desire (volume 2), meaning (volume 3) and belief (volume 4) as they relate to this psychology, and to do so in a bit more detail than I have been able to do in this volume. Volume 4, in particular, returns to many of the questions in this volume, but tackles them from a more psychological point of view, particularly drawing on evidence from cognitive biases and showing how they depend on the absolutisation avoided by the Middle Way.

However, this volume is probably the fullest and clearest philosophical account I have yet managed of the view of objectivity I am offering in Middle Way Philosophy. Obviously there will be some overlaps in content with some of my previous work, but all the text is entirely new and written for the purposes of this book. Nevertheless it is still part of an ongoing project that is subject to change and revision. Up to date information about new writings and developments can be found on the website of the Middle Way Society, a society I founded to involve others in development and practice of the Middle Way. Constructive feedback which aims to further improve the objectivity of the judgements made in Middle Way Philosophy will always be welcome, and can be emailed to robert@middlewaysociety.org.

This book contains sets of arguments that are probably better seen as interlocking than as sequential: a jigsaw rather than a journey. Thus it may not be crucial for everyone to begin at the beginning with section 1 and read sequentially to the end. The conception of the book makes that a reasonable approach for those from a philosophical background, who begin by asking philosophical questions and want reasoning from first premises. However, not everyone who picks up this book may have that background. Those approaching it from Buddhism, for example, may find it more engaging to start with section 3 and then go back to read sections 1 and 2. There are also some chapters addressed to those with certain specific concerns that will be of less interest to those without those concerns, such as 1.g, which is mainly addressed to those from a theistic or theological background. These kinds of sections can be skipped where not relevant to you, without great loss to the overall sense.

I hope that you will be able to use this book, and the planned ones that follow it in the series, in a way that stimulates and supports your own path towards objectivity and integration.

Robert M. Ellis
Malvern, December 2011

Note on the second edition (2015)

After writing and publishing the remainder of the volumes in the series, this second edition of volume 1 sets out to iron out the inconsistencies that have unavoidably crept in during the journey. This new edition of volume 1 now takes into account the change in my original plans from a 5 volume series to a 4 volume one. Any arguments that I think I can now improve upon have been revised, and some internal forward references to the other volumes have been inserted. Internal references use the format of volume number (in roman numerals), followed by section and chapter number, so chapter a of section 1 of volume 1 is I.1.a.

1. The avoidance of metaphysics

This section aims to clear the ground for the positive understanding of the Middle Way that I hope can be built up in the longer term. I will begin in a critical and sceptical vein, in order to avoid misunderstandings at the outset and lay the groundwork for a new account of objectivity without interfering metaphysical assumptions.

This section is about how we can distinguish Middle Way Philosophy from various kinds of metaphysics common in Western tradition. This is a largely negative but nevertheless a crucial function. I will begin with sceptical arguments simply to show why we should not accept metaphysical claims, but nevertheless argue that consistent scepticism liberates us to hold provisional and incremental beliefs that relate to our experience. After heading off some of the likely objections to this project that might be offered by analytic philosophers and theologians, I will then also focus on some specific metaphysical beliefs that can distort our whole approach to objectivity: the fact-value distinction and assumptions about the self.

A. Sceptical arguments

Sceptical arguments are the best place to start in presenting the Middle Way, because they enable a philosophical argument about its justification to be built up. To start by facing up to all our uncertainties, and then consider what positions we can justify in spite of them, is a pattern of presentation that has often been used in Western philosophy (for example, by Descartes and Hume, who both attempted to confront scepticism after it had re-arisen in Western civilisation). What this approach reflects is a concern with *justification* which I share with Descartes and Hume, even though of course I disagree with them in other ways.

A concern with justification is ultimately a practical concern. If we do not face up to the challenges of justification, we may remain deluded in ways that could have been avoided, and those delusions may well catch us out with practical consequences in the future. I want to argue that much Western thought has turned its back on this concern with justification, because of a set of interrelated unnecessary assumptions about it, and that this has had negative practical consequences.

So, I am going to begin with an account of a range of sceptical arguments. Many of these arguments are well known and are often taught on introductory philosophy courses. The first of them were introduced to Western Philosophy by Pyrrho of Elis, the founder of the Pyrrhonian school of scepticism in Hellenistic philosophy, but they are also found in Indian philosophy, which may have influenced Pyrrho. These arguments set up a basic challenge in Western philosophy that the most prominent philosophers have been struggling to address ever since. What all of these arguments have in common is the casting of doubt on all claims of knowledge.

Middle Way Philosophy 1: The Path of Objectivity

1. **The ten modes of Pyrrhonism** (first given by Aenesidemus[4]) give a range of reasons why our senses do not necessarily give us correct information about objects. These are
    a. that different animals have different sense organs, so therefore animals perceive objects differently from humans
    b. that different humans have different sense abilities (e.g. some have visual impairments) and thus perceive objects differently
    c. that different senses perceive objects differently (e.g. I may be able to hear something I cannot see)
    d. that differences in circumstances lead to different perceptions (e.g. a hand put in hot water and then cold will find the cold colder through contrast)
    e. that differences in spatial position relative to an observed object (e.g. a distant landmark) lead to different perceptions and to perceptions that may be mistaken
    f. that our perceptions of an object will be altered by what we see it with or near, which may lead us to see it differently (e.g. camouflage)
    g. that the same object will vary in the way it is perceived when in different quantities or when composed differently, making it impossible to identify the object with certainty (e.g. wheat grains look different from flour, but are composed of the same substance)
    h. that if objects are claimed to be absolutely existent this claim is still only understood relative to other claims
    i. that the constancy or rarity with which something appears changes our perception of it (e.g. comets are rarer, and thus seeing one is more significant to us, than stars)
    j. that moral claims also differ between people (one person's good child is another's bad).

---

[4] Sextus Empiricus (1996)

In general, then, these arguments point out that all our perceptions are relative, because influenced both by the specific circumstances of our perception and of the object we are (or may be) perceiving. This means that any perception may be in error.

2. **The dream argument** considered by Descartes[5] and others, suggests that we cannot tell with certainty that we are not dreaming (or that our whole experience is not otherwise illusory) at a given moment, and therefore that our perceptions are not erroneous. This argument is problematic if applied to all our experience through time, as it then deprives us of any contrast between 'dream' and 'reality', but we could consistently maintain this distinction to assert that at least some of our past experience must not have been a dream, and yet not be certain that our current experience is not.

3. **The error argument** points out that even if our whole experience at a given time is not erroneous, particular objects that we think we perceive may still be so. Past mistakes in perception show that mistakes are possible, and we were not aware of those mistakes at the time we made them, so we may not be aware of our current mistakes. This argument can be applied to current perceptions and also to memory, to point out that with a past perception we may have made a mistake in the original perception or in our memory of that perception.

4. **The time lapse argument** used by Bertrand Russell[6] suggests that we cannot be certain of the object of perception because the conditions of that object may have changed by the time we receive the perception (e.g. the sun may have ceased to exist 7 minutes ago, but due to

---

[5] Descartes (1912)
[6] Russell (1940) p.13

the distance from the sun and the time it takes light to traverse that distance, we wouldn't know about it yet).

5. **The relativity of cultural background.** Earlier sceptical arguments acknowledged all the physical reasons for the relativity of perception, but more recent psychological and linguistic research tells us more about the mental reasons. Our cultural background may lead us to perceive objects differently: for example, perceivers of the Müller-Lyer Illusion (see figure) make a bigger misjudgement about the relative lengths of the lines if they are accustomed to environments with rectilinear architecture[7].

6. **Problem of Induction.** All generalisations based on specific observations lack certainty, because the observations do not provide enough evidence to cover the possibly infinite number of instances referred to in the generalisation. For example, if I claim that all physical objects have mass and are subject to gravity, I have not checked all the physical objects in the universe to ensure this.

7. **The infinite regress of justification.** There is no possible claim for which one could not ask for further justification (i.e. there are no self-evident claims). However, if a justification is offered, one could then ask for a justification of the justification, and so on ad infinitum. This argument works not only for empirical claims but for a priori ones. For consideration of possible self-evident claims which might be claimed to undermine this sceptical argument, see 1.b

8. **The relativity of linguistic categories.** Even if we were able to overcome the above sceptical arguments in other

---

[7] Segall et al (1963) pp. 769-771

respects, the language out of which we represent claims about objects in the universe does not have an absolute relationship with the objects themselves, either as they may exist in themselves or even as we experience them. We cannot be certain either that another person understands the same as we do by a particular proposition about the world, or even that we mean the same ourselves when we return to our previous utterances after an interval of time[8]. Even if we were to weaken the requirement to one of identical representation of our experiences to ourselves after a few seconds, we cannot be sure that our mental representation of that experience has not changed, and thus that the language does not mean something different from what it meant to us beforehand. Claims of certainty depend on the absolute consistency of language used to represent those claims, otherwise any certainty that might apply to a statement at one instant will immediately be lost at the next instant, even for the person who made the statement.

9. **The vagueness of linguistic categories**. Any possible representational term out of which a claim of certainty might be made is also inadequate for the representation of any reality (or even any experience) because of its vague relationship to that reality or experience. The terms used for representing objects (even abstract ones) are nouns, and any given noun is vague in terms of the scope of what it represents either in experience or the object of experience. For example, if I use the word 'pen' to

---

[8] This is the scenario considered by Wittgenstein in his 'Private Language Argument' (Wittgenstein 1967 §258), which I discuss in Ellis 2001 pp.258-62. I argue that although Wittgenstein is correct in pointing out the lack of standards of correctness based on defeasibility in private language, this is no different from the situation with public language. Standards of correctness are not absolute in either case because meaning is not purely representational, but this does not deprive us of a degree of meaning (see volume 3 for much fuller discussion of meaning).

describe an object, and even if I give a precise and unique description of that pen, giving measurements and physical co-ordinates, what I am referring to is vague both in terms of space (some molecules or even smaller particles may not be clearly defined as part of the pen or not) and time (any interval of time I may specify for my statement about the pen will have duration, and during that duration the pen may change). If, on the other hand, I make no claims for the object which take up any space or time, my claims will be uninformative. It might be claimed that *a priori* claims such as those about numbers avoid this vagueness, but when applied to any claim about the universe these numbers depend on counting and measurement, which are unavoidably vague (see 1.f for more discussion of *a priori* claims).

Together these sceptical arguments provide a huge over-determination of the sceptical case. We do not need them all. Only one of them has to be successful to prove that there can be no certainty attached to any claim of knowledge. It is not surprising that philosophers have often been concerned with questioning the assumptions behind these sceptical argument rather than refuting them directly in their own terms. In their own terms they are unanswerable. However, as I will argue in the rest of section 1, it is the assumptions of those who attempt to undermine the sceptical approach that are unnecessary.

Before I go on to defend the basis of these sceptical arguments further, and then develop an account of their implications, I should re-iterate that my purpose in doing this is ultimately practical. I am not defending scepticism in order to assert the relativity of all judgements. In fact, I think that sceptical arguments of the kinds listed above offer us the key to avoid relativism and assert that some judgements are better than others – but only if sceptical arguments are consistently and unflinchingly applied, and we do not try to dodge scepticism nor ever cease to take it seriously.

B. The failure of philosophical arguments against scepticism

Philosophical arguments against scepticism have come in broadly five types, as far as I can identify:
1) The assertion of self-evident truths (e.g. Descartes)
2) Arguments that scepticism is practically unsustainable, and thus that dogmatism is unavoidable (e.g. Hume)
3) Arguments that scepticism involves practical inconsistencies (e.g. Burnyeat, Nussbaum)
4) Arguments that scepticism is unjustified because it only offers negative grounds of judgement (e.g. Moore and other positivists)
5) Arguments that scepticism makes invalid semantic assumptions (e.g. Wittgenstein)

I shall argue here that each of these lines of criticism itself involves assumptions that we do not necessarily need to make in approaching the subject. The case for not making these assumptions is not merely sceptical, but also pragmatic.

1. If self-evident truths exist then this would obviously undermine scepticism, as there would be a foundational certainty from which other certainties might then be deduced. Descartes' *cogito*, in which the certainty of the thinker's existence is deduced from the experience of a thought, is the classic example of a self-evident truth[9]. In 1.g I will provide a more detailed response to the claim that *a priori* propositions such as mathematics or the laws of logic provide self-evident truths.

But for the moment let us accept for the sake of argument that there might be self-evident truths such as that I, a thinker, exist at this instant. Since it is not empirical, this claim avoids the first six sceptical arguments listed in the previous chapter,

---
[9] Descartes (1912)

and it avoids the seventh, the infinite regress, if its foundational claims are justified. However, this claim and any other foundational claim are still subject to the last two sceptical arguments that point out the relativity and vagueness of linguistic categories. "I, a thinker, exist at this moment" is relative to each thinker because it can only be interpreted according to the linguistic understanding of each individual thinker. If you tell me that you exist at this moment, to me that obviously means that **you** exist at this moment, which means something rather different from **me** existing at this moment. Unless this statement has an absolute unchanging meaning for all who may comprehend it – which it clearly does not – it can hardly have an absolute unchanging justification. The same point would apply to mathematical or logical claims (see 1.f), if considered in accordance with the account of meaning that will be presented fully in volume 3.

The ambiguity of statements supposedly offering self-evident truths creates contradictions in the very claims involved. "I, a thinker, exist at this moment" for example, either means that a thinker exists over a short period of time, or at a genuine instant of time with no duration. If the former, the thinker can have thoughts (which always take up a certain amount of time), but by the time the thinker gets to the end of her thoughts, she may be different from when she started them and thus no longer "exist" in the absolute, unchanging sense required. On the other hand, within an instant without any duration, no thoughts can take place and thus it seems that a thinker cannot exist.

All these kinds of arguments (the sport of philosophers, but very tiresome after a while) are merely different ways of showing that we, being non-absolute creatures, cannot handle absolutes without constantly contradicting ourselves. Our physical experience and our language shrug off absolutes as water shrugs off oil. Philosophers should know better by now than to go in for any kind of absolute, and self-evident truths are unavoidably absolute in their claims.

2. Hume's argument about scepticism, on the other hand, attempts to adopt a no-nonsense practical approach to it. After admitting that we cannot refute scepticism on its own terms, Hume seems to be saying that there is no way that we can, in practice, accept those terms. It is 'nature', he says, that drives us to belief, rather than reason, because when we engage with objects in the world around us we do so on the basis of a practical assumption of their existence and form. Scepticism is all very well in the abstraction of a study, but there is no way we can keep it up in ordinary life:

'I dine, I play a game of backgammon, I converse, and am merry with my friends; and when after three or four hours' amusement, I would return to these speculations, they appear so cold, and strained, and ridiculous, that I cannot find in my heart to enter into them any farther.'[10]

Hume makes an unjustified assumption about the implications of scepticism here: indeed, he gets the whole matter the wrong way round. Scepticism casts doubt on any claims to certainty, but this does not imply that to take it seriously means that we must be constantly straining to disbelieve what we encounter in everyday experience. On the contrary, our everyday experience involves uncertainty, and scepticism, far from relying on 'cold' and 'strained' calculations, uses this everyday experience as its point of departure. It is claims of certainty, and the attempt to justify them, that go far beyond everyday experience and become cold and strained.

This point is closely related to another that I will consider more closely in 1.e: namely the distinction between denial of claims and denial of certainty about them. If we were to assert the

---
[10] Hume (1978) p.269

opposite of everything we take for granted in everyday life, e.g. that there is not a table in front of me, that the world does not exist etc, then this would indeed be a cold and strained exercise. However, there is no reason why we should have to interpret sceptical arguments in this way. Scepticism denies certainty, and thus leaves us in a position lacking certainty, rather than asserting the opposite of our accepted beliefs. To assert the opposite would be at least as uncertain an enterprise. Hume, however, (along with many of his successors) seems to confuse these two positions.

3. Burnyeat and Nussbaum, on the other hand, respectively accuse scepticism of other kinds of practical inconsistency. Burnyeat claims that it's impossible to maintain the degree of detachment from one's views that scepticism demands[11]. Nussbaum argues that the classical sceptics are dogmatic about the value of *ataraxia*, which in classical Pyrrhonian scepticism is the relaxed state of detachment from opposing certainties[12]. Both these objections could be seen as versions of what is sometimes called 'the paradox of scepticism': namely, that sceptics are certain about uncertainty. This supposed paradox can be presented either as a direct contradiction or at least as a practical inconsistency.

Both of these thinkers are commentators on the classical sceptics and make these remarks in the context of discussing classical Pyrrhonism. I am purposely avoiding too much discussion of the scholarly issues about historical schools of philosophy here, but am attempting only to isolate what we do or do not need to think about sceptical arguments based only on the implications of the arguments themselves[13]. Burnyeat's and Nussbaum's arguments may or may not be true of classical Pyrrhonism, but my argument is that their criticisms

---

[11] Burnyeat (1980)
[12] Nussbaum (1994)
[13] A similar argument to mine, but grounded more in the historical context, is found in Kuzminski (2008) ch.1

distract us from the useful insights offered by this line of sceptical argument in the modern context.

Both of these objections fail to take sufficiently into account the distinction between the denial of claims and the denial of certainty about claims. If we assert the opposite of a given claim, we raise the same issues of certainty about it as with the original claim. If we merely deny the certainty surrounding a claim, however, we modify the way in which that claim may be held rather than setting up a new claim. If we understand the modification of the way we hold a claim in **psychological** terms, rather than merely in terms of opposing propositions, this becomes clearer. I will explore this point in more detail in 1.c. A claim not held with certainty is held in a more provisional and a more relaxed fashion, which may also affect our subsequent judgements about how to assess it. Contrary to Nussbaum's assumptions, the value of such a provisional state is not one that we have to accept absolutely and all at once, but is a matter of incremental recognition (a point that interlocks with various other arguments about value to be found throughout this book).

Burnyeat overestimates the degree of detachment required to take scepticism seriously, because he shares the confusion between denial and provisionality with many modern commentators. We do not need the amount of detachment that would be required to seriously adopt a position of denying all our beliefs in order to merely hold them provisionally. Nor does it require a certain fixed amount of detachment in order even to hold them provisionally. If we think about provisionality in an incremental rather than an absolute way (see 1.e) then we can think of the process of giving up attachment to certainty as a gradual and dynamic one. This process then becomes practically achievable in a way that a sudden demand for massive detachment would not.

4. Another, positivist type of response to scepticism is to assert that only positive justifications for belief are acceptable, and that negative doubts about a claim not accompanied by definite evidence against the claim are inadmissible[14]. The logical positivists and their allies in the early twentieth century saw this as a way of protecting evidence-based scientific investigation against the encroachments of metaphysics. Those who deny commonly accepted empirical beliefs, after all, often do so only on the basis of speculation.

Much as I sympathise with the logical positivist attempt to distinguish metaphysics from claims that can be justified through experience, the positivist route does not succeed in doing this. Positivism prevents us from taking negative doubts seriously, and simultaneously makes its own metaphysical assumptions unassailable. We need negative doubts in order to be able to consider conventionally accepted beliefs from an adequately critical perspective. The positivist dismissal of negative doubt leaves us dependent upon conventional beliefs and unable to break out of the set of assumptions that are currently accepted in our context. Logical positivism, and its successors in analytic philosophy, remain dependent on analysis of conventional positions or commonly shared intuitions, and unable to reach a justified critical standpoint beyond those conventional positions.

Like many of the previous criticisms, too, positivism confuses denial with the mere acceptance of uncertainty. Negative doubts require us to accept the *possibility* of currently accepted beliefs being wrong, not to accept the alternative claim that they are definitely wrong. Speculative metaphysics puts forward new claims that are beyond experience – so sceptical argument is a crucial tool that should be used for combating metaphysics, not discarded at the very point when it would be most useful.

---

[14] E.g. in Ayer (1946)

A more specific version of this positivist argument is that used by both Moore[15] and Wittgenstein[16] in slightly differing ways to assert the existence of their hands as a basic certainty. Their reason for dismissing scepticism about something as certain as the existence of one of their hands was not just that mere negative doubts were inadmissible, but that any evidence that could be used to support the assertion that their hands existed would be less certain than the existence of their hands. For positivists, then, some kinds of claim have to be taken as certain and basic to all other discussions. Without those basic assumptions, it is argued, the discussion could not take place.

This argument, even if it is valid in other ways (and there are many other ways that its assumptions can be disputed), can only be directed against the error argument, and other sceptical arguments that raise one specific doubt whilst taking a wider context for granted. It does not apply to the dream argument, or the infinite regression argument, or the linguistic arguments. The dream argument does not require us to take one kind of fact for granted in order to cast doubt on others, only that there be some unspecified factual basis to use as a ground of contrast with a current uncertainty. Similarly, the infinite regression argument can be used against any claim of certainty whatsoever, regardless of its relationship to other claims, and the relativity and ambiguity of the linguistic composition of these claims remains regardless of its relationship to other claims.

5. Finally, Wittgenstein's objections to sceptical argument were also based on the alleged linguistic privacy of sceptical argument, and his objections to linguistic privacy in the so-called private language argument[17]. However, he was mistaken on both counts. Not only is scepticism not necessarily based on linguistic privacy (assuming that we can

---

[15] Moore (1962)
[16] Wittgenstein (1969)
[17] Wittgenstein (1969). See note 8 above.

The failure of arguments against scepticism

even make sense of the idea of linguistic privacy), but there is no reason to assume that language developed in linguistic privacy is meaningless.

The Cartesian version of scepticism, in which I can entertain the possibility of being the only real thing in the universe, does not depend on solipsistic assertions but only on the *possibility* of solipsism (the same confusion we have already noted). However, all the other types of sceptical argument mentioned above, including the modes of Pyrrhonism and the linguistic arguments, could just as well be applied to a publicly shared context as to a 'private' one. I might be wrong about my perceptions, but we might also be wrong about our collective perceptions, for very similar reasons. The publicity or otherwise of the language makes no substantial difference to these kinds of arguments.

The concept of linguistic privacy, completely and absolutely distinguished from linguistic publicity, seems dubious in the first place to me. We use language to communicate with others, but we also use it to communicate with ourselves over time (as in a private diary) and perhaps even to articulate without communicating (as when we talk to ourselves to clarify our thoughts). Wittgenstein simply assumes, without further justification, that the only acceptable function of language is communication. He then asserts that when using purely private language (i.e. a symbol whose significance is known only to me) in a private diary, when using it later I would have no clear criterion of meaning. However, I would have a relative criterion of meaning based on my memory of previous experience which the symbol represented. A falsely absolute distinction is made if it is assumed that the private criterion is relative whilst a public one is absolute, for there is no guarantee that a publicly used piece of language, even within a particular language game (i.e. social context where that language is shared) is not equally ambiguous.

Middle Way Philosophy 1: The Path of Objectivity

Like the other attacks on scepticism, then, Wittgenstein's do not apply to all the arguments, and also confuse lack of certainty with definite denial. Like the other attacks, it is based on a confusion about the purpose and implications of scepticism, as should become clearer as we go on. A complete reversal of the assumptions in all these attacks on scepticism is required. Scepticism is not a dragon to be slain, but rather a knight in shining armour. It is certainty that is the dragon.

C. Provisionality

Now that I have established the justification of sceptical arguments, it is possible to move on to the much more interesting business of their implications. Scepticism removes certainty, and without certainty we have, instead, provisionality. Since we can no longer justify holding any beliefs absolutely, we can only justify holding them more lightly.

The idea that beliefs should be held with a degree of conviction that is proportional to the evidence is one that goes back to Hume[18]. The implications of this, however, are more profound than Hume seems to recognise. Philosophical justification by itself does not offer an account of what it would be like to hold a belief provisionally and to a certain degree, because a priori reasoning can only tell us about the contradictory nature of absolute beliefs, not the positive calibration of the non-absolute beliefs we might use to replace them. Instead, the justification of specific non-absolute beliefs depends on a complex interplay of different factors of context, character, language and intention. A priori reason deals only in invariable generalities, so using it to describe variables is like using an unreliable nuclear weapon to make a minor adjustment to your bicycle gears: the nuclear weapon either destroys everything or leaves it exactly as it was, when what is needed is gradual and subtle change. Only experience itself tells us what provisional beliefs are like, and any description of them is a psychological description, not ultimately a philosophical one.

That psychological description could be based on a theoretical model of the relationships between parts of the psyche that explains how provisionality works. This is what I will attempt in

---
[18] Hume (1975) pp 110-111

Middle Way Philosophy 1: The Path of Objectivity

detail in IV.2. There I argue that provisionality is distinguished by offering *optionality*: that is, at the moment we make a judgement, there are alternative possibilities available to us. This forms a contrast with the repression of alternatives created by absolutisation, in which the supposed complete justification of one belief blocks all alternatives. This optionality also creates antifragility[19] – that is, the ability to benefit rather than suffer from a range of unexpected conditions. To maintain optionality, we also need what Daniel Kahneman calls 'slow thinking'[20] at the right moments when circumstances make it possible to use it. In this way we avoid the cognitive errors that follow from rigid patterns of 'fast thinking' that may be adapted to some situations but are not sufficiently flexible in the wider range we are likely to encounter.

Alternatively, provisionality can be explained using a physiological model in terms of the relationships between the two hemispheres of the brain. Since it is the left hemisphere of the brain that maintains all our linguistic representations of the world and a sense of certainty about those representations[21], provisionality can be seen as the maintaining of sufficient awareness of the perspective of the right side of the brain to limit that left-brain certainty. The right hemisphere provides all contextuality in our awareness[22], and it is contextuality that is required for an awareness of fallibility. It is only if our beliefs exist in a functional vacuum, with other possibilities not being actively considered, that we can start to attach certainty to them.

Sceptical arguments, then, can act as a prompt to remind us that our brains have two hemispheres, and that if we have slipped into the mode of left-hemisphere dominance, this is not

---

[19] A term coined by Taleb (2012)
[20] Kahneman (2011)
[21] McGilchrist (2009) p.70
[22] Ibid. P.80

even justifiable in its own terms. We may need to take active steps to balance our mental states by taking enough account of the right hemisphere, in order for our judgements to become more objective and justified. There will be much further discussion of such steps later in this book and later in the series.

For the moment, however, I am going to focus not on the positive psychological explanation of provisionality, so much as the negative philosophical explanation of processes that interfere with provisionality. Philosophy cannot give a precise enough description to help us make subtle adjustments in our experience, but rather than working only with the destructiveness of a nuclear weapon, it can also work as an air-raid siren to warn us when a nuclear weapon is on its way, or as a bomb disposal expert to render the nuclear weapon useless. These kinds of operations are crude but vital. They provide us with a starting point, a clear field of security in which more subtle psychological work can begin to take place. In the middle of a nuclear war, we are not likely to be too troubled about the exact state of our bicycle gears.

The nuclear weapons in this analogy are *metaphysical beliefs*. It is metaphysical beliefs that fall foul of sceptical argument and are incompatible with provisionality. They are also purely the products of our left brain hemispheres, which maintain a self-referent certainty about them that repels any interference by the right hemisphere. The term 'metaphysics' is used in a variety of ways, but I am using it here to mean absolute beliefs that can only be dogmatically asserted, rather than provisionally asserted in a way that can be justifiably falsified through experience. As I will argue in more detail in 1.f, these kinds of beliefs function psychologically as apparently invulnerable rallying points for our egoistic identification – but the invulnerability is deceptive. A full survey of different types of metaphysical belief is also made in IV.3 & 4.

Middle Way Philosophy 1: The Path of Objectivity

The ideas of verification and falsification have been another of the many philosophical battlegrounds in which philosophers have tried to reach absolute beliefs about the world of experience – and have failed to do so[23]. If we could manage absolute verification or absolute falsification through experience, then we could achieve certainty, but, as I have already established, we cannot do that. The distinction between metaphysics and general theory is, most importantly, that metaphysics pretends to that certainty and fails to entertain possible alternatives, whilst general theory is justified to a degree and set beside alternatives.

Metaphysical beliefs can often be identified from their necessary source of justification (i.e. the source without appeal to which they could not be justified). If the source of justification is absolute, such as a revelation from God, an absolute law of nature, or a purely a priori framework (or the direct denial of these things – see 1.e) then their justification cannot be provisional. Even if the belief in question claims to be a scientific theory, if it makes absolute claims this will fall foul of the problem of induction unless the theory is made provisional (and also remains consistently provisional in the further implications it is judged to have).

Even if the belief is claimed to merely provide a prior condition for other widespread beliefs, if it is claimed to be the only possible a priori framework that could be used it becomes metaphysical. So, for example, the observation that we *generally* rely on an a priori framework of space and time is not metaphysical, but the absolute assertion that all experience *must* use a framework of space and time is a metaphysical assertion (because without evidence of the absence of other possible frameworks, it must dogmatically appeal to the uniqueness of the one we have).

---

[23] For example, in Ayer (1946) – the verificationist approach, and Popper (1959) – the falsificationist approach

Another way that metaphysical beliefs can often be identified a priori is through their *dualism*. Metaphysical beliefs tend to come in opposed pairs, where the same claim is either affirmed or denied, and dualism is the tendency to be restricted to these opposed pairs without awareness either of further alternatives, or of the equal justification that can be given to the opposing claim. For example, theism and atheism, realism and idealism, determinism and freewill (or determinism and indeterminism, depending on which features of determinism you highlight), and mind and body are each opposed pairs of metaphysical dualisms. If the application of a different explanatory framework makes a denial just as likely or unlikely to be correct as an affirmation, and this point is completely unrecognised by the person making the claim, then we are dealing with a metaphysical belief. For example, a theistic set of beliefs may superficially appear convincing even in the face of evil if we accept that only God knows his own justification for allowing evil events, but if we don't accept this framework of explanation we could just as easily conclude that God does *not* exist because his goodness and omnipotence (which are usually seen as essential features of God) are contradicted by him permitting evil. Someone who puts forward this defence for believing or disbelieving in God without recognising the equal plausibility of the alternative is doing metaphysics. Another incidental feature of such dualism is that the third alternative – agnosticism – is not taken seriously, but for more on this see 1.e.

Metaphysical claims can often be readily seen as incompatible with scepticism because of their dogmatic justification and dualistic form, whereas provisional beliefs without these features are just as clearly not threatened by scepticism – not because they are proof against it but because they take it into account. If I claim that I have seen a blackbird in the garden several times, I rely not on a dogmatic source of justification, but only on my own observation on several occasions, and my memory of those occasions. I may be wrong (I may have misidentified the species, or misremembered the previous occasions, for example), but I could freely admit to discovering that I was wrong without it having the further implications that would undermine an absolute source of information. Similarly, I could confidently assert that I saw a blackbird several times without needing to defend this claim against a sceptical threat. However, if alternatively I asserted that the blackbird *exists,* I would have to assert that it did so regardless of my experience, and in the process repress alternatives. To distinguish that the blackbird really existed as opposed to the fact that I observed it, I would need to dogmatically assert that it could not have been an illusory blackbird, even though this would be just as coherent an account of the event.

It might be objected here that there are perhaps an infinite number of possible explanations of any experience, so that it is impossible to distinguish experiences with multiple possible explanations as metaphysical as opposed to those without such, for this would be a false distinction. It is not the possibility of multiple interpretations that is the point that makes the difference, but our awareness of them. When I thought I saw a blackbird, I could possibly have seen a disguised alien spacecraft, a hologram, or a hallucination. However, a self-consciously limited claim allows for these alternatives, whilst still confidently asserting that, as far as I can tell on the evidence available to me, I saw a blackbird, not a hologram. It might need further discussion to establish explicitly that my claim is intended to be provisional, because it takes into account these other possibilities without refusing to make a claim at all. If I go on to make the metaphysical claim that the blackbird *really existed*, however, my claim does not allow for these alternatives, but is arrogantly extended so as to actively deny any contesting claim that the blackbird did not exist.

This self-conscious limitation (an aspect of justification that I call *agnostic foundationalism*) will be discussed further in 1.e., and it is a relatively easy way in which provisional claims can usually be distinguished from metaphysical ones. Of course, we have to investigate closely the issue of meaning here (discussed in volume 3) and take into account the intentions which would enable us to distinguish claims with attached metaphysical assumptions from those without them. We cannot just pounce on every use of the word 'exists' and assume it is metaphysical, or conversely assume that every statement apparently just describing or generalising from observation is not. Claims accepted from the testimony of others also may or may not be accepted for dogmatic reasons. If the claim is made philosophically explicit, though, or if other philosophically explicit metaphysical claims are deduced from it, we can become clearer about whether it is metaphysical or not.

To use a different analogy, metaphysical claims are like old oak trees in a storm, that are so stiff they cannot bend to the wind. They either stand or they break. Provisional claims, however, are like young oaks, flexible enough to change when the conditions change, and thus always able to stay adequate to those conditions. The difference in flexibility between provisional and metaphysical assertions is determined psychologically by the awareness of the possibility of different conditions, which is only generally rather than precisely reflected by the terminology used.

D. Incrementality

Just as scepticism does not prevent the justification of provisional statements that take into account the possibility that they may be wrong, similarly it does not prevent the justification of incremental statements that are a matter of degree. However, scepticism does create a reason for us to be much more careful and consistent in making all our claims incremental rather than absolute. I use the term 'incremental' rather than 'relative' here to avoid an unfortunate ambiguity in the term 'relative'. If a statement is 'relative' it can mean either that it makes limited claims, or that it is equally justified with all other statements. 'Incremental' on the other hand, can be used to mean the former without the latter.

Incrementality can be used as a further way of distinguishing metaphysical claims from provisional claims. Metaphysical claims are concerned with truth, either by claiming that a certain state of affairs is true or that it is untrue. Provisional claims, however, only deal with a degree of justification. I say 'a degree of *justification*' rather than 'a degree of truth' here, because the very idea of truth cannot be incrementalised. A degree of truth has to be guaranteed by knowledge of the whole truth, just as we cannot go half the distance to Edinburgh without knowing where Edinburgh lies. Without knowing where Edinburgh lies, what we take to be half the distance to Edinburgh may be in a completely different direction to Edinburgh, and similarly a degree of truth cannot be distinguished from complete falsity. Given that our very language and physical limitations rule out the possibility of knowing that we know the whole truth, we also have to abandon the belief that we can ever know a degree of truth. This does not mean, however, that we cannot have a degree of *justification* based on variable criteria from experience, because a level of justification can be based on the degree of adequacy of our approach rather than any measure backwards from a supposed reality (for more on this see 1.e).

Metaphysical claims cannot be incremental, both because of their concern with truth and because of their dismissal of error. If we only have a degree of justification this also implies a degree of error, but error is the condition for learning in human experience. We become relatively more justified, not only as we detect errors and learn from them, but also as we display the capacity to do so[24]. Metaphysical claims involve a fundamental rejection of this attitude to human progression, because they try to take shortcuts to a complete account of the truth. In this they reflect Plato's belief that a partial justification is no justification at all[25].

Incrementality also provides us with a crucial method for understanding aspects of our experience which have traditionally been discussed only in dualistic metaphysical terms. We are not obliged to think in metaphysical terms if we make the effort to think through an incremental alternative. The basic method here is to adopt a strict agnosticism as regards metaphysical claims (see next chapter) and to consider what qualities in our experience are referred to when we use dualistic metaphysical terms. I will give a few brief examples of incrementalised metaphysical dualisms in the remainder of this chapter to illustrate this method, but this is far from an exhaustive list. These and other examples of dualisms will be discussed in more detail in IV.4.

- One of the most important areas where Western thought has tended to think in metaphysical dualisms has been **universal ethics**. Either we have a dogmatic source of universal ethics such as God or an a priori deduction, it is thought, or ethics is merely relative to different societies,

---

[24] For a superb account of this process, with a wide variety of excellent examples, see Schulz (2010)
[25] Plato (1987) §504c

groups, or even individuals. However, I will be arguing throughout this book that the incrementalisation of ethics is psychological integration of different desires identified with by the ego (or left hemisphere) at different times. For more on this see I.7 and IV.4.b.

- The dualism of **mind and body** is created by mind being seen as having qualities such as self-consciousness, freewill, or intentionality that cannot be incrementalised. This dualism is not resolved by ignoring these qualities or treating them as unimportant in the way that physicalists and behaviourists tend to do. Instead, we need a critique of metaphysical accounts of the self (see 1.j), and to substitute a dynamic psychological function – what I call the ego – for a metaphysical absolute (the self). Instead of certainty about our identity, we substitute a flexible awareness of identifications. Apart from self-consciousness, though, some other features of mind are primarily features of uniqueness or situatedness. The meaning of a symbol for me, or the specificity of a sensual experience (like my individual experience of the red of a tomato), seems to be unique to my individual awareness because it is concentrated in the particular location associated with an individual brain: but situatedness is an incremental quality, not an absolute one, even if awareness is very sharply concentrated in one place and very rapidly falls away as we depart from the complex brain-conditions required to maintain it. Incrementality is not a quality unique to physical types of object (e.g. my pain, a mental quality, can get incrementally worse as I focus increasingly on the most affected spot), so that incrementalising mental properties in this way should not be confused with reducing them to physical properties. Mental properties are thus more or less identified with and more or less situated in my brain and body, regardless of whether they are 'inside' or 'outside': a pain in my toe, for example, is probably a bit less 'mental' on these criteria than a pain in my head.[26]

- The dualism of **ideal and real** is created by absolutising a quality of character which we experience as incremental – i.e. objectivity. I will be discussing objectivity, including the relationships of scientific, moral and aesthetic types of objectivity, and the ways I think it can be understood in terms of integration, in section 4 of this book. Also see IV.4.d for more discussion of idealism and realism.

- The dualism of **freewill and determinism** is related to those of mind-body and ideal-real, and can partly be resolved in the same way. However, the concept of responsibility or its absence is also central to the discussion of freewill. Responsibility is an incremental quality that can be understood in terms of psychological integration, because the more integrated I am, the more reflective my actions become (so as to take more conditions into account) and the less constrained. For more details on this, see I.7.b, IV.3.f and IV.4.c.

- The dualism between **belief in God (theism) and denial of God (atheism)** needs to be incrementally understood in relation to the meaning of God as people encounter it in experience, with a rigorous agnosticism refusing to enter into questions of God's existence. My suggestion is that God is primarily encountered in religious experience in relation to integration of meaning, a concept that will be explored fully in III.4.e. I shall argue there, along Jungian lines, that we encounter a God archetype more fully the more meaning is integrated. For more detailed discussion of theism and atheism see IV.4.f.

---

[26] For a more detailed discussion see IV.4.e

In terms of the brain, all of these approaches to metaphysical dualisms can be seen as finding ways of moving our understanding of these concepts out of absolutist left-hemisphere dominance and more into effective contact with the right hemisphere. The right hemisphere has to engage with incrementality constantly as a feature of time and space[27], whilst the left hemisphere can only grasp incrementality in an abstract conceptual way. Incrementalisations usually have the common property of requiring some sort of imaginative representation across time or space: for example, integration involves the idea of different desires, meanings or beliefs at different points of time or space being unified. Even an incrementalisation of colour into shades of grey tends to make us implicitly imagine a spectrum that stretches across space, rather than just the single ideas of black or white. For this reason, incrementalisation is also part of the key to provisionality. We are forced to connect with the more provisional right hemisphere by being incremental in our interpretation of concepts.

---

[27] McGilchrist (2009) p.76

E. Distinguishing negative metaphysics from agnosticism

I have already mentioned the importance, when interpreting sceptical arguments, of distinguishing the denial of positive claims from the casting of uncertainty on those claims. This is a distinction that goes back to that between the arguments of Academic and Pyrrhonian types of sceptic in ancient times. Academic sceptics made assertions about the relativity of knowledge, whereas Pyrrhonians merely doubted the existence of knowledge and refrained from making claims about it. It is not clear, however, that the Pyrrhonians followed through their agnostic attitude in every respect[28]. I am concerned here not with historical claims about the Pyrrhonians, but with the possibility of making the distinction clearly and consistently.

In the modern context, it is the distinction between negative metaphysics and agnosticism that is crucial for distinguishing Middle Way Philosophy from naturalism, scientism, atheism, existentialism, nihilism, postmodernism, relativism, or any other theories that in one way or another deny metaphysical claims. The nature of metaphysical claims is such that the mere denial of a metaphysical claim only sets up another, converse, metaphysical claim that is equally distant from experience.

This point can be seen more closely if we analyse more fully what is meant by the denial of an assertion. If I deny a claim that is within experience (e.g. "I can see a dog in the room"), then the converse is also within my experience ("I can't see a dog in the room"). When looking for the dog, I can take into account the possibility that the dog may or may not be seen in the room, without having to pre-judge the question. In contrast,

---

[28] See Ellis (2001) 4.b

a metaphysical statement ("God exists") is neither easier nor harder to support through experience than its denial ("God does not exist"), because in either case, I can only interpret any particular experience as evidence for or against God by not taking into account the possibility of that evidence being interpreted the opposite way. For example, I can only take the evidence of the complexity of the eye as proof of God's design if I ignore the ways it can be explained as due to a long process of random genetic mutation and environmental selection[29]. On the other hand, I can only take that explanation as disproving God's design if I ignore the ways in which random genetic mutation and environmental selection can still be explained as the results of divine creation.

In the case of God, it can be illustrated relatively clearly and easily how the denial of a positive metaphysical claim only sets up a dualistic opposition and does not advance the discussion. Rancorous debates between theists and atheists are common, and in all cases each side merely proceeds by casting doubt on the metaphysical assumptions of the other, but nevertheless drawing the opposed metaphysical conclusion[30]. This can only be done when one fails to understand the difference between metaphysical assertions and assertions within experience, and that metaphysical assertions remain untouched by evidence.

One rather glaring example of this is found in Richard Dawkins' *The God Delusion*: his rejection of agnosticism contains much rhetoric and only one argument, which is this one:

If he existed and chose to reveal it, God himself could clinch the argument, noisily and unequivocally, in his favour.[31]

---

[29] Dawkins (1996) ch.5
[30] For example, Dawkins (2006) vs. McGrath (2007), which put together provide a veritable armoury of arguments for agnosticism
[31] Dawkins (2006) p.73

Presumably Dawkins envisages a voice booming from the heavens saying "I am God" or something similar, so that everyone on earth could hear. We could hardly envisage metaphysical claims being proved in any way more explicit than this. But would it convince everyone? Should it convince everyone? Hardly. The experience of a big voice indicates that some being or thing has produced a big voice, not that a perfect and infinite being is producing it. No possible finite experience can provide the evidence to support an absolute claim – either about an infinite being or about an alleged truth that is said to be the case throughout the universe – it's a simple as that[32].

Even if one appreciates this point in relation to the debate about God, it is less widely applied to other issues, but exactly the same considerations apply to metaphysical dualisms in philosophy of mind, the debate about freewill, in ethics, in political ideology, in scientific realism, and for other kinds of religious metaphysics (such as Buddhist claims about enlightenment). In all these areas, philosophy and related areas have often got fruitlessly caught up in disputes which admit of no possible resolution, because they consist only of one dogmatic assertion followed by an equally dogmatic counter-assertion. These assertions are backed up by the selective use of sceptical arguments which undermine the opposing position, whilst those which undermine one's own are ignored.

The alternative to denying metaphysical propositions is to remain agnostic about them. Agnosticism involves a recognition that we do not know, and is the outcome of sceptical argument applied equally to all sides. As I have been arguing in the previous chapters so far, these sceptical

---

[32] I owe this point originally to Sartre, who points out our responsibility for the interpretation of all 'signs' of God as being such. See Sartre (1948).

arguments do not leave us unjustified in making any assertions whatsoever, but only unjustified in making metaphysical assertions, whilst provisional assertions remain justifiable. It is not possible to make a metaphysical assertion provisionally because a metaphysical assertion is necessarily absolute, and impossible to either justify further or to incrementalise.

As it is impossible to make a metaphysical assertion provisionally, soft agnosticism, in which one awaits further evidence for metaphysical claims, is practically mistaken. One would be waiting infinitely, simply having failed to get the message that metaphysical assertions do not admit of evidence. So the type of agnosticism I am recommending is hard agnosticism, in which one recognises that no evidence can ever be available on metaphysical claims. Such agnosticism is in no sense indecisive, but actually involves a decisive refusal of involvement in fruitless metaphysical disputes.

One possible objection to this position is that it involves agnosticism about trivial metaphysical positions as well as those that people are actually attached to. I need to be just as agnostic about the Flying Spaghetti Monster as about God, even though nobody seriously believes in the Flying Spaghetti Monster, so it may be claimed to be not worth being agnostic about. However, I think this confuses the question of what discussions are worth our attention from metaphysical agnosticism as a general approach. I can be in principle agnostic about the existence of the Flying Spaghetti Monster (if it comes up), even though it is far more important to be agnostic about God, because a lot more people believe or disbelieve in God and their belief or disbelief has a lot more practical implications.

Another argument that has been used against hard agnosticism is that it is contradictory in "dogmatically" rejecting both positive and negative metaphysics. Here one needs to distinguish between dogmatism and a decisiveness justified by practical requirements. A belief is dogmatic if it is absolute, represses alternatives, and is thus inaccessible to counter-evidence, but hard agnosticism decisively rejects metaphysics precisely in order to maintain an accessibility to evidence which would be obscured if it were to accept metaphysics. Hard agnosticism itself is not a metaphysical belief, but rather is the avoidance of metaphysical beliefs, in order to make practical progress by focusing on non-absolute beliefs.

In order to be maintained consistently, however, hard agnosticism requires a psychological state of provisionality. In practice, agnosticism even on important topics is difficult to maintain consistently because of the phenomenon of *sceptical slippage*, where positions that are in principle agnostic easily turn into positions of metaphysical denial the moment we lose a psychological state of provisionality. I will be discussing this further, with the ways in which many modern philosophies are subject to it, in 1.h.

More positively, it is the balancing of sceptical agnosticism between positive and negative types of metaphysical claim that forms the basis of the *Middle Way* – which is, of course, a defining feature of Middle Way Philosophy. For more about the Middle Way see section 3 of this book.

F. Against *a priori* arguments for metaphysics

I am now going to offer a more detailed argument in this chapter against the claims of those who will continue to insist that some claims must be accepted as certain on *a priori* grounds. This chapter is aimed at the likely objections of some analytic philosophers and Kantians, whilst the next is aimed in a similar fashion at theologians. If you are not especially interested in either of these categories of argument you might find it helpful to skip these two chapters and go directly to 1.h.

I have already argued in 1.b against the idea of self-evident truths that are not subject to scepticism, dealing there particularly with the idea that Descartes' cogito is a self-evident truth. At that point I stated that mathematical and logical self-evident truths could be accounted for in a similar way. In order to clarify why mathematical and logical truths are not examples of justifiable metaphysical truths I will need to adumbrate the account of meaning that will be tackled in more detail in volume 3.

The case for self-evident truths *a priori* begins with claims that must be universally true, or true in all possible worlds, because of their definitional nature. Thus a bear is an animal, whether or not there are any bears or any animals, whether or not people understand that bears are animals (or whether or not people even exist to have such understanding). The claim is alleged to be absolutely universal because it is hypothetical – *if* there is a bear (in the sense we usually understand 'bear'), then that bear must be an animal.

Hume's empiricist response to this kind of claim is to point out that, although such claims are indeed universal, they are also uninformative and trivial, because they tell us only about the way in which we categorise the universe, rather than the

Against *a priori* metaphysics

universe itself – they are analytic as well as a priori, and Hume alleges that all *a priori* claims are analytic. This is the basis for Hume's 'fork' in which only analytic and empirical types of knowledge are allowed[33].

Whilst I find Hume's fork a very useful starting-point in dealing with *a priori* claims, it does not quite complete the job Hume wanted it to do, which is that of making experience the only source of justified belief. This is because it is too strong in one respect and too weak in another. It is too strong in claiming that all *a priori* claims must be analytic, because this would rule out the Kantian *a priori*, in which *a priori* claims tell us about the prior conditions for experience (and which I will turn to presently). On the other hand it is too weak in allowing *a priori* claims even the status of trivial knowledge.

As we saw in 1.a, sceptical argument need not stop at casting doubt on knowledge through the senses. It can also challenge even *a priori* arguments by requiring further justification, and it can also employ the final two linguistic arguments. However, simply asking for further justification for *a priori* claims will not convince those who think they are self-evident. It is the linguistic arguments that can do the sceptical work more fully here, because they point out the assumptions made about meaning by those who appeal to *a priori* certainty.

The main problem with *a priori* claims to metaphysics, then, is that they assume linguistic categories that are both absolutely consistent and that have unambiguous boundaries. Without such consistency and such boundaries, if you read "a bear is an animal" the terms "bear" and "animal" mean something different to you to what they mean to me. Indeed they may already mean something different even to me now as I write this paragraph to what they meant when I first brought in this example five paragraphs back. They may be different in terms

---

[33] Hume (1975) p.163-5

60

Middle Way Philosophy 1: The Path of Objectivity

of what counts either as a bear or as an animal, or in terms of what is bear or animal and what is not. We are not only dealing with academic zoological disputes between Linnaeans and Claddists (who have different accounts of species taxonomy) here. For example, is a genetically engineered creature with 95% bear genes a bear? Is a piece of fur on the point of falling out of a bear's coat "bear"? We may have different answers to these questions, and our answers may vary with context, purpose, and feelings.

One analytic response to this is to continue to insist on the purely hypothetical nature of the claim "A bear is an animal". Ambiguities in identifying particular bears or animals, or vagueness about their boundaries, it may be argued, make no difference to the claim that *if* we are agreed that a particular thing is a bear, *then* it will also be an animal. However, this purely rational insistence would allow a bear to somehow be an animal even if all the things we actually called "bears" were not actually animals. A bear "in the usual sense" now, might in a future context have quite a different sense, yet the usual sense now would still be asserted to be true in all possible worlds and times. More generally, to maintain the metaphysical insistence on the certainty of *a priori* claims we might have to completely disconnect it from human experience. There can be fewer clearer instances of the *abstracted turn* in philosophy, where the goal of philosophy in reasoning for the clarification of the beliefs of people is lost, due to attachment to a particular theory with no connection to that goal.

It is also an example of what in other contexts would be called *ad hoc* reasoning, sticking to a proposition that one insists must be universally true regardless of the practical circumstances. Compare these two scenarios:
1. Jock asserts "No true Scotsman eats his porridge with sugar." It is pointed out that Hamish is a Scotsman, but he

Against *a priori* metaphysics

eats his porridge with sugar. "Hamish is not a true Scotsman" asserts Jock.

2. Aldous asserts that "A bear is an animal" is true in all possible worlds where "a bear" is used in the usual sense. It is pointed out that in possible world x "bear" is used to mean anything that is not an animal. "In this possible world 'bear' is not used in its usual sense" says Aldous.

What these two scenarios have in common is that 'true' in the first and 'usual' in the second are entirely abstracted from the context in order to defend a particular claim. The problem with Jock's idea of a true Scotsman is not just that it hasn't been fully specified in advance, but that it is impervious to *any* possible evidence, just like Aldous's use of 'usual'. What one takes to be 'usual' cannot be specified in advance because it is the result of custom in a particular area rather than definition. Thus *a priori* claims about things that are necessarily true when we take the words in them in their 'usual' sense turn out to be merely asserting the conventions of a particular time and place without any particular reason for doing so. Certainty ascribed to *a priori* claims is thus just as metaphysical as that ascribed to 'God exists'.

An even more abstracted case than that of a categorical statement like "a bear is an animal" is that of the laws of logic. It may be claimed, for example, that "a=a" is an absolutely certain proposition. However, one does not get beyond the inconsistency and ambiguity of linguistic categories by using algebraic constants. To be correct, "a=a" must be true for any term inserted in the place of a. Even in the time it takes me to think that "a=a", any term that I may insert in the place of *a* may change its meaning by the time I get to considering its equivalence to itself. For example, if the meaning of 'bear' is constantly changing, and I insert 'bear', then the bear I consider at the beginning of the statement is no longer precisely equivalent to itself by the time I get as far as considering its equivalence. More obviously, if I insert "Proteus", a creature who completely changes form every millisecond, Proteus has obviously changed during the time elapsed in reading the proposition. It does not matter if the change in meaning is miniscule, because the equivalence has to be absolutely perfect for the law of logic to be absolutely true in the way asserted.

Similar points apply to the assertion that mathematical claims are certain. 1+1=2 is only true *a priori* by virtue of the fact that whenever we find two objects that we regard as singular and put them together, there will be two of them, regardless of what the objects are. However, by the time we complete this reflection, the meanings of the object terms that we regard as singular may have changed. One what? Two what? What makes any object discrete other than a set of conventions that are subject to change? Even two people can become one, if the wording of some traditional marriage services is to be believed, and one person can become two, by a different convention, if they have multiple personality disorder. If this is the case for people, how much more flexible might be the conventions attached to the singularity of stones, blades of grass, or electrons!

What I have been doing here is trying to show some of the ways in which the theory of meaning assumed by *a priori* metaphysics is self-contradictory. The theory of meaning assumed, under which the traditional assertions appear to make sense, is a truth-conditional theory in which the meaning of a proposition consists in the conditions according to which it would be true. This theory is inadequate for all sorts of reasons, which will be discussed more fully in volume 3. Chief amongst these is its complete abstraction from what we actually take to be meaningful in experience, which in brain terms involves the dominance of the left hemisphere to the exclusion of the right. The reason it is proving self-contradictory here, however, is because it is a static theory that assumes meanings to be fixed and eternal, rather than a changing property of living human beings. But it is our right

Against *a priori* metaphysics

hemispheres that engage with experience, including that of changes in time. As soon as we introduce temporal changes of meaning into a system that relies on this exclusive left-hemisphere fixedness, the whole system collapses. This is a further indication that scepticism is on the side of the humans against the angels, not the other way round.

There is an alternative way of understanding meaning, which you will need to read in detail in volume 3, and which forms an important link in the coherence of the alternative approach of Middle Way Philosophy. Briefly for now, this approach to meaning recognises that meaning is not just a cognitive matter, separated falsely from emotive meaning, or 'meaningfulness', and from physical experience. Instead, the theory of George Lakoff[34], which relates meaning to physical experience, can be used to unite cognitive and emotive aspects of meaning into a single type of explanation. If meaning arises from our physical experience, it is certainly variable and dependent on our complex individual states. However, one other effect of this account of meaning is to remove the eternal certainty from a priori propositions.

This approach does not deny all usefulness to mathematics, logic, and taxonomy, but merely limits the more arrogant claims for universality that might be made for them. If the meaning of terms used in mathematics, logic or taxonomy is dependent on our physical conditions, then we have to share enough of those conditions for those ways of working to be useful to us when communicating. Mathematics remains useful for those who share a sufficient understanding of it, for practical purposes where the ambiguities that might obtrude are not practically speaking a problem. Similarly, logical reasoning (such as the reasoning in this book) remains valid, but only to those who share enough of the same cultural basis

---

[34] Lakoff 1987

to find it so. Even those may understand and apply it in very different ways.

One other sense of the *a priori* must be considered here – the Kantian. In these terms, *a priori* claims must be considered certain because they identify the conditions required for our experience and/or judgement to occur. For example, "Objects exist in space" might be considered metaphysically true, just because existing in space is a necessary condition for any object we can conceive.

One long-standing problem with this kind of assertion, identified by Körner[35], is that we cannot prove the uniqueness of our particular transcendental deduction: in other words, spatiality may be necessary for all objects for us, but we cannot prove that there may not be other creatures who perceive objects without spatiality. We cannot say anything about such alternative categorial worlds, because (if they exist) they lie beyond even the categories upon which our imagination is founded. Yet there may nevertheless be such categorial worlds for other beings.

The linguistic sceptical arguments we have already discussed also apply to this kind of *a priori* claim of certainty as much as to the more traditional kind. The meanings of the terms 'objects' and 'space' may differ between me and others, or even for myself at different times. If I am going to create an *a priori* metaphysical certainty that is true in all circumstances, I need not just consistency of experience but also consistency in the language used to describe that experience.

Again, that does not prevent Kantian discussions of the conditions for experience being extremely valuable, but it means that they should be judged as theoretical claims to be judged by their consistency with experience like any other

---

[35] Körner (1967)

theory. The requirement of provisionality applies to theories of the Kantian *a priori* very much as it does to empirical theories, with the conditions theorised about just being those required for all experience so far rather than being about the objects of that experience. To theorise about the conditions of experience is, after all, just an extension of theorisation about the conditions for anything else: for example the conditions for life or the conditions for combustion. Just as sceptical argument successfully undermines all claims about "Laws of Nature" that are said to apply across the universe despite the limitations of the evidence used to support them, similarly Kantian theories about the *a priori* amount to generalisations about all experience so far, but it would be an over-extension of the justification of such theory to claim that they were true of all possible evidence whatsoever.

G. Against revelatory metaphysics

Apart from philosophers, the other major source of metaphysical claims in the world is religious. I do not identify religion solely with revelation and metaphysical belief, so it is not religion as a whole, or even any specific religion as a whole, that I am commenting on here. However, religion is a sphere where revelatory metaphysics is often found. In this chapter I am going to try to head off some common defences for it.

By 'revelation' here, I mean a metaphysical claim that is justified by appeal to an absolute authority. Very often such revelations are believed to come from God, but God is not the only claimed source of revelations. In the Buddhist tradition, revelations come from enlightened beings, and in polytheistic traditions, from gods or other spiritual beings. Even when revelations are believed to come from God they also need a proximate authoritative source to convey them, such as a religious leader, a scripture, a 'sign', or the inspired will of a community. These revelations become metaphysical when they gain absolute authority because of their source, rather than being judged as theory according to their relationship to experience.

Here we need to distinguish the idea of absolute authority from a source and credibility from a source. If we have trusted a source before and found it reliable, then we have greater justification in trusting it again, based on experience. We are also likely to trust sources in a secondary way because they are recommended by people that we know as trustworthy, or are widely assumed to be trustworthy. So, for example, many people throughout the world (including me) trust the BBC news as offering a reasonably objective report of world events. However, this is far from an absolute reliance. If I began to experience the BBC as less reliable, I would lessen my trust in

Against revelatory metaphysics

them and perhaps switch to other sources of news – if I could find better ones. An absolute revelatory authority, however, is not subject to this kind of review in the light of experience. A religious believer who trusts God, or trusts the guidance of the Buddha, cannot withdraw or even reduce that trust when it proves unreliable, because there are no circumstances in which it can be accepted to be unreliable. If the BBC allows an uncritical account of a despotic or corrupt regime in a distant country, we can soon find out by consulting other sources about that regime. If, on the other hand, we are given a one-sided account of Jesus or the Buddha by religious scriptures or modern religious teachers, the absolute claims made for these figures, and the lack of an effective critical tradition within religious traditions, means that challenges will be taken as attacks on the religious group as a whole and ignored or reinterpreted so as to be compatible with continuing faith in the revelation.

Credibility is not only based on direct or indirect experience to begin with, but it is also subject to continuing scrutiny by comparison with alternative sources of information. Revelation may sometimes be accepted on the basis of experience, but the partiality and limiting assumptions that are used to interpret that experience can only be recognised with great difficulty once the revelation has been accepted, because of the lack of ongoing critical scrutiny. Critical scrutiny becomes redundant once an absolute source of truth is believed to have been discovered, simply because the motive for believing in that source of truth is no longer conceived as investigative.

It is the dualistic features of revelatory metaphysics that have been most obvious to atheistic critics making a moral case against 'religion'. Revelation puts the emphasis on a source of authority, which often has the effect of polarising the response between those who obey or disobey that authority. This polarisation is strongly illustrated by the episode in Exodus where Moses leaves the Israelites to ascend Mount Sinai, and when he returns finds that they started to worship a Golden Calf image in disobedience against God's law.

Moses saw that the people were out of control and that Aaron had laid them open to the secret malice of their enemies. He took his place at the gate of the camp and said "Who is on the Lord's side? Come here to me"; and the Levites all rallied to him. He said to them, "The Lord God of Israel has said: Arm yourselves, each of you, with his sword. Go through the camp from gate to gate and back again. Each of you kill brother, friend, neighbour." The Levites obeyed, and about three thousand of the people died that day. Moses said, "You have been installed as priests of the Lord today, because you have turned each against his own son and his own brother and so have brought a blessing this day upon yourselves."[36]

This episode has been echoed in a host of religious conflicts ever since, the defining feature of which is the revelatory assumption of one true account of 'God's word' and the falsity of all other beliefs. If evangelical certainty no longer results in such massacres in all cases today, it can hardly be revelatory beliefs themselves that are responsible for the development of tolerance. Rather it is the countervailing development of awareness that other views may, after all, have something to be said for them because they are expressive of other experiences that have engaged differently with conditions, or perhaps with the recognition that slaughter does not address the conditions of belief as well as persuasion does.

Those that receive revelation assume a special status, which can in some cases apparently justify any action up to and including the massacre of those without that status[37]. Revelation also puts the emphasis on revealed moral

---

[36] Exodus 32:25-29: Oxford Revised English Bible
[37] This can be seen not only in the above example from Exodus, but also in the Israelite conquest of Palestine as recorded in the book of Judges, and the well-known 'Sword verse' of the Qur'an (9:5), discussed further below.

Against revelatory metaphysics

instructions to be followed to the letter, which makes it easy for these moral instructions to become an end in themselves regardless of the wider moral context. For example, the Jewish dietary regulations given in Leviticus 11 seem largely motivated by the need to distinguish the Israelites from other tribes.

In all of these kinds of cases, it is revelation that is the problem, not 'religion', for religion includes many other beliefs, attitudes and practices, and amounts to a whole sphere of life, not a particular set of beliefs. Religious art, ritual, story, community, meditation, ethics or social action does not have to be either revelatory or metaphysical, though these aspects of religion can be focused on or motivated by metaphysics to a greater or lesser extent. It is revelation that makes religious attitudes metaphysical, whereas in other cases religious beliefs and practices can merely provide a context for passing on theories that can be tried through experience, whether these consist in moral attitudes, rituals or meditation technology.

Just as positive metaphysics is dualistically opposed by negative metaphysics, revelation is dualistically opposed by anti-revelation: that is, by the denial of the content of revelation because of the authoritative claims made for it. A Middle Way response to revelation, then, denies the authority of the revelatory claims, but examines the content of revelatory scriptures or other instructions in the same way as other content, neither giving it higher nor lower status than other texts (except where greater credibility can be based on experience). Obviously this is easier to do with some texts than others. It is hard to interpret the passage from Exodus quoted above in other than revelatory terms, but if we focused on, for example, the content of Jesus' moral teachings or the Buddha's meditational instructions aside from the claims of authority ascribed to them, these can provide a rich source of religious technology or religious inspiration regardless of revelatory claims.

Theologians through the ages have offered various kinds of justification for revelation, some of which I will try to address here:
1. Human sinfulness makes reliance on 'reason' unacceptable
2. Revelation can be wholly or partly supported through 'reason'
3. Revelation arises from, and is justified by, the power of religious experience
4. God would not allow us to be influenced by the wrong revelation

1. Firstly, the belief that human beings are universally sinful is itself a metaphysical belief which can have no justification in experience. No matter how great our experience of the evil or the corruptibility of individual human beings, this would not justify us in extending an assumption of absolute sinfulness to all human beings. Any theory of universal absolute sinfulness that was open to observation would immediately founder on every example of human goodness. If only a degree of sinfulness is encountered, though, it would not make us utterly unjustified in using reason. Human sinfulness, then, is not a justifiable foundation for accepting revelation.

Further unjustifiable assumptions are also made in this line of argument, even if it were accepted that we are universally sinful. If sinfulness merely makes our use of reason fallible, this is a fallibility that needs to be embraced rather than rejected, for the reasons outlined in 1.d. If our reason is flawed by sinfulness, in any case, this does not necessarily mean that we should depend entirely on revelation as an alternative. Since there is no further reason for accepting revelation beyond the authority of the source, accepting revelation because of doubt about our own capacity to think through the issues correctly is a bit like jumping off a cliff because you can't see any way to climb down it.

Theological arguments of this kind tend to share a conception of 'reason' with analytic philosophers that unhelpfully separates the conceptual aspects of human experience from the emotional – a distinction tackled in I.1.i and III.1.a. For the moment I am using the common term 'reason' with scare quotes, but really do not accept the narrow assumptions that are often attached to the concept of 'reason' used as a synonym for thinking justified by human experience. In drawing conclusions from evidence or assumptions, we use our emotions as much as our logical faculties, and such 'reasoning' is only ever as good as the assumptions it depends on. The acceptance of revelation itself involves 'reasoning' in which one abstract representational belief is justified by another, and it is the false dichotomy between revelation and 'reason' that needs addressing here rather than asserting one over the other.

2. Given that revelation attempts to provide an absolute justification for belief, in its own terms there is neither need nor justification for using 'reason' as a basis of judgement. There is no need because revelation has already answered our questions with absolute authority, and no justification because the use of reasoning based on experience to justify beliefs might undermine that authority. Of course, in practice religious believers through the centuries have indeed supplemented or supported revelation using reasoning based on experience, but one presumes because that this is due to understandable limitations in their faith in the revelation. The re-emergence of the perspective of human experience in a religious context dominated by revelation seems unavoidable, because the complexity of that human experience is simply not fully addressed by revelatory certainties. The adoption of increasingly liberal perspectives within a revelatory religious

context increasingly sidelines the revelation until it becomes almost irrelevant.

One area where it might be argued that the use of reasoning based on experience is always necessary is in the interpretation of revelation. Any verbal statement of revelation, in a scripture, a leader's words, or elsewhere, will either be highly generalised or written for a specific context different from the one where it is used. The terms used will also be interpreted differently by the audience from the speaker and will contain many ambiguities. For example, take the 'Sword Verse' from the Qur'an:

But when the forbidden months are past, then fight and slay the pagans wherever you find them, and seize them, beleaguer them, and lie in wait for them in every stratagem (of war). But if they repent, and establish regular prayers and practise regular charity, then open the way for them: for Allah is Oft-forgiving, Most Merciful.[38]

The context of this verse, as moderate Muslims point out, is one of treaties between Muhammad and the pagans of Makkah. The preceding verses appear to give Allah's blessing to the breaking of treaties with pagans that are believed to have broken their obligations or become hostile to the Muslims. So, the verse could be taken to mean that Muslims should only fight pagans who showed hostility first. It could be used to stop Muslims waging holy war during Ramadan or against those who have surrendered to Islam. On the other hand, it still supports the use of violence, in at least some circumstances, to force people to convert to Islam. What this means today, then, particularly for a Muslim surrounded by unbelievers or a Muslim nation in contact with non-Muslim nations, is highly ambiguous. Who broke a contract first, for example, is often highly disputable, as is the more basic moral

---

[38] Qur'an 9:5 (translated Abdullah Yusuf Ali)

Against revelatory metaphysics

issue of whether we should praise Muslims for their restraint in limiting warfare against pagans to certain defined conditions, or blame them for engaging in it at all.

What this tells us is that there is a basic incoherence in the very idea of propositional revelation, not that the use of 'reason' can somehow preserve the absolute status of revelation despite these difficulties. Given the relativity of linguistic communication, no absolute truths can be communicated in words, so that if we use reasoning based on experience to interpret utterances that are supposed to be revelation, we are actually treating them merely as advice and weighing them on their own merits. If all religious believers admitted that this was what they were doing there would be no problem about it, but when fundamentalists and other religious conservatives use 'reason' to interpret revelation and then attach the supposed absolute authority of the revelation to their own interpretation, we have major confusion and self-deception.

The alternative to a propositional revelation is a non-propositional revelation, which may occur, for example, in a wordless mystical experience, in a vision, in an experience of nature, or through the character of a great religious leader. Some of the issues around religious experience will be considered under the next point, but generally there are even more difficulties surrounding the idea of non-propositional revelation than around propositional revelation. Given the requirement on religious believers to do all the interpretation from a deeply ambiguous communication, how can non-propositional revelation be distinguished, in practice, from inspiration? It is difficult to see how those claiming non-propositional revelation are not merely trying to attach the authority of revelation to beliefs acquired through their own judgement and experience.

Middle Way Philosophy 1: The Path of Objectivity

On the whole, then, revelation and reasoning based on experience are oil and water. They can supplant each other but they cannot mix. Any appeal to revelation prevents judgements being based on experience because the revelation, if it is as absolute as is claimed, must always override the perspective of experience. Any judgement made on the basis of experience to supplement or interpret revelation, on the other hand, removes the revelatory authority and substitutes a fallible human perspective.

3. Religious experience is an important dimension of human experience, and there is no justification for reductive treatments of these experiences. They remain potent, mysterious and inspirational for those who have them (or even, indirectly, for others). However, I want to argue that the religious tradition of trying to make revelatory capital out of religious experiences is just as crass as the attempt to explain them away as 'merely' chemical imbalances in the brain or the product of psychiatric disorders.

One basic argument against the possibility that religious experiences could communicate absolute truths is simply the impossibility that perfection could be experienced in a context of imperfection. Whatever experiences of rapturous emotional positivity, empathy, intuitive insight or apparent certainty religious experiences may offer, these cannot be experiences of a perfect being or even a perfect perspective, because they are imperfect. What has happened is that a human being has experienced an inspired and integrated state, but nevertheless still a fallible state. To attribute godlike qualities to a fallible human experience is a type of (what in the theistic traditions has been called) idolatry, not very different in effect from attributing godlike qualities to a carved piece of wood. In terms of brain hemispheres, it takes the open and intuitive experiences of the right hemisphere and reduces them to the linguistic certainties of the left hemisphere.

Against revelatory metaphysics

Sometimes traditional accounts of religious experience take the gap between perfect and imperfect into account. For example, the Israelite elders who are said to have seen God on the top of Mount Sinai can see and comprehend the pavement he stands on, not God himself[39]. Muhammad in the Cave of Hira is told to recite the words of the Qur'an that arise in him spontaneously, so the words are not said to be expressive of his revelatory state at all – he is merely a channel for God[40]. However, even if we grant that religious experience merely provides a context for the communication of divine words, rather than the divine words being justified by the experience, we are still left with the contradictory idea of divine words. Such words, if they were ever capable of expressing a perfect point of view, will immediately lose that perfection when understood and interpreted.

4. A final theological strategy to defend revelation is to appeal back to God's perspective. If we doubt whether we have the right revelation, and point out the imperfection of our interpretation of revelation, it is argued that God must be guiding that interpretation. Indeed, given that God is both omnipresent and good, God *must* be guiding our interpretation, and would not leave us alone in error.

If you were to use this argument to support belief in the existence of God, it would obviously be circular: we believe in God because he has revealed himself to us, and we know the revelation to be correct because God exists. However, if you believe in God's existence already, it would certainly be within God's power and consistent with his assumed personality to ensure that we understand revelation correctly.

The bigger problem with this argument, then, is the abstracted turn that it shares with analytic philosophy (see previous

---

[39] Exodus 24:9-11
[40] Qur'an 96:1

chapter). This argument does not appeal to God as an experience at all, but to a conception of God that is metaphysical and thus beyond human experience. It would be possible to believe in such a God, and that he was guiding our revelations, even if our experience appeared to completely contradict such assertions, for example if his revelation involved instructions for deliberate destruction of the earth and mass suicide, or if every individual on earth had a different revelation which brought them into violent conflict with all the other individuals.

Finally, then, it must be re-emphasised that the decisive rejection of revelation is not anti-religious. The problem is metaphysics, not religion, and revelation is simply metaphysics applied to religion. However, it has to be accepted that religion provides us with many of the most striking examples of the drawbacks of metaphysics.

H. Sceptical slippage and modern forms of negative metaphysics

Sceptical slippage is my term for the way in which agnostic positions justified by sceptical uncertainty have a tendency to become positions of denial. There are a number of possible reasons for this.

One is that the distinction between agnosticism and denial is a subtle one – but that at least can be remedied by study. Agnosticism involves rejecting a positive metaphysical position just as denial does, but it equally involves rejecting the converse position. At the same time one accepts whatever either position has to offer in relation to experience – only rejecting the metaphysical assumptions. The information that one rejects one position conveys little by itself unless one can also think more positively what alternative is embraced. In the case of metaphysical agnosticism the alternative embraced to either acceptance or denial is the possibility of progress in understanding the conditions that relate to the claims made on either side. We can only start to make that progress if we avoid thinking merely in terms of metaphysical affirmation or denial.

Another reason for sceptical slippage is the social fact that groups find it easier to unify around concepts that are readily understood, and to have clear points of disagreement with opposing groups. For example, psychological research has helped to establish the tendency of the members of one group to exaggerate the homogeneity of other groups, who are assumed to have consistently wrong beliefs rather than a variety of different beliefs with differing degrees of correctness.[41] The definite denial of the clearly identified and supposedly consistent beliefs of opposing groups thus gains support more

---

[41] Ostrom et al (1993)

readily than agnosticism can. In political terms, this can be revealed in a polarisation effect, where media bias is reinforced by public preferences for simplified alternatives and party interest in maintaining those alternatives[42].

This tendency for easily identifiable positions that maintain a group to be defended can even lead to the *unholy alliance effect*: that is, for those with vested interests in maintaining a simple dualistic model of a situation to unite in condemning what they see as the obfuscations of agnosticism. For example, politicians to the extremes of a political spectrum may unite against the challenges posed by the centre in order to maintain the conditions for their shared supremacy: a situation that continues in the democracies of both the US and the UK. In the UK, an unholy alliance of Labour and Conservative Parties until recently repressed all forms of electoral reform to create a more proportional electoral system, which would mean increased sharing of power in coalitions with the central Liberal Democrat party. The counter-dependency of each major party on the other and on the conception that it offered the only alternative to the other is reflected in Margaret Thatcher's statement that "There'll always be a Labour Party". The opposed two-party system, especially in its heyday in the 1970's, was closely associated with dichotomies of class and regional support and a perception of diametrically opposed economic policies (though fortunately this polarisation began to weaken in the 1990's) and these polarisations in turn were often perceived as based on absolutely opposed values such as individualism vs. socialism, or social conservatism vs. social progressivism. In this kind of atmosphere, it was hardly surprising if those who tried to think about the best ways of addressing political conditions found themselves subject to strong social pressures towards one political group or the other, and a questioning of

---

[42] See Bernhardt et al (2008) in relation to US politics

Sceptical slippage

the Conservative approach tended to lead one either to the Labour Party or to marginalisation.

A third likely reason for sceptical slippage is semantic: if we (implicitly or explicitly) think of claims as either true or false according to their representational relationship with an out-there reality, rather than as incrementally justified in relation to our whole experience (in the way outlined in 1.d above), then there is little room for the Middle Way. To understand the very possibility of metaphysical agnosticism requires us to shift our understanding of what is being asserted in a theory, from that of a "real world", right or wrong, to that of a more or less useful metaphorical construction that we may be able to fruitfully relate to our basic experience to a greater or lesser degree. To be agnostic about the claims of a metaphysical set of beliefs, we do not have to reject the whole set of representations of the world that it has built up, only the idea that this set of representations has an absolute validity. Indeed it is important *not* to reject the set of representations itself, just to start taking those representations much more provisionally: as a story rather than as a truth. To treat them provisionally, as a story or a hypothesis, is to defuse their metaphysicality, rather than creating a rival metaphysicality through complete and absolute rejection. For example, in rejecting the metaphysical claim that Jesus was the son of God one does not reject the stories about Jesus, or even the significance of him being the son of God in those stories: only the abslute truth or falsity of such an assertion.

As often, the debate about God's existence provides a particularly clear example of these issues. Hard agnosticism about God's existence is difficult to maintain in the face of both theistic and atheistic expectations. Both sides tend to try to exploit the sceptical arguments that support agnosticism for their own purposes, and to sweep agnostics either into their own camp or the opposing camp. Both theists and atheists have contributed to sceptical slippage here by labelling agnosticism "negative atheism"[43], on the assumption that anyone who doesn't believe in God can be lumped together with those who deny the existence of God. Atheists sometimes assume that God's existence is an empirical matter, and thus, on the basis of empirical standards of proof (which will be discussed in section 2), reject God as non-existent because of the lack of empirical evidence[44]. This tends to make agnostics just look like people who can't make their mind up in a case where the evidence is clear, rather than people who take God's existence to involve metaphysical claims which are immune from evidence. Alternatively, atheists may attack the a priori justifications for believing in God using sceptical arguments which only support agnosticism[45], thus acting as a spoiler for arguments for agnosticism and further confusing the issues.

At least in the debate about God the concept of agnosticism is recognised, even if it is widely misunderstood. Try being an agnostic in the debate about the mind-body problem, for example, or in the debate about the absolutism and relativism in ethics, and you may as well be talking Klingon – even the idea that agnosticism is a serious, coherent option that is not just 'sitting on the fence', let alone the idea that it might be the key to objectivity, is completely alien both to most philosophers and to the wider public. Their response, then, is either to reject it as on the other side, or incorporate it into their own, despite the fact that many practical responses to these issues begin with such agnosticism. For example, any legal resolution to the moral dispute about the permissibility of abortion other than a total ban or free abortion on demand (such as those adopted in the UK by the 1968 Abortion Act or in the US by Roe vs. Wade) must implicitly assume that a foetus is neither wholly a person nor wholly not a person, for

---

[43] It seems to have been an atheist (at the time), Antony Flew, who first used the term: see Flew (1994).
[44] E.g. Dawkins (2007)
[45] Ibid

the state would otherwise either become accessory to murder or be interfering unjustifiably in women's property rights. Metaphysical agnosticism is the obvious practical solution, yet it often does not even appear on philosophical horizons. Our theory has often yet to catch up with our practice.

Western thought since the enlightenment is full of figures who seemed to be breaking the mould in their time, because they questioned metaphysical orthodoxies, but who failed to break the final orthodoxy of dualism. Sometimes they achieved some measure of popularity, because they seemed to relate to at least some of the suppressed experience of the people of that time. However, because their scepticism was only selective and there were further conditions in experience that their approach prevented them from addressing, they became new figures of a counter-orthodoxy. So it was with Descartes and Hume, with Kant, Hegel, Marx and Schopenhauer, with Mill, the Logical Positivists and Wittgenstein, with the Pragmatists and Existentialists and Postmodernists[46]. All of these figures rejected revelatory metaphysics, but many of them substituted a priori metaphysics. Rather than coming fully to terms with uncertainty, they merely attacked the certainties of their opponents, whilst relying on new certainties of scientific fact, of mathematics, of historical inevitability, of individual freedom or of relativism. Even that Protean arch-ironist, the indefatigable critic of metaphysical certainties, Nietzsche, relied upon an aesthetic elitism[47]. Some philosophers, like Nietzsche and Wittgenstein, even adopted an anti-systematic style, but this was no indicator of a lack of metaphysical assertions in their thinking[48]. Irony, also, that last refuge of the nihilist, is no indicator of philosophical progress, but merely a lack of confidence in putting forward even provisional

---

[46] All of these figures are discussed in detail in Ellis (2001) chapters 3 and 4.
[47] Ibid 4.g
[48] Ibid 4.e. and 4.g

assertions that supports negative assumptions about whatever one might put forward.

There have been two main ways in which modern philosophers have clung onto metaphysical beliefs. One tradition, beginning with Hume and inherited today by analytic philosophy (as well as academics in many other subjects) depends on the fact-value distinction (which I will deal with in the next chapter) to give a status to scientific knowledge that it does not give to ethics. In analytic philosophy, metaphysical assumptions are thus made about the relativity of ethics, the 'objective' nature of scientific truth, and also about the absolute status of a priori claims (dealt with in 1.f). Another, 'continental' tradition, going through the existentialists to the postmodernists, often takes a relativist view of scientific beliefs as well as moral ones[49].

Relativism of any kind requires the denial of a metaphysical belief in absolute and universal standards of truth – a denial that is just as metaphysical, and in the process involves just as many contradictions, as the affirmation. First amongst the contradictions is the relativist's paradox – that a relativist is making a universal and absolute statement of relativity. In the process of denying universal values, other equally metaphysical values must also be affirmed (given that we cannot be value neutral), which means that relativists end up by default affirming the justification either of their society's values or of the choices of individuals. For further discussion of relativism see 7.a.

Sceptical slippage is a pervasive problem for anyone seeking to put forward metaphysical agnosticism. One battles against the difficulty people have even in understanding agnosticism as an alternative. If you have read thus far and think that Middle Way Philosophy is 'really' absolutist or relativist, really

---

[49] See Ellis (2001) 4.a, 4.g. and 4.i for a fuller discussion.

in one camp or the other – perhaps that it is just a new manifestation of relativism or secularism or naturalism – then you will not have understood it yet. I would ask you to continue to give me the benefit of the doubt for the moment and let the cumulative advantages of the agnostic position unfold a little further.

I. Against the fact-value distinction

The fact-value distinction is, unfortunately, widespread wherever there is serious thinking about science, ethics or aesthetics in the Western world. It is based on the logical argument used by Hume[50], that a value claim cannot be implied by a factual claim – you cannot derive an 'ought' from an 'is'. For example, according to this approach even the claim "Everyone believes murder is wrong" would not, if true, imply "murder is wrong."

This logical distinction is based on the assumption of different justifications for believing factual and value claims. Factual claims are taken to be justified either through observation or through *a priori* reasoning, whilst value claims are taken to be conventionally agreed within a group or society. By this means, 'facts' become in principle absolute – verbal claims that have been tested for their precise correspondence to reality – whilst 'values' become in principle relative because they lack this correspondence. Even many thinkers who do not accept the relativism of Hume's account of ethics have accepted the fact-value distinction, though they have offered different kinds of justifications for a universal ethics, such as revelation or intuition.

The effect of the fact-value distinction has been disastrous for Western ethics, because it has consigned all thinking to the dualism between absolutism and relativism. If one accepts Hume's account of the matter (as many analytic philosophers have) ethics can consist only in the analysis of what people happen to think about ethics in your context, with there being no further way to show that this ethics has any universal validity. If, on the other hand, you challenge Hume's relativism but still accept the fact-value distinction, the justifications for

---
[50] Hume (1978) p.469

ethics that you can offer can only be based on the dogmatic over-extension of intuitions or *a priori* reasoning. Ethics has become either the preserve of mere conventional analysis or of extravagant metaphysics.

The fact-value distinction has also been disastrous for the status of science. Although it might seem that in the short term the distinction gives scientific claims a superior status separated from 'subjective' values, in the longer-term this has undermined appreciation of the degree of objectivity offered by science, by making its claims appear merely dogmatic when its pretensions to represent reality were punctured. Once sceptical arguments are applied to science, and the relativity of scientific claims starts to be appreciated, the dualism created by the fact-value distinction leads to the sudden loss of the credibility of science rather than an incremental calibration of that credibility in accordance with the evidence, and the falseness of the distinction, being revealed, leads to scientific 'facts' being seen as mere relative 'values'. Those who now believe that creationism is a scientific theory to be treated on equal terms with evolution theory, or that homeopathy is a medical treatment to be given parity with mainstream Western medicine, do so by assuming that science, too, is 'just' a value judgement. Science is now getting (if you can excuse the pun) a dose of its own medicine, as an effect of previous support for the fact-value distinction under the illusion that the distinction helps to maintain objectivity. To get rid of the fact-value distinction would be in the interests of science, by enabling the public to grasp the basic point that justification is a matter of degree.

There are some philosophers who have attempted to challenge the fact-value distinction, but these have mainly done so using analytic methods, and by trying to find exceptions to the general rule, where it is claimed that our intuitions tell us that a value claim is implied by a factual claim. Thus Searle, for example, claimed that factual claims about promises implied value claims about the normativity of keeping them[51], and MacIntyre argued that the context of a 'practice' such as football, farming or sociology was one in which facts about certain kinds of effective actions within that practice implied values[52]. However, the ways that this approach is circumscribed make it impossible for it to challenge the absolutism vs. relativism dualism Hume created. Searle and MacIntyre were merely identifying occasions when people assume, disputably, that certain kinds of actions are good, not identifying any justification for believing that they *are* good in a more universal sense. Analysis by itself will only ever provide you with a description of what people believe, not with grounds for prescription. The very distinction between description and prescription is one established by the fact-value distinction, so that accepting analysis as the only legitimate ('factual') method of philosophical investigation into this problem is itself to implicitly accept the fact-value distinction.

Instead, we need to question Hume's assumptions and look at the problem more widely. The prime questionable assumption made by Hume is that facts and values are justified in entirely different ways. This in turn assumes that value claims are subject to sceptical argument in ways that facts are not. Hume's response to scepticism about empirical facts was naturalistic – he thought that we could not defeat the sceptical argument, but that we were simply not able to take it seriously, and should rely on observation as the most informative basis of judgement available. I have already commented on this argument in 1.b, pointing out that Hume has falsely assumed that the difficulties we would have in maintaining actual disbelief in our everyday perceptions should stop us taking a sceptical argument seriously, when sceptical arguments only deny us certainty about them.

---

[51] Searle (1964)
[52] MacIntyre (1985)

Against the fact-value distinction

If Hume's assumptions about scepticism are wrong, so is his assumption about naturalism. We do not have to ignore sceptical arguments about factual claims in order to develop and use science, just to take factual claims provisionally. Although in practice many scientists do take their claims provisionally, the interpretation of the status of factual claims is inconsistent because of the influence of Hume's arguments, because they can be taken to be either absolutely or provisionally correct. Furthermore, when factual claims are compared to value claims, sceptical arguments which apply just as much to the factual claims as to the value claims are not usually taken into account. "The dog is hungry" is just as subject to sceptical doubt as "You ought to feed the dog." given all the possible mistakes we could make in interpreting the dog's behaviour as well as issues of responsibility for animal care.

So, if we compare the justification of factual claims to that of value claims in the light of the full range of sceptical arguments, we find that they are not very different. The last of the ten modes of Pyrrhonism, for example, points out the relativity of moral claims, but all the others are concerned with empirical claims. All the other sceptical arguments considered in 1.a apply equally to factual and value claims – for example, both require further justification giving rise to a possible infinite regression, both are subject to the error argument, and both are subject to linguistic scepticism. There are no clear examples here of types of sceptical argument that apply to value claims but do not apply to factual claims. Both, therefore, are equally uncertain in principle, and both equally open to provisional assertion.

The fact-value distinction is also a result of the abstracted turn discussed in 1.e. Hume's argument cannot be contested in its own terms in the abstract, but it does not apply to any actual examples of people's judgements about facts or values. In the concrete situation, facts and values are never found in isolation. Whenever we assert a fact, we have a motive for doing so, which implies the value of doing so. Even a claim as apparently neutral as a mathematical claim, in the context of a mathematics classroom, comes with values attached about the value of studying mathematics (or, for younger students, perhaps the value of conforming to society's expectations that every child will study basic maths). Facts do not exist in isolation from people who believe them. Whenever we assert a value, on the other hand, there will also be implied background facts that are assumed for that value to make sense. For example, "You should eat green leafy vegetables every day" is a value claim that assumes the existence of green leafy vegetables and the capacity of the auditor to eat them (apart from, very likely, beliefs about the relationship between the nutrients found in green leafy vegetables and health).

Without the abstracted turn, the fact-value distinction is irrelevant to us, and yet it is still assumed in many arguments about ethics, particularly in the widespread perception in the West that ethics is a personal matter, a mere matter of opinion. However, if we were to apply provisionality and incrementality to ethical claims just as much as to factual claims, it could be appreciated that 'personal' opinions can be justified to a greater or lesser extent. Philosophers bear a lot of the responsibility for not thinking harder about this topic in its concrete context, and for the social results of their failure.

The fact-value distinction makes even less sense if we are prepared to reform our account of meaning in the way I will be proposing in part 3. If the meaning of a claim does not just consist in a representation of the circumstances in which it would be true (or even of the social rules surrounding the language in the claim), but rather consists in the related experience of a physical organism, both cognitive and emotive, then there is no clear distinction between the type of meaning of factual statements and that of value statements.

Against the fact-value distinction

One can no longer argue, as A.J. Ayer did on the basis of his truth-conditional theory of meaning, that moral statements are strictly meaningless, because they do not correspond to any possible state of affairs[53]. Given that the meaning of a factual statement is not purely representational in its meaningfulness to us in the first place, Ayer's emotivism is built on a set of unnecessary narrow assumptions.

One objection to such criticisms of the fact-value distinction attempts to distinguish between strong and weak versions of it, claiming that these criticisms only apply to a strong version of it, perhaps a 'fact-value dichotomy' as opposed to a 'fact-value distinction'. A weaker distinction, it can be argued, can still be made on the basis of analysis of our everyday distinctions between facts and values. Even if our claims involve a mixture of facts and values, we still distinguish them in practice as fact or value claims. A physicist's claim about the properties of hydrogen would not normally be thought of as a value claim, and "We should always tell the truth" would not normally be thought of as a factual claim.

In analytic terms this is obviously correct. We make a conventional distinction in practice between these different kinds of claim. However, when we consider the justifications for this distinction rather than merely the convention, there is not even a weak justification for the convention, given that in all possible concrete examples, facts and values remain mixed. There is also a pragmatic argument for not hardening this convention into a supposed philosophical truth, even of a weak kind. We will always recognise what is happening in practice more fully, and thus respond to it more adequately, if we take into account the ways in which facts and values are inextricably combined, and thus respond to both in any claim, rather than limiting the conditions we address by only considering one. If I recognise that the physicist's paper about

---

[53] Ayer (1946) ch.6

hydrogen is not just about hydrogen, but also the value of researching hydrogen, then I will respond better to the physicist if I take this point into account than otherwise. If we are even trying to move beyond a merely descriptive ethics, there is no point in trying to defend even a weak fact-value distinction.

Claims to have weakened the fact-value distinction or to have gone beyond it are also not fully convincing unless we can develop an alternative to it, and show how moral objectivity is not strengthened but weakened by the abstraction of values to separate them from facts. So, this chapter needs to be read in conjunction with the account of objectivity found in section 4, and the account of ethics found in section 7 – indeed, in a broader sense, in conjunction with the whole of the rest of the volumes of this book.

J. Metaphysical assumptions about the self

One more major area needs to be tackled to complete this survey of major metaphysical assumptions in Western philosophy. It is an area that interlocks with all the other sets of metaphysical assumptions: the self.

Western philosophers have sought a static quantity, or at least a clearly definable continuity, in the self. For Plato and for the Christian tradition, the self was an eternal soul, meaning that the body was contingent. For Descartes, the self was the self-conscious thinker separated from the doubtful and changing physical world. For Kant, the empirical self (that is, the self as we experience ourselves) could be distinguished from the self of apperception, the centre of experience. Even for many philosophers in the analytic tradition, who no longer take seriously the idea of an eternal soul, there is a search for continuity (whether physical or psychological) which would give a philosophically defined shape to what I mean by 'me'.

Alone in this tradition, it is Hume who consistently applies sceptical argument to the problem. In Hume's account, when I observe my inward experience, I only find various mental events (thoughts, feelings etc) which I label as 'mine', rather than any particular experience I can identify as 'me'. Hume thus concludes that there is no self, only a changing set of mental events[54].

Kantians have pointed out that Hume is looking for a self as the object of experience, when the self, they argue, is actually the *subject* of experience, shaping the very way we experience rather than being something we explicitly experience. There does seem to be a centre of experience (for more on this see section 2) – what Kantians call apperception

---

[54] Hume (1978) pp 251-263

– but this apperception is just another *a priori* condition of our experience, together with other conditions like space, time, and the assumptions of causality and substance. This is not what I think of myself as being and identify with as myself. The central distinction here is that the self of apperception is not necessarily conscious: it is just an assumed framing feature of experience. My sense of myself, however, whether directly experienced or projected onto that experience, is self-conscious, and it is this sense of myself that is subject to Hume's argument, not a possibly unconscious centre of experience.

So Hume's sceptical argument remains correct – except that, as usual, an argument that justifies agnosticism has often slipped into one of denial. Hume's argument justifies the recognition that *we do not know whether* we have a self, and have no grounds for distinguishing a metaphysically existent self from a mere assumption. It does not justify us in concluding that we have no self.

What this whole tradition of argument assumes, however, is that the self, if it existed, would be a static quantity with fixed identifiable features. Even the discussion about continuity of identity is looking for sufficient overlaps in features over time for us to be able to relate the self to a continuity. Since we do not experience ourselves as a static quantity, and we are unlikely to be satisfied by accounts of ourselves as a continuing series of overlapping features, this whole discussion appears to have missed the point. It has done this, again, through the abstracted turn which looks for cognitively identifiable objects ('facts') as opposed to recognising the meaning of terms like 'self' in terms that give due recognition to the affective and dynamic.

Experience does not offer us clear justification either for *being* a certain self, or for denying our selfhood. What we can assert on the basis of experience without metaphysical claims is that we have desires in relation to ourselves, usually to exist as a certain self (or sometimes, perhaps, not to exist). There is no sceptical problem about whether my drives and wishes are me, for it would be contradictory to say "I want some tea but I may be deluded" in a way that it could not be to say "I believe there is some tea but I may be deluded". Believing there is some tea because I want it may be wishful thinking, but I can still want it even if I do not believe there is any available. I can also be confused about what I want, but not deluded when I think I want it. I want, therefore I exist – in a sense.

Of course, this should not be taken in any cognitive metaphysical sense, but merely as a psychological point. I do not continue to exist as the same being because I continue to want, for the "I" is not anything separate from the changing wants. So Hume continues to be correct that we have no grounds for believing that the self exists as a fixed entity. Nevertheless, we experience a changing dynamic entity which we identify with – which I call the *ego*, in distinction from the self. This is merely a stipulation, a way of navigating through a minefield of contradictory usages in both philosophy and psychology. The 'self' is a term I shall be using for a metaphysical claim, whereas the 'ego' represents a dynamic experience. Some distinction of this sort has to be made, even if others would prefer to make this distinction differently or even reverse my usages of these two terms. The ego may experience continuities – of belief, of memory, of social recognition and of purpose – but these are all contingent within the experience that I call 'ego'..

This account of the self is also consistent with scientific evidence about the self-representations of the two brain hemispheres. The objectified and wilful self – what I have called the ego – corresponds to the left hemisphere's functions, whilst the right hemisphere maintains a self-view over time and in relation to others[55]. The problem of the self as understood by Western philosophers has consisted in the difficulty of reconciling these two perspectives, which will each become active when the hemisphere that promotes it is dominant, so as to explain and justify the right hemisphere view in terms of the left. This is an impossible task, because the left hemisphere has no grasp of continuity over time[56]. The self I want to be can vary from moment to moment, but the sense of the self continuing over time and relating to other wants is discontinuous with the egoistic view. Rather than asserting that either the left hemisphere or the right hemisphere view of the self is finally correct, then, it is better to think of the ego as existent within its momentary, willed limitations and to neither affirm or deny the right hemisphere self, avoiding any appropriation of it by the left hemisphere. The function of the right hemisphere is to integrate these different egos that we experience at different times, rather than either to destroy them or to give them the illusion of complete dominance.

The recognition that we cannot justify believe in a self, but that we can justifiably think of ourselves as egos with changing identifications, revolutionises a whole set of philosophical problems at a stroke. If we have changing identifications and these identifications are interdependent with our beliefs, then we can have more or less consistent and more or less adequate identifications and beliefs. The *integration* of our desires and beliefs becomes available as a criterion for objectivity that is capable of explaining the variable adequacy of our experience without appeal to metaphysics. The Middle Way becomes more than just an avoidance of metaphysics to either side, but can increasingly be understood in positive terms as a path of integration.

---

[55] McGilchrist (2009) p.87
[56] Ibid. p.76

If we understand ourselves as egos, the question of how value can be objective, so puzzling to so many Western philosophers, can be resolved. We are the bearers of value, for value is no different from desire, but desires can be more or less integrated. We do not have to destroy the ego to be moral, merely to channel it in a way that is more consistent and realistic in its demands. Nor does moral progress have any necessary connection to being "selfish" or "selfless", since ego-identifications may or may not be with one's individual body, but may be with others, or with groups or ideas.

This central point is the basis of a number of other arguments in this book, including about objectivity (section 4), justification (section 5) and integration (section 6). These in turn lead on to the more detailed accounts of different aspects of integration in volumes 2, 3 and 4. All that is required in understanding these further arguments is that you do not interpret them in the terms of the traditional metaphysical assumptions, which we should now be able to increasingly leave behind.

2. The Appeal to Experience

So far, then, I have been attempting to remove traditional metaphysical assumptions to clear the way for a philosophy built on *experience*. But what, more positively, does this mean?

This section is largely concerned with working out a relationship between Middle Way Philosophy and other movements that have appealed to experience, such as empiricism, phenomenology, and science. Middle Way Philosophy is argued to be distinct from these past movements. It also sketches out approaches to meaning, justification and integration that will be expanded in more detail later on.

Central to this presentation is the idea that experience is not just a fixed entity: not some kind of passive, neutral receptacle for what the world throws into it. Experience, rather, works at varying levels of *adequacy* which enable us to think of degrees of objective value as an inseparable part of experience.

This whole section is relatively abstract (perhaps ironically given that its topic is experience), and is directed primarily at those who might assume that Middle Way Philosophy is just a rehash of other philosophies that have previously emphasised experience, or who find my use of 'experience' so far a bit vague. Those without such concerns may prefer to skip ahead to section 3.

A. Experience and its adequacy

What is experience? In some ways the answer to this seems obvious. Experience is what happens to people: the succession of mental events associated with a particular individual. In other ways this is not so obvious. In what sense do these mental events "succeed" one another and in what sense are they "associated with a particular individual" if they are not linked by a metaphysical self (see 1.j)? Given that my experience is unique, how can I talk about it at all? Most importantly, how can we use experience to justify claims of any kind?

In the remainder of this chapter I will offer some preliminary answers to these questions. However, like the arguments against metaphysics in section 1, these answers will depend on a particular account of meaning, considered in 2.b. In the remaining chapters of section 2 I will be clarifying how this approach differs from previous approaches that have appealed to experience.

In 1.j I accepted the Kantian distinction between the self of apperception and the empirical self. This is a crucial distinction in explaining how our experience can be structured without a metaphysical self. The self of apperception is simply a framework for experience that sets the limits on what we experience and determines the format in which we experience it. Many of the limits and formats of experience appear to be universal on the evidence available to us (though, as discussed in 1.f, we cannot conclude that they are actually universal), but nevertheless, each self of apperception has an individual version of those limits and formats. For example, all of us appear to perceive objects in time and space, to assume that objects are substantial and that they relate to each other causally: however, each of us perceives a different time and space, with different substances and causes, just as different computers may each be formatted with the same software, but each use this software to process different data.

In an important sense, then, I experience my own individual universe. If this were not the case we would not be subject to many of the problems of perceptual scepticism that are due to the relativity of perspective. However, if we distinguish this universe created by the self of apperception carefully from the self as an object of experience, there is no need to draw solipsistic conclusions. Solipsism is a negative metaphysical position, which assumes that because we have no absolute proof that there are others in the universe we experience, therefore there are no others. This is an example of sceptical slippage from uncertainty into denial of a kind that should now be familiar (see 1.h). It is enough that there *seem* to be others, and that our apperceptional universes *appear* to interact. We are also released from any requirement to identify other metaphysical *selves,* if we can let go of the idea of others being selves and instead think of them as egos (in the sense discussed in 1.j). There is no 'problem of other minds' if we refuse to get hung up on worries about the *reality* of other minds but merely investigate experience.

There are also obviously ways in which our experience interacts with the ways in which we signify it. We do not need to think only of experience happening first and then us describing or representing it, but also of representations influencing the way in which we experience our universe. One simple example of this is the selectivity of perception when we are searching for something. We have a representation in our minds of what we are seeking, which, put together with our drive to seek that thing, causes us to concentrate only on experience that may aid our search. If I am looking for greenfly on a rose, I am not likely to be admiring its bloom at the same time. Various psychological experiments have indeed shown that people can ignore bizarre and unexpected events when they are intent on something else in the field of view.[57]

This influence from our representations does not prove that there cannot be any experience that is independent of our representations and the expectations that they create, only that there is an interplay. We can always be surprised, and our representations may lead us to be more or less prepared for such surprises. If we believe that we know the universe, for example, surprises may be much more damaging than if we manage to maintain a degree of provisionality in our beliefs about it (see 1.c). In terms of the brain, if we stay in a state of left-hemisphere dominance we will assume certainty about the universe we represent to ourselves, but if we allow sufficient interaction with the right hemisphere we will be alert for threats to that universe. There seems to be good evidence that the right hemisphere does remain alert for such threats without the conscious linguistic activity of the left hemisphere being involved[58]: but it is still possible for a dominant left hemisphere to completely ignore its promptings.

We can try to *signify* experience, then, because the signification is linked to the experience in our minds. We can *tag* a set of words, a symbol, a mental picture or even an entirely abstract code, to our memory of a particular experience. However, as previously argued (1.a) we cannot be sure of any precise relationship between the experience and the signification, beyond the moment that we link the two. We may make mistakes ourselves about the link due to lapses in memory, and clearly others may attach a quite different signification to a particular set of words or symbol to what we intended. When I "talk about" my experience, then, all I do in effect is make a fallible mental link between the experience I am trying to signify and the experience of the signs I use to tag it in myself or in others.

---

[57] See Chabris & Simons (2010)
[58] McGilchrist (2009) p.107

Middle Way Philosophy 1: The Path of Objectivity

To create a claim about an experience, I not only make this significating link, but associate that link with representational belief. Within my private universe of experience, I construct a smaller universe, the universe I believe I inhabit. This smaller universe is made out of propositions or other representations.

So what could justify me in putting forward propositions that are claimed to represent "the universe"? Not any certainty of its relationship with an actual universe, nor even any certainty of relationship with the universe of experience, as I have already explored. Instead, it must be the adequacy with which those beliefs have been formed, and the provisionality with which they are held.

If my beliefs merely state pre-conceptions, or pre-conceptions that are only modified slightly by experiences from beyond those preconceptions, they are not very adequate. If my experience itself has been shaped to a large extent by pre-conceptions, then the experience itself will not be very adequate, even if I report that experience fully. If I investigate thoroughly with an open mind, and represent my experiences as faithfully as I can, but then am not open to modifying my claims subsequently in the light of further experiences, my justification also loses adequacy.

So, more generally, adequacy can be understood as the openness with which the universe is experienced and represented, not just at one time but over a period of time, taking into account the limitations of our experiences and representations. Physiologically, this will correspond to the extent of effective links between left and right hemispheres, that have not been inhibited by excessive left hemisphere dominance.

Adequacy can be limited both by things that we expect to find that unduly dominate our experience and representations (positive metaphysics), and by things that we do not expect to find that we are thus not open to experiencing and representing, because we reject any theoretical conception of them (negative metaphysics). So positive metaphysics tends to limit our experiential adequacy through confirmation bias, and negative metaphysics through disconfirmation bias. A believer in angels will look for them and see them in the architecture, whilst a denier of angels will not even look for them and is thus extremely unlikely to see them. Both are equally mistaken in the ways they limit their experience. Those with more adequate experience still need to be looking for something – whether angels or litter-bins – but will do so more flexibly and with a greater openness to the unexpected.

However, there is also a further aspect of experience that needs to be incorporated into this complex, balanced picture. This is the demand of action. Our experience does not occur passively in a vacuum, but is rather a function of our active behaviour in shaping our environment. Adequacy of experience must thus include not just adequacy of judgement in relation to what we represent as being the case in our constructed universe, but also adequacy of judgement as to how and when to act. Since action cuts off contemplation, our suspension of judgement often must have a time limit. I cannot look too hard for angels when I have to find bread for my family. My maximising of experiential adequacy must be maximising in the practical circumstances.

Very often our motive for accepting a certain provisional account of things is practical. My physical desires drive me to seek food, shelter, social status, stimulus or respite. To seek these things I must provisionally accept an understanding of the world in which they both exist and are important to me. Nevertheless, my search for bread need not bar me from distinguishing between types of bread that are more or less nourishing and acceptably produced. My anxiety about social status need not prevent me from being an empathetic observer of others as far as I am able. Nor need my need for stimulus lead me to accepting either distracting trash or baffling obscurity, when the need for stimulus itself can help me to understand the world around me at a level I can understand and absorb. Positive and negative metaphysics potentially interfere with the adequacy of my experience not just in moments of scientific investigation or disinterested philosophical contemplation, but also in everyday practical decision-making. I gain in adequacy by neither idealising bread, (or people, or entertainment), nor on the other hand being undiscriminating, and thus my experience is at a very basic level a differentiable ethical experience.

So, experience is not, as the early empiricists suggested, a blank slate on which we represent a precise set of impressions of the universe as it enters our senses. Nor, on the other hand, is experience a clouded mirror, a necessarily confused approximation of eternal truths known through reason, as the rationalists claimed. Instead, experience is more like a net, from which we sample the variety of the ocean's fishes, and incidentally make our livelihood. It is a net with a size of mesh that we have some influence over, and that may catch too much or too little of interest. When we create theories from our experience we also use a second net to fish a selection from the first. If either of our nets is too big or too small, is practically too easy or difficult to haul, or has too fine or gross a mesh, or has holes in it, or is vulnerable to damage, or we do not take into account the limitations of our sampling and vary the fishing grounds, we become much less effective fishermen.

B. Experience and meaning

The above theoretical account of adequacy can be strengthened further by introducing the account of meaning that has already been mentioned at several points in section 1. Although a detailed account of this theory of meaning must wait until volume 3, an outline has already been offered: meaning needs to be understood as based on physical experience, and that physical experience unites cognitive and emotional aspects of meaning. Not only should our account of the breadth of human experience influence our account of meaning, but also vice-versa.

Our experiences are clearly influenced most basically by our desires. Although things may impact on our experience that we don't want, our experience is also driven by desires, which lead us to act in ways that create further experiences. For example, I choose a holiday because of my desire for that holiday, and then my experiences are determined by it. What we signify from that experience, however, is not only influenced by what we want to signify, but by the limits of our sense of meaning.

The limits to our sense of meaning take two distinguishable (but inter-related) forms: the cognitive limits of what I am able to represent through language, and the affective limits of what I am motivated to express. Both aspects of meaning are necessary when we signify our experience. For example, I cannot talk about my experience of looking at the circuits inside a computer with anything like the specificity that a computer engineer could bring to discussing it: I do not have the specialised vocabulary or sufficient understanding of what I am looking at, so here I encounter cognitive limits. I also do not enthusiastically start a conversation with a friend about the fact that the stones used to build my house are still mortared together in the same pattern they were yesterday: this is normally just not of sufficient novelty to evoke interest (except perhaps as a special mindfulness exercise), even though I do have the technical capacity to describe it.

If we were to take a purely representational view of language, like the truth-conditional theory routinely used by analytic philosophers, then the affective elements of meaning would simply not be taken into account. My selection of experience to express in the form of words or symbols could be explained only by my technical ability to represent it, if it could not be explained by my desires or my beliefs. This would be inadequate, because the motives to use certain signs to represent my experience that I experience as affective meaningfulness are only a subset of my wider desires, and these motives are not always formulable as beliefs. To create meaning I combine affective desires to express with a technical capacity to represent, with a combined result that is reducible neither to desire, to belief or to an ability to represent.

For example, suppose I am invited to a friend's house for a meal. I am generally motivated by hunger (as well as politeness and social expectation) to eat the meal, but the aspects of my experience of that meal that I choose to signify (even to myself) are limited. I may comment on a particularly tasty dish, or the method used to cook the potatoes, but my signification is selective. That selectivity is not explained by my technical ability to talk about these things – I could have done so in detail had I wished to do so. It is also not entirely explained by my beliefs. There are all kinds of implicit and explicit beliefs that relate to the experience of the meal, such as beliefs about my relationship with the friend, the nutritional properties of the food, the moral status of eating particular foods, and so on. However, my selection of features to signify is a prior condition (though not a sufficient condition) for the explicit expression of beliefs, and my implicit beliefs may form a condition for signification but do not necessarily lead to it.

For example, it might be the fact that I chose to talk (or even just think) about the cooking of potatoes that led me to express my belief in the culinary superiority of waxy potatoes over floury-textured ones. This belief is dependent on my signification of the cooking of potatoes. Perhaps my implicit belief that I had correctly identified these vegetables I was eating as potatoes forms part of the necessary background to my talking about them, but that implicit belief would not have necessarily led to my talking about them. Instead, it was the affective meaningfulness of the potatoes – the way they impacted on my emotional experience – that made them an interesting topic of conversation or reflection, and it is this interest *combined* with my articulate use of the right grammar and vocabulary to signify these things that made my talk about potatoes meaningful.

The meaning of potatoes in my experience is thus distinguishable from beliefs about potatoes and also from the desire for potatoes. My talk about potatoes required not only a technical ability to use language signifying potatoes, but also a desire to use that language, which put together created meaningfulness that would not have existed had the cognitive or affective meaningfulness been separated out.

Thus a purely representational account of meaning, concentrating on our capacity to create verbal pictures that are capable of representing 'truth', completely neglects an important dimension of the way we conceptualise our experience – namely affective meaningfulness. This in turn leads to an inadequate epistemology and an inadequate ethics based on the fact-value distinction (see 1.i), as these depend on a theorisation of how we process experience.

Meaning in the truth-conditional account inheres in propositions, whilst in the Wittgensteinian account it inheres in language according to its communicative function in a language game. Neither of these limiting assumptions needs to be made here about the relationship between meaning and signs. If meaning can be both cognitive and affective, the signs we use to represent meaning do not have to be cognitive propositions – they are still meaningful for affective reasons if they are just exclamations, or even if they are abstract pictures or musical notes. Nor do meaningful signs have to be communicative: it is the mere act of linking an experience with a sign that makes the sign meaningful in our experience, whether or not we choose to try to communicate using that sign, and whether or not others understand and share our experience to any extent. Signs are thus an aspect of experience, rather than a separate phenomenon that attempts to comment on experience from outside. The adequacy of our signification is seen as part of the adequacy of our experience, without going to the other extreme of treating experience as entirely reducible to signs.

A parallel point can also be made about the alternative (but less common) approach to meaning that I call *expressivism*. Expressivism explains meaning only in affective terms, and does not recognise the cognitive elements in meaning. However, if we analyse our signification from experience only in these terms, we take no account of the capacity to make mental representations of different aspects of our experience. However, there are also occasions when representational ability is at a premium in communication, and any account that leaves it out would obviously be impoverished. For example, when a scientist writes up an account of an experiment, the extent to which she contributes to the advancement of understanding by doing so depends not just on being motivated to select salient features of the experiment, but having the capacity to do so precisely, probably using highly technical vocabulary. This capacity is likewise not fully explained either by the beliefs of the scientist or by her drives.

One can also think of this account of meaning in terms of the relationship between the brain hemispheres. Cognitive or representational meaning is the preserve of the left hemisphere, whilst affective meaning is the preserve of the right hemisphere[59]. Without the activity of the left hemisphere, I would have no way of linking my experiences together to form a representation of the world in which to act, but without the activity of the right hemisphere, those representations would become closed and affectively meaningless, like the words of the headteacher in the school assembly that I mentioned at the beginning of my introduction. Left hemisphere meaning is part of a self-referential closed system of truth or usage conditions, whilst right hemisphere meaning depends ultimately on physical experience, which can give life to abstractions through metaphor. As McGilchrist puts this: "Everything has to be expressed in terms of something else, and those something elses eventually have to come back to the body."[60] Rather than seeking ultimate status for either of these sorts of meaning, we need to combine them and treat both as necessary.

In order to explain our selection of experience for signification, then, we need a theory that combines both cognitive and affective elements of meaning, and that also considers meaning in distinction from desire and belief, even whilst recognising the complex interrelationships between desire, meaning and belief. The details of how a Lakoffian theory of meaning can be used to support such an account will be given in volume 3. Such a theory, however, also has a further great usefulness in providing a fuller account of the idea of the adequacy of experience mentioned in the previous chapter.

As mentioned above, experiential adequacy is the extent to which we are open to experience and able to learn from it, using provisional theory to support us but not limited by rigid prejudices. There are three levels at which we could analyse

---

[59] McGilchrist (2009) p.110-126
[60] Ibid. p.116

that adequacy further – desire, meaning and belief. Desire obviously shapes the adequacy of our experience by conditioning both situation and focus. Belief affects the adequacy of experience by being more provisional or dogmatic (for more on both these other kinds of adequacy, see 6.g, and more broadly volumes 2 and 4). Meaning, however, also plays a key role in determining what we signify about our experience and how we signify it – which then feeds back into conditioning what we actually experience.

The more capacity I have to signify, linked to an interest in signifying, the more my experience will be able to take into account experiences it would otherwise neglect. The trained scientist experiences the object of his investigation differently partly because he can talk about it in a way that makes distinctions others are oblivious to. The poet not only finds new forms of expression, but maintains an affective openness to experiences that is conditioned by the process of turning those experiences into poetry. Even the musician experiences musical sounds differently because they are part of her means of expression. Each of these figures has extended meaning in a way that also extends experience, taking it beyond the norm in specific appreciable ways.

I have already proposed an incremental view of both desire and belief: desire being more or less adequate as it is more or less consistent and sustainable over time, and belief being more or less adequate as it is more or less provisional. However, I am also going to propose an incremental view of meaning. This will come as a surprise to Western philosophers who are used to treating meaning as a set of discontinuous representational conditions, but it begins to make sense when you consider the full implications of treating meaning in both cognitive and affective terms. The adequacy of my experience is extended both by the extent to which I can represent what I experience and by the affective meaningfulness of what I experience, each of which are interdependent incremental features that can be treated quantitatively. Together these incremental features create adequacy of meaning.

Thus the adequacy of experience can be analysed in terms of the adequacy of desire, the adequacy of meaning and the adequacy of belief, each of which contributes necessary conditions to my ability to learn from experience and justify my claims on the basis of experience. My claims about the universe can be justified, not by the way in which these claims represent an inaccessible reality, but by the extent to which I (and/or my society – see 6.f) have developed these kinds of adequacy. In section 4 I will be developing my account of how this experiential adequacy can be understood as objectivity, in section 5 as a basis of justification, and in section 6 as integration.

C. Theory in relation to experience

Moving on from the relationship of meaning to experience, let us now start to consider the relationship of belief to experience. A mere signification about experience begins to become a belief when it involves theory: the positing of a representation of the world we believe exists, or at least of the one we coherently encounter. By 'theory' here, I mean quite a wide band of beliefs, from the most general (say, the theory of gravity) to the specific (there is a rose outside my window). I am also encompassing what scientists would call a 'hypothesis' when it is more provisional, or what they would misleadingly call a 'law' when it is less provisional. Even the most specific of theories involves a degree of generalisation: to conclude that there is a rose I put together my experiences over more than one instant, and of more than one feature of the flower (I have to put together the size, the colour, the shape and distribution of petals etc, to conclude it is a rose). To draw specific conclusions I am also often making comparisons with other objects to enable me to classify new ones. We really can't avoid a degree of generalisation, and hence of theory, whatever we assert.

I cannot justify my claim that an object is a rose only from my experience at one instant, because a lot more is assumed than my experience at one instant. If I were to put together my experiences of similar flowers on a number of occasions and generalise ("I will call this thing a rose") I would have a degree of justification depending on the number of occasions, but subject to uncertainties of memory and of the correct identification of the flower. In practice, with many such everyday objects, I have been taught to identify a rose since childhood and depend on other people's labelling, identification, and indeed cultivation of roses. The degree of uncertainty that comes from others' testimony here has to be balanced against the amount of experience from others that is being drawn on, which in this case seems to make it overwhelmingly likely that my belief that there is a rose outside my window is correct.

In this approach I am following Hume's view that verificatory experiences give no certainty to a theory, but that they do add incrementally to its probability – a probability that needs to be understood psychologically. However, I do not agree with Hume that we have no control over this process (Hume was a determinist or 'involuntarist' about beliefs). We are not forced by further experiences to believe the theory that they support, because we are capable of changing the theory to fit our prior assumptions, and even changing our interpretation of the implications of past experiences when we change our theory. Probability is not a kind of score-card kept by the gods, who reward us with total belief when we have totted up enough confirmatory experiences. On the contrary, it is our own attempt to measure incremental justification, and just as fallible as any other judgement.

To make our assessments of probability as reliable as possible, it is not only the number of confirmatory experiences and testimonies that need to be taken into account, but also the degree of adequacy of those experiences (and of the experiences that support the testimonies). The amount of evidence is one factor, but the quality of evidence is another, and may outweigh the quantity. If the evidence is likely to be affected by metaphysical assumptions, this is a major point against it, making it more likely that evidence will have been selected or interpreted prejudicially to fit the theory – or to not fit the theory in the case of negative metaphysical assumptions. For example, on the subject of religious experience, by far the most useful evidence comes from those who approach the subject neither with the assumption that God speaks through it, nor with the opposing assumption that it can be reduced to a material explanation.

Middle Way Philosophy 1: The Path of Objectivity

In empirical investigations, it is common to take credibility criteria into account where other people are concerned – which may involve roughly estimating the adequacy of their experience. For example, do they have a vested interest? Do they have relevant expertise or direct experience to offer? However, we do not usually apply credibility criteria to ourselves. To consider the justification of our use of experience to support theory, this is exactly what we need to do – that is, not just assess the strength and coherence of the evidence available to us, but our chances of being wrong about it. For more detailed discussion of the implications of this, see section 5.

The complexity of the response that we need to experiences that confirm a theory is given a further twist when we come to disconfirmatory experiences. We can no more prove that an experience falsifies a theory than that it confirms it, even though a falsification, once accepted, is much more decisive than a verification, as it means that the theory if wrong. If my theory is that all Scotsmen like porridge, I only have to find one Scotsman who does not to explode the theory. But is he really a Scotsman? His grandmother was English, after all. And does he really not like it? He might just be lying due to a complex about his Scottish identity, but secretly eating porridge in private. The scope for ad hoc modification of the theory or re-interpretation of the evidence is still great.

Popper's requirement for criteria of falsifiability stipulated in advance will go a long way towards freeing a theory from ad hoc manipulation. But (applying linguistic scepticism again) no such criteria are ever going to be completely free of possible category disputes and ambiguities. In the end it is recognising the falsifiability of the theory (an aspect of its provisionality) that increases the adequacy of our use of experience in supporting it. This recognition is a psychological criterion rather than the purely rational one that Popper hoped to find. Because there are no definable rules that we can apply with certainty to determine whether falsification has occurred, we are reliant on relative judgement. It is thus the objectivity of the right hemisphere and its integration of judgement, rather than the left hemisphere's quest for certainty, that will provide the crucial final move in justifying a theory.

Whilst the philosophy of science has much to contribute to an understanding of the ways in which experience can justify theory, there is one tradition of scientific method that appears to rest only on dogmatic foundations and so must be dispensed with in Middle Way Philosophy. This is the tradition of an absolute requirement for public observability. The public observability and/or reproducibility of the evidence for a theory makes it scientific according to the conventions of science, but it is only one factor contributing to judgements about the justification of theories for individuals. Some theories held by individuals may only be about privately observable matters, but this does not disqualify them from being the subject of theory. In some such cases, the adequacy of the experiences that support a theory may be much more important than the fact that they are publicly observable. This is particularly the case with meditation, where records of individual experience may provide a lot more justification for theoretical conclusions than brain scanners – not because brain scanners are not informative at all, but because 'internal' experience is the main focus of meditation and the main source of evidence about it.

So, the public observability of evidence forms only one non-essential element of the way we can use experience to justify theory. The quantity of evidence forms another aspect of this justification in finding a theory increasingly probable, but the adequacy of the experiences that provide evidence for it are the most important element. I shall be returning to these points and developing them in more detail in my account of justification in section 5.

D. The phenomenological use of terms

The phenomenological method was devised by Edmund Husserl, and consists in an attempt to use reflection and analysis to purge our language of metaphysical assumptions, and reach a point of certainty through a process of "universal epoché with respect to the being or non-being of the world"[61]. Husserl was trying to reach a point where our language reflected only experience or the necessary structure of that experience, without prior assumptions interfering with its adequacy. In a sense, whenever we reflect on experience so as to try to avoid both positive and negative metaphysical assumptions in Middle Way Philosophy, we are engaging in a process that in some ways resembles Husserl's and could be called 'phenomenological'. However, some important distinctions also need to be made.

Husserl's approach was based on what he took to be the major insight of Descartes, that if we can manage to make deductions based on experience and its conditions alone, then we will have achieved sceptic-proof certainty. However, in 1.b I have already argued that this is not the case. Descartes' claims are still subject to linguistic scepticism which points out the possibility of changes in meaning over time or ambiguities in the term "I". Husserl was engaged in the same fruitless quest for certainty, although he used Kant's apperceptional self as the basis of his deductions rather than the empirical self. However, linguistic scepticism means that any deduction whatsoever, even a=a, is uncertain, as I argued in 1.f. Far from enabling us to reach certainty, breaking off our assumptions with respect to being or non-being is a way of removing false certainty and leaving us with uncertainty.

---

[61] Husserl (1960) section 15

Nevertheless, phenomenological analysis can be useful as a way of removing metaphysical assumptions to the best of our ability, and thus making our claims better candidates for a degree of incremental objectivity. Some kinds of claims stand up better to phenomenological analysis than others, as even though they are not certain they have avoided forms of metaphysical assumptions that commonly hamper us. For example, in 1.j I suggested "I want therefore I exist". This is not philosophically true if "I" is taken to be a self rather than an ego, but its aim is to divert our view of ourselves from the fixed self to the changing ego, and thus to avoid the particular problems associated with metaphysical fixation on the self.

It will not help me very much to turn object-language into phenomenological language, and very often this is only a formalistic exercise which fails to take into account the limitations of language in the first place. If instead of "I see a white convolvulus flower", I were to write "I see a soft white irregular cylinder shape flared out at one end", I have gained only in verbosity and ambiguity, and the attempt to rule out object-language is no less subject to scepticism than the ordinary English. The dropping of all mention of object nouns or mentions of existence misses the point that noun-language can be used just as well to describe our provisional representations of a theoretical universe as it can to describe an absolute metaphysical claim. Metaphysics is created, not just by language, but by intentions and contextual interpretations that are only roughly represented in language.

The use of terms in Middle Way Philosophy, then, needs to be understood as phenomenological only in the sense of its "universal epoché with respect to the being or non-being of the world". The process of removing our reliance on metaphysical claims, however, is not merely a matter of phenomenological analysis (in fact, not very much a matter of phenomenological analysis at all!) but rather a psychological process in which the way we hold a belief becomes more provisional. Changing our language to make it phenomenologically compatible involves the removal of obviously metaphysical points for identification (such as 'God', 'Nature' etc, or their denials) but not noun-extraction, and the result of our phenomenological approach is not a Cartesian absolute but a provisional standpoint.

E. The limitations of empiricism

By appealing to experience, Middle Way Philosophy might be labelled as a type of empiricism. However, great care needs to be taken in applying that label – and, to avoid confusion, it is probably best not to apply it to Middle Way Philosophy at all. The various forms of empiricism in Western philosophy have been laden with almost as many unnecessary metaphysical assumptions as the rationalists. Before closing this section on experience, it is as well to ensure that the appeal to experience in Middle Way Philosophy is not confused with those made previously by empiricism.

One of the major metaphysical assumptions made by empiricists since Hume has been the fact-value distinction, already tackled in 1.i. However, this assumption arose in association with others. Facts could only be assumed to be justified in a different way to values if it was assumed that there was a definite way to prove them. There are three common ways to do this, which could be described as the Aristotelian and Humean forms of naturalism, and positivist phenomenalism.

In Aristotelian naturalism, the universe is taken to be structured in such a way that we can gain understanding of it. Every object in the universe, for Aristotle, has a distinct form that is intelligible, even if its ultimate matter is not so. This is still the basis for one possible form of empirical realism, but it is obviously based purely on dogma – we have no way of knowing that the universe is human-shaped in this way[62].

Humean naturalism, the more recent and sophisticated form, admits that there is no response to scepticism, but nevertheless argues that we cannot help believing in what the

---

[62] For further discussion see Ellis (2001) 4.b.ii

senses present to us. We believe in the facts presented to our senses despite scepticism, because (as was discussed in 1.b) Hume thinks that we cannot continue to take it seriously. As I have already argued, this is based on a misunderstanding of the implications of scepticism. It is also based on an involuntarist account of how we form beliefs (see 2.c) that presupposes determinism, a dogmatic metaphysical belief that goes far beyond experience. We *can* help what we believe to the extent that we can evidently respond to it in differing ways.

In terms of its practical effect in promoting belief in science, there is not much difference between the Aristotelian and Humean brands of naturalism. However, it is Hume's version which has given rise to the fact-value distinction, which Hume himself first made (see 1.i), and has been much more influential over modern analytic philosophy.

Hume's supposed respect for scepticism is also sharply at odds with his theory of ideas and impressions, which attempts to provide grounds for foundational certainty from sense-experience. He does this by analysing ideas into impressions, alleging that all ideas must derive solely from sense-experiences, and analysing all impressions into simple atomic packets of sense-data. Each of these simple impressions, it is reasoned, provides a definite source of information from the universe, even if it is then assembled by the mind into complex and abstract forms[63]. Although the precise form of Hume's theory has not stood the test of time, the concept of phenomenal atomism has not gone away (being turned by the early Wittgenstein into a logical atomism[64]). Any form of atomism, however, runs into the problem of linguistic ambiguity. How do we know which way the universe is meant to be cut up, and how do we know when we have reached the final atomic units, even if we are dealing with atoms of

---

[63] Hume (1978) pp.1-7. For further discussion also see Ellis (2001) 4.c.ii
[64] Wittgenstein (1961)

The limitations of empiricism

experience or its analysis rather than atoms of substance itself?

Logical atomism gave way to the third type of empiricist response – the positivist phenomenalism of the logical positivist movement. Rather than attempting to prove the existence of a world that we observe, or even arguing that we can't help believing in it, the logical positivists developed a phenomenalist sense-data theory that denied the existence of a material world beyond potential packets of sense-data, and used linguistic methods to give a privileged status to theories about scientifically-observable sets of sense-data over other theories. Verificationism depended on the assertion that unverifiable propositions are strictly meaningless. The dogmatism now, then, is not materialistic or deterministic but linguistic. Whatever your experience of the meaningfulness of moral or religious expressions, the logical positivists were obliged to impose a blanket meaninglessness on them. This was a major mistake because, as I have argued (see 2.b) meaning is affective as well as cognitive, so the logical positivists simply cast aside a whole dimension of our experience of meaning and tried to define it into nothingness. The problem with metaphysics is not its lack of meaning but its lack of relationship to experience – a point that the logical positivists had some inkling of but were unable to theorise usefully.[65]

Apart from the doomed atomistic project and logical positivism, the main recourse of modern empiricists has been convention. There is no answer to why we should accept information from the senses apart from the fact that we do. Analytic epistemology, rather than attempting to solve the problems of scepticism, is now overwhelmingly concerned with merely definitional issues, where the basis of any solution consists only in identifying intuitions that we conventionally accept.

---

[65] For further discussion see Ellis (2001) 4.d.iii

Middle Way Philosophy 1: The Path of Objectivity

The overwhelming reason for rejecting contemporary empiricism, then, is that it is mired in dogma, and in turning to conventionalism has effectively given up on the main challenges of philosophy. Middle Way Philosophy is not 'empiricist' in any of these senses, because it begins by taking sceptical arguments seriously and by rejecting the fact-value distinction. Hume can still be an inspiration because he set much of the agenda on the crucial issues, but his theories are too deeply flawed and too contradictory to be in any way a foundation for further progress.

Some other further features of empiricism are its rejection of *a priori* reasoning as a basis of knowledge, and its reliance on the five senses. Here its account of 'experience' as a basis of knowledge also seems unnecessarily narrow, and indeed compares unfavourably with phenomenology. Internal experience of physical pleasures and pains, emotions, thoughts, imaginings and other mental events are just as much sources of information as the five senses. Indeed, as we have seen through the sceptical arguments (1.a) and the complexity of experience (2.a), the products of the senses are often not distinguishable from the influence of mental events. The boundary between 'internal' and 'external' is a fuzzy one that can hardly be made the basis of rules that distinguish acceptable judgements.

Reasoning is also an aspect of experience, both because reasoning is something that we experience doing, and because we can hardly distinguish 'experience', often heavily conditioned by reasoning, from reasoning about experience (much of which may in any case be processed unconsciously). This reasoning may be about the *a priori* conditions for experience, or about mathematics or logic. If we include the *a priori* within the purview of experience, accepting its *general* but not *absolute* validity, we immediately defuse the centuries-old conflict between empiricism and rationalism. The

The limitations of empiricism

unnecessary narrowness of empiricism consisted in trying to exclude it, and the narrowness of rationalism from privileging *a priori* reasoning above experience and giving it a falsely absolute status.

Thus Middle Way Philosophy is also distinguishable from empiricism in the very much wider scope it gives to its account of experience. Experience, after all, is just what happens to people. This wider scope for experience is a crucial aspect of the way in which it attempts to overcome dualism by incrementalising metaphysical absolutes.

3. The Middle Way

We have now perhaps covered enough philosophical ground to introduce the key term that gives its name to Middle Way Philosophy – the Middle Way. The fact that this term comes originally from Buddhism generally means that a fair amount of background explanation needs to be given first, in order to avoid instant presumptions either of Buddhist scholarship or Buddhist apologetics. However the first two sections should have made it clear that I am not doing either of these, but rather practical philosophy which begins from first premises and assumes a Western context of thought. Even now, I am not about to start invoking the Bodhisattvas or offering gnomic quotations from Tsongkhapa.

Nevertheless, the Middle Way is a shaping influence of Middle Way Philosophy that needs to be acknowledged. I also need to make it clear what I think the Middle Way is, how it relates to themes explored so far such as the avoidance of metaphysics and adequacy of experience, and to what extent I agree or disagree with Buddhist conceptions of it. This section, then, explains not only the origins and modification of the idea, but also how the Middle Way is integral to some of the other key concerns of Middle Way Philosophy.

A. Buddhist inspiration without Buddhist justification

As far as we know, the key concepts of the Middle Way were first explicitly recognised and formulated by the Buddha – that is, the historical religious leader Siddhartha Gautama, who lived in what are now the states of Bihar and Uttar Pradesh in northern India around 500 BCE. This does not mean that the Middle Way was not implicitly recognised independently elsewhere both before and after this point, as it can be implicitly developed merely by the steady application of reflective awareness in practice. I will suggest in 3.c some ways in which the Middle Way can be implicitly found in both Christian and Islamic traditions.

Recognising the Buddhist origins of the Middle Way here is largely a matter of politeness, in accordance with the academic conventions for recognising a source. Some referencing is justificatory, giving further evidence researched by somebody else to back up one's own theory. In this case, however, the fact that the Buddha first made it explicit is not relevant to its justification, any more than belief in gravity is justified because Newton first formulated scientific theories about it. To establish justification for believing in Newton's theories about gravity, one does not make references to Newton's writings and then leave it at that: one gains an understanding of the theory and then tests it out in experience. Similarly, when one is dealing with a general theory like the Middle Way, that theory is justified by the consistency of evidence about it in the experience of everyone who is capable of understanding the discourse, not by an absolute source of knowledge through *a priori* reasoning or revelation (see 1.f and g). In the same way that Newton's writings are now a historical by-line in scientific investigation, read largely only by historians of science, in the same way, the Buddhist origins of the Middle Way should soon become largely a historical by-line mainly of interest only to specialists. The trouble is that Buddhists don't tend to see it that way.

The Buddhist tradition has frequently confused the Middle Way as general theory with the Middle Way as revelation, with the result that a great many metaphysical beliefs have entered Buddhist tradition with alleged revelatory justification, such as beliefs about an enlightened state, universal conditionality, and karma and rebirth[66]. Often this belief in revelation is presented as trust in the Buddha's personal testimony, but the Buddha is far too remote a figure, mediated by millennia of transmission, translation and interpretation, for his teachings as they are recorded today to be given the moral authority of someone we know personally or have well-justified beliefs about (see 7.e on moral authority). In any case, even if the Buddha did have moral authority, this would not justify the revelatory use of his teachings by a large section of the Buddhist tradition.

In the case of the Buddha, the source of assumed revelation comes from the Buddha's alleged status as an enlightened being, and the belief that the Buddha being enlightened somehow guarantees the truth of his teachings. Even if the Buddha had somehow gained absolute knowledge, the idea that his teachings could convey it in words runs counter to linguistic scepticism (see 1.a). The recourse to a tradition of wordless intuition (emphasised a good deal in Zen, for example) is not subject to linguistic scepticism, but offers a tradition of inspiration rather than revelation. A tradition of wordless intuition passed on from the Buddha can hardly justify verbal revelations from spiritual masters further down the line of inspirational transmission without inconsistency.

So, the Buddha's words need to be examined and tested in the same way as anybody else's, but nevertheless in the rest

---

[66] See Ellis (2011a)

of this chapter I will, out of politeness, indicate some of the most important sources of the Buddha's teachings about the Middle Way. This is not meant to indicate either that the Buddha did not say contradictory things elsewhere, or that my interpretation of what the Buddha said is the only possible one. I am not interested in scholarly disputes about what the Buddha really said, or what he really meant by what he said – whatever you think he said, the question is whether you can incorporate it into a consistent and practically helpful account that will be of long-term help to the world. The following particular selection and interpretation of the Buddha's teachings in relation to the Middle Way seems to me a helpful one – whilst those that assert, for example, that the Buddha really knew metaphysical truths but kept them esoterically hidden, may or may not be correct but are not helpful.

1. The Middle Way is first introduced alongside the Eightfold Path in the the *Dhammacakkapavatanasutta* (Sutta on turning the wheel of the Dharma) in Samyutta Nikaya 56.2. Here it is made clear that the Middle Way is a practical path which avoids the extremes of eternalism and nihilism (see 3.d). The practical nature of the path is made clear by its linking to the Noble Eightfold Path, which gives eight areas of practical development: wisdom, aspiration, concentration, mindfulness, effort, action, speech, and livelihood. These eight areas link together philosophical understanding with practical activity and psychological work on mental states.

2. The parable of the raft from the *Alagaddupamasutta* (Majjhima Nikaya 22:13-14) offers a famous teaching of the importance of provisionality in the holding of beliefs. The Buddha compares his teachings to a raft which is used for a certain practical purpose – the crossing of the river Ganges – but would only be an encumbrance if carried further after the river crossing. This suggests that a belief starts to become metaphysical when we hold onto it only due to our egoistic

identification with it, regardless of its practical usefulness or relevance.

3. The 'silence of the Buddha' (*avyakata*) occurs at several points in the Pali Suttas (e.g. in the *Culamalunkya Sutta*, Majjhima Nikaya 63). Here the Buddha refuses to answer questions about metaphysical questions that are of no practical relevance, such as the origins of the universe or the existence of the soul. When pressed, he says that either affirming or denying positions on these topics would not be helpful. Here is an indication that the Buddha meant the Middle Way to involve hard agnosticism about metaphysical positions: though amazingly, Buddhists often only apply this to the metaphysical positions specifically mentioned in the scriptures, rather than the ones that affect us most today (or, of course, the ones widely believed in by Buddhists!). This failure to relate a specific teaching to an obvious more general principle is a bit like arguing that Jesus' parable of The Good Samaritan only applies to helping injured travellers and not to other acts of compassion.

4. The simile of the ocean in the Udana 5.5 stresses the importance of incrementality, comparing the teachings to an ocean that gradually slopes down and can be entered to different degrees. Since incrementality is one feature found in experience that is never present in metaphysical claims, this provides a further indication of the importance of keeping theory compatible with experience (see 1.c).

5. The *Kalama Sutta* (Anguttara Nikaya 65) shows the Buddha responding to a group of villagers who are confused by the multiplicity of contradictory claims by different religious teachers. They are seeking epistemological advice – how should they judge who to believe? The Buddha emphasises the importance of experience as the basis of judgement ("When you yourselves know..."), but the criteria for judgement using experience include reference to the wise. This suggests

that the Buddha did not support revelatory claims, but accepted that moral authority of a kind that gives increased credibility to a teacher depends on direct trust, which in turn has to be based on experience rather than remote, traditional claims.

6. The Middle Way is also symbolised (rather than explicitly taught) in the traditional story of the Buddha's life before he was said to have achieved enlightenment. This has a clear dialectical structure (see 3.k). The Buddha first lives in an enclosed, protected environment as a privileged prince, but becomes dissatisfied with the conventional values of that environment. He then leaves home and is taught by a succession of spiritual teachers, whose limitations he quickly comes to perceive, and associates with a group of ascetics, whose values he also rejects after trying them out. The Buddha is here going through a practical process of learning by trying out lifestyles dominated by opposed metaphysical views (particularly the belief in absolute moral values accepted by the teachers and ascetics, in contrast to the relativist conventionalism of his home background). He becomes dissatisfied with both extremes, and manages to make progress by going beyond the sets of assumptions each represents.

In this final story, a key point about the Middle Way is presented. It is exploratory. It involves a process of moving on from the limitations of one's starting point in pursuit of greater objectivity. In the process one is more successful in gaining objectivity if one learns from opposing claims and accepts their limitations, rather than wholly committing oneself to one or the other.

B. The limitations of traditional Buddhist presentations of the Middle Way

Although the Buddhist tradition is our chief explicit source of Middle Way theory, on the whole it says far too little about the Middle Way. Hundreds of books are published about Buddhism every year, but I have yet to come across a serious attempt to update the Middle Way or explore its implications amongst them. Although it is accepted as a key part of what the Buddha taught, it is not given much emphasis by any contemporary school of Buddhism, but in introductions to Buddhism is often simply identified with the Eightfold Path or with conditioned arising[67]. If it is identified with the Eightfold Path we are told what areas to work on, but not how to work on them or how to make judgements as to what would actually constitute Right View, Right Speech, Right Effort etc. The distinctive insights that Buddhism has to offer about what sorts of views, speech, effort etc would be helpful to us are not given prominence when Buddhism is presented in this way.

As for identifying the Middle Way with dependent arising (or conditioned genesis, or however else you translate *paticcasamuppada*): as a general principle this is either so basic to our experience as to be completely uninformative, or it is an over-extended absolute metaphysical claim about interdependency. Either way, a presentation of interdependency in no way substitutes for a presentation of the Middle Way. The former is a metaphysical claim with no obvious practical implications, the latter a whole approach to

---

[67] Many introductory texts on Buddhism could illustrate this point, but to take two popular ones: Rahula (1959) just identifies the 'Middle Path' with the Eightfold Path (p.45), and Harvey (1990) identifies the practical Middle Way with the Eightfold Path – for monastics only (p.23) and the philosophical Middle Way with conditioned arising (p.58 and other places).

judgement that makes a huge practical difference in any context[68].

The Middle Way does play a more prominent role in the thought of the Madhyamaka school of Mahayana Buddhism, but here again it is often identified with interdependency or emptiness. The work of Nagarjuna and Chandrakirti of the Madhyamaka School is usually treated as a new more subtle and somehow 'better' metaphysics than that of their predecessors the Svabhavikas. The problem here is that there can be no such thing as a better metaphysics, given that all metaphysical claims are beyond experience and thus non-incremental and absolute. I will return to this below.

Even when they do get around to discussing the Middle Way, a long way down their priority list, both Buddhist teachers and scholars of Buddhism generally confine themselves to scholarly presentation of the traditional teachings, which at best present the Middle Way applied in a very different context from our own, rather than the exploration of Western thought in relation to the Middle Way that is required to apply the Middle Way more fully to Western life.

The Middle Way in Buddhism is often presented as two distinct ways: a practical Middle Way and a philosophical Middle Way. The practical Middle Way is presented as the Middle Way between asceticism and self-indulgence, as illustrated in the Buddha's life. The philosophical Middle Way is presented as the Middle Way between eternalism and nihilism, where eternalism (*sassatavada*) is defined as the belief in the eternal existence of the self, and nihilism or annihilationism (*ucchedavada*) is defined as the belief that the self is destroyed at death.

---

[68] For further discussion see Ellis (2011a) ch.5

Middle Way Philosophy 1: The Path of Objectivity

One of the few Buddhist writers who does develop some ideas about the implications of the Middle Way as distinct from other key Buddhist teachings is Sangharakshita. Sangharakshita makes the links between the practical and philosophical Middle Ways explicit, but in the process goes in for sweeping dogmatic claims:

How absolute is the dependence of the Middle Path in ethics upon the Middle Path in metaphysics and in psychology...should now be apparent. The belief that behind the bitter-sweet of human life yawn only the all-devouring jaws of a gigantic Nothingness will inevitably reduce man to his body and his body to its sensations; pleasure will be set up as the sole object of human endeavour, self-indulgence lauded to the skies, abstinence contemned, and the voluptuary honoured as the best and wisest of mankind. Similarly, the contrary belief that the macrocosm is grounded upon absolute Being, whether personal or impersonal, is automatically adumbrated in the sphere of psychology as the belief that above and behind the microcosm, the little world of human personality, there exists a self or soul which is on the one hand related to an absolute Being...which...is independent of the physical body.....The object of the spiritual life will be held to consist in effecting a complete disassociation between spirit and matter, the real and the unreal, God and the world, the temporal and the eternal; whence follows self-mortification in its extremest and most repulsive forms.[69]

Sangharakshita here seems convinced that belief in absolute being *necessarily* leads to belief in the eternal self, which in turn *necessarily* leads to asceticism, and its denial *necessarily* leads to denial of the self and self-indulgence. These are not very difficult claims to refute: all one needs to find is some counter examples to completely destroy these absolute claims that have allowed for no modulations or exceptions. It would be quite easy to find someone who does not believe in the

---

[69] Sangharakshita (1987) pp.162-3

Limitations of the traditional Buddhist Middle Way

eternal soul who is ascetic (say, a lean workaholic materialist scientist) or who believes in the eternal soul but is self-indulgent (say, a jolly bibulous catholic). I believe (without mentioning any names) that I have met specific examples of both these counter-example types. There are also plenty of people who are materialists about the human body and do not believe in an afterlife, but do not thereby believe in "the all-devouring jaws of a gigantic Nothingness". Marxists, for example, are materialists who have been driven by the inspiration of a Communist Society, and if anything in the process have often been rather puritanical, seeing self-indulgence as a betrayal of the people's revolution.

The odd thing about Sangharakshita's account is that it provides an insight into a relationship that seems to have largely held in the time of the Buddha, but he does not seem to have thought at all about its relationship to the variety of people around him in modern Western society, their beliefs and psychologies, and the complex relationships between them. The assumption that the Middle Way is metaphysical cuts out investigation into how it actually works in human experience, and ironically leads thoughtful Buddhists like Sangharakshita into exactly the trap they believe the Middle Way will help them escape from – that of dualistic metaphysics. One should not conclude, because the sweeping claims made by Sangharakshita about the relationship between beliefs, ethics and psychology are wrong, that there are not any such relationships: but a more cautious theoretical approach is needed to understanding these relationships, using an epistemological and critical rather than a metaphysical theory so as to de-absolutise the claims. It is this process of investigating eternalism and nihilism, initially inspired by Sangharakshita (whilst also struck by his limitations), that I first undertook in my Ph.D. Thesis, *A Buddhist Theory of Moral Objectivity*[70].

---

[70] Ellis (2001)

Middle Way Philosophy 1: The Path of Objectivity

Traditional forms of Buddhist presentation tend to take specific features of the Middle Way that were highlighted in the Buddha's context, and take them to be generally definitive of the Middle Way, rather than deriving a more general but flexible principle from the Buddha's indications. There may have been instances in the Buddha's time of people who were too ascetic because of their belief in the eternal soul, such as the five ascetics in the life-story of the Buddha, but surely the more general principle is that metaphysical beliefs of whatever kind can give support to inadequate or unintegrated attitudes, by providing rallying points for dogmatic identification? The problem for Buddhists, however, is that once you admit this point all Buddhist metaphysics must itself be dropped, and the Buddhist tradition has failed to offer a clear alternative philosophical approach that avoids metaphysics.

The Madhyamaka School has a different way of presenting the Middle Way. Here eternalism is identified with the belief that the world really exists independently of conditions, and nihilism with the belief that it does not exist[71], with the Middle Way identified with a recognition of conditional interdependency (*paticcasamuppada*). However, this is an attempt to define the Middle Way metaphysically, a metaphysical appropriation of the Middle Way (see 3.I). If you merely substitute a supposedly correct metaphysical description of how things are for the two metaphysical extremes, you leave the method of investigation untouched. The Emptiness doctrines of the Madhyamaka are neither idealist nor realist, but that does not necessarily make them adequate expressions of the Middle Way by themselves: I will explore this point further in IV.4.d.

---

[71] An account given explicitly for example, by Burton (2001) and Sangharakshita (1987) p.160

Limitations of the traditional Buddhist Middle Way

It would be quite possible to accept the idea that everything was conditionedly interdependent merely on the basis of the Buddha's revelation, but that would not lead us to change our attitude to how we address conditions in our experience. Just as with any ultimate causal claim, we do not know whether or not all phenomena are conditioned, and we do not need to speculate in general – only to theorise about the relationships between specific conditions in practice. Interpreting the Middle Way as a third metaphysical position leaves Buddhist philosophy subject to scepticism, and misses the epistemological and moral insights offered by the Buddha's rejection of metaphysics and his advice to the Kalamas. Instead, the Middle Way needs to be seen as an epistemology and ethics providing a basis to criticise metaphysics, not as a new form of metaphysics.

There can be no such thing as an anti-metaphysical metaphysics. Rather in order to get us out of metaphysics one needs to understand it in ways that are open to change and are not inevitable, and one needs to focus on the kinds of pragmatic approaches and values we need to adopt to avoid it. To my mind, the 'Emptiness' talk of the Madhyamaka rarely succeeds in doing this. However, it is of course possible to interpret it in ways that do, and I have myself been partially inspired by the Madhyamaka to seek clearer accounts of the insights it seemed to be trying to articulate.

The Buddhist attitude to the Middle Way today seems to act more as a spoiler than as the genuine basis of a critique of metaphysics. Nagarjuna and the Buddha give many Buddhists the reassuring impression that the issues of metaphysics have been dealt with – but then they are brought right back in again by the back door. If the sceptical arguments found in the Buddhist tradition were applied consistently, however, they would require the complete re-examination of many aspects of Buddhism currently taken for granted, starting with doctrines on enlightenment, karma, and conditionality. This is the subject of one of my other books, *The Trouble with Buddhism*[72], where these arguments are dealt with in more detail.

One reviewer of the first edition of this book seemed to take it as obvious that the Madhyamaka approach to the Middle Way is not metaphysical, and thus claimed that in this book I am plagiarising Madhyamaka ideas and falsely passing them off as my own – "a pompous rehash of Madhyamaka ideas in Western philosophical clothing". If only this were correct! It would have been a great deal easier to take Middle Way Philosophy off the shelf, merely extract it from scholarly or Buddhist books, and then just practise it, than to try to cultivate the seeds of understanding that I felt they offered in the more laborious way I have been doing. I would be grateful if this reviewer, or anyone else, can contact me and tell me exactly where, in Nagarjuna or Chandrakirti, or in their modern interpreters such as Jay Garfield or David Kalupahana, they find any of the basic features of Middle Way Philosophy. Where do these people write about provisionality, incrementality, or integration? Where do they offer an adequate approach to ethics that avoids relativism? How do they account for both the limitations and the successes of Western science? How do they relate the Middle Way to the structure of human brains and the cognitive biases discovered by psychology? Show me these things in the 'Emptiness' literature, and I'll happily withdraw all my books and settle down to quiet practice, rather than attempting to disrupt the academic consensus. But neither these things, nor any functional equivalents to them, are, in my experience, found in such literature. Where references to the Middle Way are found, it is almost always put in terms of something else, usually relying on a metaphysical claim, rather than explored in its own terms.

---

[72] Ellis (2011a)

Limitations of the traditional Buddhist Middle Way

Because the Madhyamaka literature says so little of real use about the Middle Way, I had at some point to cease reading it and engage instead in Middle Way Philosophy, drawing to a much greater extent on the much more fruitful resources I found in Western philosophy and psychology. I can only apologise to those who see this as a necessarily arrogant undertaking, but it seems that I cannot avoid the appearance of arrogance (for some) whilst attempting to create a basis of adequacy.

If I were also to take up any challenge to prove my contentions about the inadequacy of the account offered in the Madhyamaka in scholarly terms, I am aware of the kind of quagmire I would be entering. Any assertion I might make on the basis of my own reading or experience would probably be deemed inadequate because of insufficient reference to primary sources. If one accepts the terms of the academic conventions involved (enslaved as they often are to the Original Language Fallacy – see IV.3.I), one might be then swallowed up into decades of work in a range of oriental languages, after which one would have learnt a lot that was merely incidental, but most likely nothing new that was central to our understanding of the Middle Way in universal human experience. Any synthetic work which attempts to bring in new criteria of judgement to a scholarly field is also automatically rejected by the scholars who control what is deemed acceptable within that field. I do not make statements about the limitations of the Madhyamaka lightly, and they are indeed based on past study of the Madhyamaka and its interpreters. But one cannot reference an absence, so I will make no further attempt to justify such statements. Instead I offer an alternative, that I hope will be read properly in its own terms before anyone else jumps to the conclusion that I am 'plagiarising' Madhyamaka because I dare to use the term Middle Way.

C. The Middle Way in Christianity and Islam

If the Middle Way is a general theory, available in universal experience as far as we can tell, as I propose, then it would not be at all surprising to find it implicitly in other contexts than the Buddhist tradition, even though it seems that it is there that it has been tackled most explicitly. In fact, wherever human beings have been able to theorise on the basis of experience it would be surprising not to find some evidence of implicit models of the Middle Way. We have already discussed ancient Greek Pyrrhonism, which in many ways has an explicit version of the Middle Way, and in discussing the relationship between the Middle Way and objectivity in 3.e below I will be suggesting ways in which the Middle Way can be implicitly found in modern scientific method. There is also a case, which I will discuss in volume 5, for seeing implicit aspects of the Middle Way in the development of Western democracy.

This means that we would also expect to find implicit signs of the Middle Way in religious traditions such as Christianity and Islam. I have already indicated that I do not accept the assumption that religions are wholly defined by their metaphysical beliefs. Religions include a wide range of practices, stories, symbols and communities that may to some extent reinforce metaphysical beliefs, but in other respects reflect more exploratory and provisional beliefs. Even in the case of religious symbols that seem on the surface to only represent metaphysical claims, we have to bear in mind that the meaning of these symbols is not merely representational. God, for example, can in some ways represent a metaphysical claim, but in others a mere recognition of conditions that lie beyond the control of people (as in 'an act of God') or in Jungian analysis an archetype of integration (see discussion of archetypes in volume 3). A belief in the existence of God is to some extent separable from the meaning of God – a distinction that we sometimes glimpse when atheists admit to enjoying hymn-singing, or when Christian mystics with a close experiential relationship to God appear agnostic about his existence.

I am going to quite briefly suggest ways in which I see the Middle Way reflected in Christianity and Islam respectively. The main point of doing this is to drive home the idea of the universality of the Middle Way and its lack of necessary relationship to its explicit formulation in Buddhism. It is not intended to involve any claims that these are the 'true' or 'essential' interpretations of these religions, or that there are not huge metaphysical forces also present in both religions. However, I do think that religions are human institutions that can be steered in the direction that humans wish to steer them.

In Christianity, mediation between the ideal and the real is a central theme surrounding the incarnation of Jesus. Whilst God the Father represents a perfection which was unattainably set in the Jewish law, human sinfulness and inability to live up to this ideal (often represented by Adam) is the opposing pole of denial. Jesus as a symbolic figure can be seen as mediating these polarities by combining human and divine elements in one frame, encouraging Christians to maintain awareness of both human and divine in tension. At least some of his teachings, such as those about love, the avoidance of hypocrisy and a flexible attitude to rules (see 7.f) can be interpreted as helping with the practice of the Middle Way, so as to maintain the inspiration of the ideal whilst fully recognising the conditions of the real. Jesus' crucifixion and resurrection can also offer a potential Middle Way symbology to relate to human experience. In the crucifixion, the reality of suffering and our passive inability to change evil appears to triumph, but then in the resurrection, the optimistic triumph of ideals over conditions is again asserted beyond hope. The Middle Way here involves holding both crucifixion and resurrection in tension – facing up to conditions but at the same time allowing ideals to inspire us in not being limited by those conditions.

In Islam, too, there is a tension between the ideals of the divine and the reality of the human, with a rigorous attempt to bring the whole of society into line with an ideal (for example with prayer five times daily) balanced by legal principles that make some allowances for human limitations, such as the principle that hardship should not be unnecessarily inflicted (As it says in the Qur'an Sura 185, "Allah intends for you ease and does not intend for you hardship").

In Islam, too, the principle of *shirk*, sometimes translated as idolatry, offers a basis for criticism of metaphysics. Shirk means the association of things that are not God with God, and derives in turn from *tawhid*, the prime principle of Islam, that 'there is no God but God', i.e. we should not confuse other things with God, or reduce the transcendent to the worldly[73]. Applied consistently, this should mean that all attempts to attribute the perfection of God or the authority of his will to human utterances are, in a sense, blasphemous. By claiming to know about God, let alone claiming to know revelation, we make an important mistake. Instead, if we recognise the limitations of our humanity and seek God incrementally through addressing conditions, we might actually encounter the meaning of God as it relates to human experience. *Shirk* could certainly be interpreted in a way that prohibits metaphysics by respecting the unknowability of the transcendent. However, just as Buddhists need to face up to an inconsistency between the Middle Way and their metaphysical doctrines such as *karma*, so do Muslims need to face up to the inconsistency between *Shirk* and the belief that the Qur'an is revelatory.

---

[73] For a helpful discussion of *Tawhid* and *Shirk,* see Murata & Chittick (1994) pp 47-52

D. Defining the poles avoided by the Middle Way

In traditional Buddhism, as we have seen in 3.b, the Middle Way is seen as the path between eternalism and nihilism, understood as the affirmation or denial of the eternal self (or in the Madhyamaka version, of Reality in general). This formulation has the weaknesses of not accounting for the practical complexity of the relationships between our beliefs and motives, and not clearly differentiating the Middle Way from metaphysics. When I first started working on the Middle Way in my Ph.D, thesis, *A Buddhist Theory of Moral Objectivity* (a title later changed to just *A Theory of Moral Objectivity),* completed in 2001, I tried to take the concepts of eternalism and nihilism, and define them in a way that could be made adequate to the complexities of different ideologies and their effects. This led me to define eternalism in terms of its acceptance of an absolute source of ethics, and nihilism as the rejection of such a source, with other metaphysical beliefs being understood as tributary to this primary pair of poles.

This approach provided the structure for my analysis of Western approaches to ethics through the ages, where I categorised the key Western philosophers or schools of thought as 'eternalist' and 'nihilist'. I still think that this work (which provided the basis for the whole first half of my thesis), contains much that is useful. However, this approach also had some major drawbacks. The chief of these was that the classification of theories as eternalist or nihilist had to be defended even when there was a good deal of crossover or ambiguity (as I found, for example, in Marx and in Utilitarianism): this carried the danger of distracting the reader from the much more important point of the Middle Way as an alternative to metaphysics in general. Another drawback with this approach was that it involved presenting the Middle Way primarily as a theory of ethics. Although I think ethics is still an extremely important part of it, it is also just as much a theory of epistemology and critical metaphysics, as well as potentially of science, political philosophy and aesthetics. Allowing the navigation between metaphysical views on ethics to lead and structure my analysis of all other types of metaphysics carried the danger of a partial view of the whole set of relationships between metaphysical views.

Thus it is for reasons of theoretical economy and clarity that I have decided to stop using the terms 'eternalism' and 'nihilism' to represent the two poles avoided by the Middle Way. In a sense this decision is a somewhat belated codicil of my decision in 2008 to stop using the word 'Buddhist' to describe Middle Way Philosophy. The label 'Buddhist' undermined the theory's universality, and 'eternalism' and 'nihilism' were chosen in the past, not because they would provide the clearest way of understanding the Middle Way, but because they were used in Buddhism. I am beginning to see them as a piece of unnecessary baggage from the Buddhist tradition.

Instead, in this book I am sticking to the terms 'positive metaphysics' and 'negative metaphysics' to describe the two opposed poles between which the Middle Way navigates. These terms are not in any way synonyms for eternalism and nihilism, but also indicate a shift in conceptions from a single pair of essential poles to a plurality of inter-related poles. There are many forms of positive metaphysics, and for every form of positive metaphysics there is at least potentially an opposed form of negative metaphysics. These different metaphysical beliefs are also inter-dependent in complex ways, many of which are discussed in the first part of *A Theory of Moral Objectivity*. For example, belief in an absolute source of value is often closely associated with belief in cosmic justice of some kind, whether involving afterlife beliefs or the inevitability of eventual justice in history[74]. Conversely, the

---

[74] Ellis (2001) 3.b.i & ii

Defining the poles avoided by the Middle Way

denial of an absolute source of value is usually accompanied either by a denial of cosmic justice, or of the belief in freewill that often accompanies it[75]. However, to understand the ways in which metaphysics undermines experiential adequacy, and the ways in which different forms of metaphysics are interlinked, we do not have to impose the theoretical structure of one overriding or essential principle on each side, merely to note dominant patterns of interrelationship between metaphysical claims.

To take an example – Marx and Marxism provide interesting crossovers between types of metaphysical belief that are not so commonly associated. Marx was a materialist and a determinist, but at the same time believed he had found a source of absolute moral value in the Communist Society that would redeem humankind, known through the 'scientific' analysis of dialectical materialism. His belief in the inevitability of the Communist Society fulfilled a similar cosmic justice function to beliefs in afterlife states of reward and punishment in other religious contexts. Marx thus offers a good counter-example to the naive traditional Buddhist version of the Middle Way, showing that the 'eternalist' features of absolute ethics and cosmic justice can be combined with the 'nihilist' features of materialism and determinism. However, if one tries to classify Marx as either an eternalist or a nihilist at all one is struck by how easy it would be to argue the other way instead. In *A Theory of Moral Objectivity* I classified him as an eternalist because of my strategy of defining eternalism and nihilism primarily by their absolute or relative views of moral value: but even Marxist ethics has to be largely inferred from the way that Marxists behave, given that in theory Marxism doesn't have an ethics, for ethics is seen as merely a bourgeois construct.

---

[75] Ellis (2001) 4.a.i & ii

Middle Way Philosophy 1: The Path of Objectivity

So I have concluded that a more adequate account of the metaphysics of Marxism should merely identify different positive or negative metaphysical features of Marxist doctrine, show their inter-relationships, and show the relationship of these Marxist metaphysical beliefs to failures to address conditions. The Marxist failure to address conditions – which we can see fairly clearly in the history of what Marxists have actually done – can be seen as an ethical failure, but it can also be seen (rather as Popper saw it[76]) as a failure of the very scientific method that Marx invoked.

The poles to be avoided by the Middle Way thus need to be understood anew in each new situation of judgement, where the positive and negative metaphysical options to be avoided on each side can be understood in relation to the specific representation of the situation made by the person who needs to make that judgement. There will be positive metaphysical beliefs that are potentially inter-dependent in that situation, with negative metaphysical beliefs opposing them. Those beliefs may be ones about the world, ourselves, authorities, causes, values, boundaries in time and space, or even what counts as meaningful: a fuller categorisation of the possibilities will be found in IV. 3 & 4. But those metaphysical beliefs will all be distinguished by their absoluteness. Beyond that, we do not need to speculate about essential links between groups of metaphysical beliefs, and thus 'eternalism' and 'nihilism' are unnecessary constructions.

---

[76] See Popper (1957) and (1945)

E. Pragmatism and the feedback loop

So, how does the Middle Way address conditions? By 'conditions', I mean everything that happens in our experience apart from what we experience as choice or decision-making. This would include physical, social, and economic conditions of the outside world, the physical condition of our bodies, and our psychological states both cognitive and emotional. To 'address' them, I need to understand them with as much adequacy as possible. That means that the desires, meanings and beliefs that are my response to conditions need to be as unconstrained by prior positive or negative assumptions as possible. I am not suggesting here that we have total control over our desires, meanings and beliefs, or that we have no control – only that the degree of control we experience needs to be maximised through awareness. This is a point that will be developed further in 7.b when discussing responsibility, and in IV.3.f and IV.4.c when discussing freewill and determinism.

Another metaphysical view to be avoided here is the fact-value distinction (see 1.i). When saying that I 'need' to maximise the adequacy of my response to conditions, I am being deliberately ambiguous in terms of facts and values. On the one hand I 'need' to maximise adequacy in order to understand conditions, and on the other I 'need' to maximise adequacy because I ought to do so. See 7.c for an account of this 'ought': my argument there is that all our existing ways of understanding 'ought' imply this maximising of adequacy.

The value of understanding and the value of ethics cohere in pragmatism: the belief that our most justified responses are supported through experimentation in practice rather than metaphysically. What is meant by the term 'pragmatism' in Western tradition varies hugely because much pragmatism is still affected by metaphysical assumptions rather than being

144

based only on practical requirements – typically making the practical requirements short-term or egoistic, even though there is nothing particularly practical about short-termism or about failure to look beyond one current set of assumptions. Much modern philosophical pragmatism is also still influenced by the fact-value distinction, and thus assumes that practical judgement means relative judgement. The earlier twentieth-century American pragmatists were not so dominated by the fact-value distinction, and John Dewey, in particular, manages to create a philosophy quite close to the Middle Way through the combination of empiricist and Hegelian approaches[77].

One central feature of Dewey's psychological ethics is the negative feedback loop of reflection in response to blocked impulse. We (individually and collectively) get into the habit of acting in a particular way to achieve a particular kind of desire, until conditions interfere with that habit[78]. The impulse being blocked forces us to use reflection to consider not just other means of fulfilling the same desire, but perhaps even different ways of channelling the desire. This may result just in learning about our environment, or it may result in effects that we might readily recognise as moral progress, or it may involve both. For example, whilst on holiday in France I get into the habit of walking to the local baker to buy bread every morning. Then one day I find the baker shut. I have learnt something new about my environment – the baker closes on Wednesdays – which means that the following Wednesday I will already have made arrangements to get my bread elsewhere and will not have had a wasted walk. If that does not strike you as a discovery with obviously moral implications, there are other examples that might. A child gets into the habit of bullying another child, with both insults and blows. However, one day this channelling of the impulse is interrupted by a teacher, who

---

[77] See Ellis (2001), section 4.f, for a more detailed discussion of Dewey and the other classical pragmatists.
[78] First found in Dewey (1896), and subsequently developed in Dewey's later writings

talks it through carefully as well as imposing a punishment; this leads to an increasing recognition that the other child is a person who suffers distress just as I do. The child's impulses are then channelled into other activities than bullying.

This pragmatic model of ethical learning bears a close resemblance to Popper's account of a similar negative feedback loop in scientific discovery, which can be summarised as theorisation, practice, feedback, and retheorisation[79]. When a scientific theory is tested out, the most important information about it is gained through falsification. If our current form of the theory does not stand the test we put it to, it becomes necessary to reconsider it and modify it, even abandon it altogether. It is the role of falsification that makes this feedback loop a *negative* one, a response to frustration of going back to a starting equilibrium. The process of responding to negative feedback seems to be a function of the right hemisphere of the brain, in contrast to the tendency of the left hemisphere to reinforce its own position through positive feedback[80] (verification as opposed to falsification). As a process it is thus more favourable to objectivity than positive feedback, bringing us back to a point of equilibrium, where positive feedback can merely entrench a prejudice by providing increasing amounts of apparent evidence that is merely a confirmation of starting assumptions.

The only effective difference between Dewey's version of the feedback loop and Popper's is one that could be imposed by the fact-value distinction (which Popper relies upon). Otherwise, the way that we learn about facts and the way that we learn about values is similar: through experimentation in practice that leads to the modification of our current desires and beliefs. The model of experiential adequacy can also be applied in either case, because the new model we will have

---

[79] Popper (1994)
[80] McGilchrist (2009) p.231-2

Middle Way Philosophy 1: The Path of Objectivity

created in response to the feedback in each case will be a more experientially adequate model than the one we had before.

This feedback-loop model can be applied equally to individual learning and to group or social progression. It can be used just as much in relation to our desires or ends (if we cannot get one thing that we want, we shift to wanting something different) as to our beliefs (if one understanding of the world fails, we modify it). I also suggest that it applies equally well to meaning (see 2.b). If one way of signifying is not serving our purposes, either by not representing what we need to represent or not expressing what we need to express, we modify it – for example, by learning new languages or technical terms, or by learning to communicate and express ourselves in a different medium or context.

The negative feedback loop also applies both to judgements at one time and to habitual responses over a period of time. On the one hand our judgements need to invest in the future success of the loop (by improving our moral and epistemic *virtues* – see 7.d), but on the other this should not be too much at the expense of the adequacy of current judgements. Optimum adequacy is thus produced by balancing long-term investment with short-term judgement.

The Middle Way, then, is a method for supporting this feedback loop and ensuring that it continues to work properly. If my desires, meanings or beliefs are fixed I may come back to the same blocked impulse again and again without changing my response to it, and thus not addressing conditions or improving the adequacy of my experience. Positive metaphysics will either block the feedback loop by making me certain that I have the right beliefs already, or by interpreting all evidence in terms of the positive metaphysics, creating positive feedback: so in either case I do not need to change the theory. Negative metaphysics will block the loop by inhibiting me from developing a new and more adequate belief when I encounter negative feedback, because the possibility of objective improvement has been denied. Very often these two processes are difficult to distinguish from each other, as if I believe that I have the right beliefs already this will also stop me developing new beliefs, and if I don't develop new beliefs I am effectively stuck with the old ones. The Middle Way involves the cultivation of attention to other options at the point where we encounter the frustrating factor, so that we no longer pursue ineffective, non-learning strategies when confronted in that way.

F. No final goals

The Middle Way involves the constant adjustment of goals in response to conditions, as we saw in the previous chapter, yet there are issues of motivation as well as of planning here. How can constantly adjusted goals motivate and inspire us, or give coherence to our course of action in life? Theists may talk here about the motivation of serving God, Buddhists about enlightenment as a final goal. Other individuals may talk of a sense of personal destiny or vocation guiding their lives.

It is here that we need to put together the concepts of incrementality and provisionality, to affirm the need for long-term goals in experience, and yet deny the need for metaphysical goals that go beyond experience.

Our desires readily attach themselves to imagined objects, but the adequacy of those imagined goals varies in proportion to the remoteness of their fulfilment in terms of time and conditions. The adequacy of more distant goals decreases because I do not yet understand all the conditions that may intervene to prevent them being fulfilled, and my long-term plans and goals are unavoidably vague and selective. If my goal is to cross the room and make myself a cup of tea in five minutes' time, barring a completely unexpected change of conditions (e.g. a power cut, running out of tea, a heart attack, a sudden desire for whiskey instead) I am very likely to fulfil that goal. However, if my goal is to achieve world peace, it is both a rather vague aspiration and one that could be achieved by apparently contradictory means (e.g. conquering the world and imposing peace, or negotiating settlements to all disputes). Still, if we did have a long-term goal of world peace together with a strategy for achieving it, and were able to break the necessary progress down into manageable intermediate goals, it is a goal that could just about be brought within experience.

Final goals, however, are not within experience, but rather depend on metaphysical assumptions. In the case of enlightenment as the final goal of Buddhism, for example, even if we accept debatable evidence about the nature of such a state, we cannot tell that it is a final state or that no progression is possible beyond it. Enlightenment is not within experience because it is not provisional or incremental, and there is no way of assessing its value within experience before it is achieved. We can assess the value of the remote goal of world peace, because we have experience of what peace is like as a relative state compared to war, but we cannot, by definition, have experience of a final state.

We also cannot realise a final goal by breaking it down into manageable intermediate goals, because we are not clear about what intermediate goals would be required. If we allow the intermediate goals to define the supposed final goal, then we are deceiving ourselves that the final goal is in fact our goal. For example, if we had a final goal to have divine love throughout the earth (even though we admittedly have not experienced divine love), then increasing the level of earthly love in our village would not be an intermediate goal to this final goal – in fact we would be constructing our final goal imaginatively on the lines of the intermediate one that is within the realm of experience.

The biggest mistake made by Buddhists here is not just to have enlightenment as a remote goal even though it is beyond experience, but to believe that this goal is necessary for value and motivation on the path that it defines. This theoretically implies that there cannot be value and motivation without such a final goal – which conflicts with our experience that people gain value and motivation from all sorts of sources. It attempts to support the Middle Way from a metaphysical position, when, as I argued in 3.b, only an epistemological and moral principle based on experience can help us to move beyond metaphysics.

In an Aristotelian context, the justification of claims according to final outcomes is known as teleology. Aristotle can only support his teleological view of ethics from his belief that every creature has its own form, which also determines its purpose. The fulfilment of the proper purpose of a creature is hence its teleology. This depends on the metaphysical idea that we can have knowledge of an essential form from which to derive this idea of our proper purpose[81]. Buddhism, similarly (despite its supposed rejection of essences) derives its idea of an absolute final goal or purpose from a metaphysical claim – that the Buddha achieved enlightenment, and enlightenment gives knowledge of the absolute truth about everyone's proper goals. So any views about the teleology of human beings as a whole (as opposed to the individual goals they may set themselves within experience) are clearly metaphysical and based only on dogmatic assumptions as to what these goals are.

Some continue to insist that, despite this point, special revelatory experiences (whether of God, or enlightenment, or other absolutes such as insight into Nature) tell us about final goals and thus they are not beyond experience. This claim is discussed more fully in 1.g above, but is basically mistaken because no finite experience can encompass absolutes. Just as a booming voice from the sky, however, impressive, might or might not be God, an experience of insight into what we believe to be the final goal might or might not be an experience of a goal that is really final – we are never in a position to judge. Simply adopting faith in such a goal does not help us, because it is in any case too remote to be a helpful object of identification.

---

[81] Aristotle (1976) 1.vii

In the case of the Buddha's enlightenment, Buddhists often argue that their own revelatory claims are different from others because they are made by a historical person who achieved enlightenment, demonstrating that any other human being can do the same. Their case is thus claimed to be different from religious claims about special people chosen by God (prophets like Muhammad, or incarnations like Jesus or Krishna) who define final goals only in terms of obedience to a mysterious divine will that will reward them after death or at the end of time. However, the case of the Buddha's enlightenment is not, in practice, epistemologically very different from claims about Muhammad being the seal of the prophets or Jesus being the son of God. If enlightenment was demonstrated by someone we know personally, we might have direct demonstration of it (though we would still have to assess the evidence for ourselves), but the final goal of the Buddha is only demonstrated to us through the mediation of a lengthy tradition and much inter-cultural translation.

Such a remote account of enlightenment might well provide symbolic meaning or inspiration where it represents more immediate goals, but it does not provide a helpful representational belief about a final goal. As Hume argued in relation to miracles[82], we have far more reason to doubt such a remote claim, on balance, than we have to accept it. Added to this is the argument that even if we did accept it, it would be of no use to us as a motivating goal, as explained above.

The final twist of argument that I have heard some Buddhists employ to defend enlightenment as a final goal is to claim that enlightenment is not a final goal, just a point on our horizon which may be intermediate to further goals beyond it[83]. Another version of this is to quote the perfection of wisdom literature as stating that enlightenment is empty and ultimately

---

[82] Hume (1975) ch.10 (p.109 ff)
[83] I have heard this view attributed to Sangharakshita, though I cannot find any written references for it.

no different from unenlightened existence[84]. These moves deprive the metaphysical account of a final goal even of the virtue of consistency. One cannot at the same time claim that enlightenment is a perfect truth known by the Buddha and that it is no more than an intermediate goal to be understood within experience. The contradiction, I think, serves mainly as an *ad hoc* spoiler to pre-empt criticism rather than a genuine piece of dialectic. It does not help us in practice to bridge a gap between absolute and relative truth, but merely asserts in effect that we should accept absolute truth even though it is contradictory and we should thus not investigate it critically.

Most importantly here, we should not confuse the value of the *meaning* of final goals with that of belief in them. Final goals, whether Buddhist, theistic, or of any other kind, may have an archetypal value for us. They may have helpful emotional associations as well as being represented in the provisional frame of stories. For example, the story of the Buddha achieving enlightenment through following the Middle Way (discussed in 3.a) needs some sort of end point which we might provisionally give the label 'enlightenment' within the context of the story, even though this represents something more like 'progress' in our experience. Stories about final goals can in effect help us to make intermediate goals more meaningful, though only because of the provisionality of the story frame in which the final goals are considered (see III.6.f for more details on stories). However, this possible value changes for us when final goals become objects of belief because they can only function as metaphysical beliefs, attracting fixed identification rather than motivating investigation of conditions.

---

[84] For example, see *The Diamond Sutra (Vajracchedikararjnaparamita)* section 7, or *Mulamadhayamakakarika* (Nagarjuna 1995) ch.25

G. Dualism and non-dualism

Dualism and non-dualism are another pair of terms used extensively in *A Theory of Moral Objectivity*[85], but they will be found rather less in this book. The term 'non-dualism', where used, roughly corresponds to 'Middle Way Philosophy', whereas 'dualism' is a position that takes metaphysical claims to be unavoidable or even desirable. Dualism in general should not be confused with 'a dualism' meaning a particular example of a pair of opposed metaphysical polarities, or a false dichotomy.

There are several different uses of the term 'dualism' in different contexts in Western philosophy, as well as in Buddhist (and Hindu) philosophy. In Western philosophy it can refer to a belief in distinct kinds of existence for mind and body, or the existence of a good and an evil god in opposition to each other. In relation to Indian metaphysical thought, though, it refers to the belief in a metaphysical difference between absolute independent being and the denial of being. Monism instead asserts a metaphysical unity, whilst non-dualism can at least sometimes indicate a more agnostic stance towards the issue (though strangely, it is not called non-monism, which it could just as easily be called if it was consistently agnostic), and alternatively non-dualism is sometimes taken to mean the same as monism.

The difficulty with the terms dualism and non-dualism even within the field of 'Indian' philosophy is that they are used in differing ways. In much of such thought, the fact that dualism is a metaphysical position that is being rejected does not necessarily indicate that non-dualism will be a non-metaphysical position. The terms 'dualism' and 'non-dualism' are also regularly conflated with 'duality' and 'non-duality'

---

[85] Ellis (2001): they are most closely defined in 2.c.ii

Middle Way Philosophy 1: The Path of Objectivity

In my stipulated use of these terms, however, dualism is distinguished from duality, because it does not refer to a metaphysical state of the universe, but to an attitude. Dualism assumes and supports the necessary existence of metaphysical positions and their denial, denies that there is any alternative Middle Way, and denies any distinction between denial and agnosticism. In this sense nearly all philosophies and religious beliefs that have ever existed are to some extent dualistic, though with varying degrees of entrenchment. Given that dualism is an attitude, it has a psychological as well as a philosophical aspect. It can also be associated with the dominant perspective of the left hemisphere of the brain, which seeks certainty through metaphysics and rejects the non-dualist contextual uncertainty of the right hemisphere.

Non-dualism involves a completely different way of understanding the universe, provisionally and incrementally, and in accordance with Middle Way Philosophy as I have described it so far. However, I dispute with traditional Buddhism the assumption that non-dualism requires a discontinuous absolute state such as enlightenment, where, having reached it, the world suddenly appears 'as it really is' – i.e. as a non-duality. This would be to completely miss the point that the Middle Way is an epistemology and an ethics, but not a metaphysics except in a critical sense. It would also throw the process of achieving non-dualism out of harmony with the supposed achievement – do we really *suddenly* achieve a recognition of incrementality, and reach an absolute state in order to see things as non-absolute? There is a serious incoherence in the whole idea of an enlightenment state as the key to non-dualism.

Instead, we must acknowledge that both dualism and non-dualism are implicitly part of everyone's experience, where either can incrementally develop. At times even those who are

Dualism and non-dualism

most philosophically entrenched in dualism will make practical judgements on the basis of provisionality and incrementality. If we never did this at all, we would be unable to learn anything about our environment. On the other hand, even those committed philosophically to a non-dualist view (such as myself) have times of unawareness when we lapse into implicit dualism in practice. For example, there are moments writing this book when I fall into despair, believing that there are too many conditions working even against it being read, let alone put into practice, and other moments when I implicitly assume that it will all be accepted without me continuing to exert myself on its clarity and presentation. In those moments I either recognise success and the absolute value of the enterprise, or failure and its absolute uselessness, and lose sight of the complexity of conditions, with a much more likely relative success for the enterprise, in between.

The development of non-dualism is thus a practice rather than just a philosophy, as should already be clear. The ways in which philosophy can aid practice and practice can aid philosophy require a lot more discussion, which will be found at various points in the whole of this series. If the distinction between dualism and non-dualism is one where psychology intersects with philosophy, it is not one that can be defined either purely philosophically or purely psychologically. Dualism, on the one hand, is a psychological state that leads us to support certain philosophical beliefs, whilst on the other, it is a set of philosophical beliefs that tend to lead us into certain psychological states. It can be identified where either of these two associations occur in experience rather than by fixed criteria from either side. Non-dualism, similarly, consists of philosophical beliefs conducive to psychological integration, and also psychological states conducive to increasingly objective beliefs.

Where we fail to identify a relationship between both philosophical and psychological aspects of the relationship, we should doubt our identification in any real case of a concrete person thinking dualistically or non-dualistically, regardless of the conclusiveness of general arguments. For example, if someone promotes a metaphysical view on the internet, I could dispute their view on the grounds of their philosophical assumptions, using scepticism: but this does not mean that all this person's thinking is dualistic, and it is much harder to make judgements about a person's psychological state using a remote medium like the internet. On the other hand, if I know someone well and have doubts about the balance of their psychological state, this does not necessarily mean that their philosophical beliefs cannot be examined for consistency in their own terms. It is only when we see metaphysical beliefs accompanied by a lack of psychological integration that we can be more fully justified in drawing conclusions about that person's habitual dualism, or if we experience Middle Way beliefs capable of provisionality accompanied by progress towards integration that we can be justified in drawing conclusions about a predominance of non-dualism. Neither, however, gives any grounds to give up on the possibility of a person's spiritual progress, since the most dogmatic person may still have moments of greater openness.

H. The Middle Way and the brain

At various points so far I have already mentioned the relationship between the two brain hemispheres and aspects of the Middle Way. Here, however, is a good point to pull some of that information together, and give a slightly fuller account of how I think the scientific evidence on the functions of brain hemispheres help to explain the Middle Way. Here I am hugely indebted to Iain McGilchrist's *The Master and his Emissary*[86], and what I can offer here is more a philosophical interpretation of his account of the hemispheres than anything directly based on the scientific research he uses. For a more detailed account of the science I would refer readers to McGilchrist's landmark book itself, and his detailed references and bibliography.

As McGilchrist underlines, to use this evidence about the brain to help us understand psychological and philosophical questions is not necessarily to *reduce* these questions to ones of brain functioning. It is not to say that the Middle Way, for example, is "just" a matter of making physical adjustments in the brain. It also certainly does not imply that the solutions to philosophical and psychological problems are medical ones. Instead, an awareness of our brain structure and its effects gives one more angle on the conditions in which we operate, to consider alongside the others available to us. Reading McGilchrist has convinced me that this angle is a helpful and informative angle, particularly as most of his findings tended to confirm conclusions that I had already reached in Middle Way Philosophy by other routes.

Although we rely on both the brain hemispheres constantly and they interact on a moment by moment basis, when one generalises about the hemispheres, their functions, and the

---

[86] McGilchrist (2009)

effects of the dominance of left or right hemisphere, it is as established by our experience over a longer period of time[87]. The two hemispheres have distinctive functions, despite the possibility of considerable duplication between the hemispheres, in the sense that each hemisphere has specialised in specific functions which it performs more effectively, and also inhibits the opposite hemisphere from performing[88]. Much of our evidence about these functions arises from observations of patients with strokes, lesions, or other conditions which have wholly or partially disabled one hemisphere, making it easy to observe in isolation the functions and limitations of the remaining one.

The left hemisphere is more self-referential and independent, having less white matter, which is suggestive of more internal rather than external connectivity. The right on the other hand has more external links, and co-ordinates action between the two hemispheres[89]. The right hemisphere can cope with left hemisphere tasks and approaches much better than the left hemisphere can cope with right hemisphere tasks. The left hemisphere tends to assume that objects will have enduring properties – it thinks in terms of types and categories. The right hemisphere, on the other hand, deals with each new experience afresh and treats every object or person as a unique individual. Meaning for the right hemisphere is contextual, whereas for the left hemisphere it is part of a closed system of representation.

The left hemisphere is often thought to be the language hemisphere, but this is an over-simplification. It handles abstract and familiar language and connects language grammatically, so it is essential for language formation, but the right hemisphere nevertheless deals with unique referents,

---

[87] Ibid pp.10 & 213-227
[88] Ibid. pp.16-31
[89] For this and all the following statements about the functions of the hemispheres, see ibid. ch.2 for more details and further references.

unusual words, new words and metaphorical relationships. The dominant tendency in the left hemisphere is to be focused and explicit, whereas the right hemisphere specialises in diffuse, implicit and unconscious processing. The left hemisphere maintains memories of facts, the right hemisphere personal memories. The left hemisphere engages in explicit sequential argument, whilst the right hemisphere is better at reasoning with an unconscious element, especially problem solving and the spotting of anomalies.

The right hemisphere engages with others as persons and with other living things as autonomous and alive, whereas the left hemisphere is much more concerned with manipulation and will treat everything as a manipulable object. This is also related to the way that the left hemisphere tends to divide things into parts whilst the right hemisphere sees things (or people) as wholes. The right hemisphere thus handles social relationships, is capable of empathy, emotional arousal and emotional perception. The left hemisphere can instead largely offer only superficial, 'willed' emotions and anger if its will is blocked. The general mood of the left hemisphere is superficial optimism, whilst the right hemisphere engages in any kind of pessimistic or 'negative' emotion, as well as the more profound positive ones.

Music is overwhelmingly processed by the right hemisphere, except by professional musicians. The right hemisphere can relate events in time and thus handles narrative, but the left hemisphere can only sequence things in a decontextualised logical way, and lacks a sense of temporal relationships between events or the continued existence of people over time. The right hemisphere also deals with motion, having control over the whole body when necessary, whilst the left hemisphere thinks of relationships between types of thing as static.

Middle Way Philosophy 1: The Path of Objectivity

The left hemisphere is dogmatic, drawing mistaken conclusions from limited evidence and sticking stubbornly to them, whilst the right hemisphere is always open to new evidence. The left hemisphere is rule governed and inflexible, whilst the right hemisphere can tolerate ambiguity and can hold different possibilities together imaginatively without premature judgement. The left hemisphere's certainty is related to its narrowness of focus – it has to limit the options in order to focus effectively and act at one point. The right hemisphere's openness, on the other hand, enables it to respond to unexpected dangers and difficulties.

Given these differing features of the hemispheres, then, it seems obvious that the source of metaphysical beliefs is the left hemisphere, and the reason for the continued dominance of these beliefs is dominance of the left hemisphere over the right. The left hemisphere's tendency to predominate follows from its function as the source of will and power. McGilchrist argues persuasively that despite the right hemisphere's crucial importance in interacting with the world, the left hemisphere tends to predominate because of its constantly self-reinforcing system of representation supported by positive feedback[90]. However, it clearly dominates more in some individuals than others, and in some places, times and cultures more than others. Given that metaphysical beliefs, with their tendency to self-reinforcement, their polarisation, their certainty, and their immunity to changes from experience, are the key tools of the left hemisphere in maintaining predominance over the right, it is clear that the Middle Way involves a central role for the right hemisphere.

The Middle Way is thus not the Middle Way between the right and left hemispheres, but rather the Middle Way between different metaphysical beliefs promoted by the left hemisphere. If we recall the left hemisphere's inability to

---

[90] Ibid. p.229-233

understand change over time, it becomes clearer what the right hemisphere must mediate between: metaphysically opposed views, or dualism of whatever sort, held inconsistently by the left hemisphere at different times and maintained tenaciously by the ego as the only truth at that time. Of course, conflicting metaphysically opposed views may also be held by different individual left hemispheres at the same time, but the mediation involved in these cases is similar.

McGilchrist discusses mental illnesses or disabilities that illustrate the effects of excessive left hemisphere dominance and right hemisphere dysfunction: schizophrenia, anorexia, autism, and multiple personality disorder[91]. What these all strikingly have in common is a fragmentation of awareness over time, leading to grossly inconsistent identifications, beliefs and behaviour. People with these conditions have partly or wholly lost the integrative functions of the right hemisphere: its contextuality, empathy, imagination, awareness of change over time, and sense of meaning based on the body. But we are all multiple personalities to some degree, as to the extent that we are dominated by the left hemisphere we maintain inconsistent desires, meanings and beliefs. It is clearly the right hemisphere in connection with the left at these different times that maintains the capacity to integrate them to a greater or lesser extent.

But it is not simply a matter of right hemisphere dominance replacing left. It would be very easy to get into a froth about the importance of defending the right hemisphere and keeping the left in its place: but this would be an expression of the left hemisphere, not the right, and in the longer-term it would serve the interests of the left hemisphere, which Midas-like turns everything it touches into a mere idea. We should not underestimate the capacity of the left hemisphere for

---

[91] Ibid. pp.403-7

Middle Way Philosophy 1: The Path of Objectivity

appropriating the right, nor trust any thinker who offers us metaphysical bouquets for the right hemisphere – unwrapped, they will not turn out to be flowers, but rather guns in the shape of flowers.

To support the Middle Way here requires an imaginative and compassionate recognition of the left hemisphere's contribution. Indeed, every single fragmented, dogmatic, wilful expression of the left hemisphere contributes its energy towards the integration which the right hemisphere merely enables. Only the left hemisphere supplies a representation of the world and enables a focused practical response to it. Only the left hemisphere enables articulation and reason. The contribution of the left hemisphere towards the development of objectivity is just as necessary as that of the right. It is peace and co-operation that will cause metaphysics and its associated conflict to wither away, not a call to arms. That is why metaphysical agnosticism, which tries to separate the dualistic from the non-dualistic aspects of left hemisphere activity, provides the way forward.

It is here that I think McGilchrist, in the final two chapters of his otherwise outstanding book, makes a few misjudgements. McGilchrist believes that the modern world of the West shows runaway positive feedback leading to increasing levels of left hemisphere dominance, with disastrous effects on Western society. His interpretation of modernity, however, focuses relentlessly on the left hemisphere features of modernity at the expense of others, and adopts a disproportionately negative approach to them. But if the Middle Way is the most effective way to address conditions, it seems to me clear that in the modern world, despite those features which suggest excessive left-hemisphere dominance, we must be following it in some ways that we have never before managed. True, we have many features of left-hemisphere dominance: alienation, bureaucracy, relativism, bureaucracy, mass production, virtualisation, disorientation, individualism, depersonalisation, passivity, and paranoia. However, we also have unprecedented degrees of health, longevity, education, democracy, observance of human rights, empowerment of women, scientific and technological development, security, communications, access to empowering information, and cultural opportunities. The left hemisphere has contributed hugely to addressing these conditions – in general it just needs to be more effectively integrated to address a few more. The Middle Way requires the recognition, amongst other types of metaphysical agnosticism, that neither the dogmas of pessimism nor those of optimism are entirely correct.

I. The Middle Way as moral good

Now we come to the crucial point of the ethical aspects of Middle Way Philosophy, which is a point that I can only put bluntly, even if it requires you to cast aside everything you thought you knew about ethics: *the Middle Way is good*. The flip side of this, however foolish it may sound at first, is also *metaphysics is evil*.

To put this in more precise philosophical language: *The Middle Way provides the best available account of objective moral good, so that all objective moral good can be understood in terms of the Middle Way, and progress in the Middle Way can be understood as objective moral good*. Similarly, *Metaphysics provides the best available account of evil, so that objective evil can be understood in terms of metaphysics and metaphysics in terms of objective evil*.

Interpreting these claims, it is important to remember that the point at which the Middle Way and metaphysics operate is *judgement*, and that 'objective' in Middle Way Philosophy does not mean 'absolutely objective' but 'incrementally objective'. The objective goodness of the Middle Way, then, means that people make judgements that are good to the extent that they practise the Middle Way so as to make maximally adequate judgements in their context, given their starting conditions. The objective evil of metaphysics means that people make evil judgements where those judgements are derived from metaphysical assumptions, and thus do not address conditions in their context but rather impose dogmatic assumptions on it. It is thus not people, or events, or even beliefs, which are capable of being incrementally good or evil, but criteria of judgement.

As noted above in 3.g, such criteria do not consist purely in philosophical beliefs, but also in the psychological states that

165

The Middle Way as moral good

lead one to apply them in a given set of circumstances. One can focus on beliefs as being good or evil only when psychological conditions lead to them being applied as criteria in practice. Then the metaphysical nature of a belief provides a fixed point of evil influence in what is otherwise a fluid process of motives adapting themselves to conditions, even though the dogmatism of the psychological state in which the metaphysics is applied is incremental and thus the negative impact of the metaphysics mitigated by the need to respond to conditions that we constantly experience. Similarly, the Middle Way as a principle provides a good counterpoint to the fixed influence of metaphysical belief, even though the extent to which that counterpoint prevents metaphysical belief through provisionality in practice is variable because it also depends on the psychological states in which we address conditions.

By way of analogy to help to clarify this model, let's imagine a film projector that is projecting a film onto a screen, though not a screen in a purpose-built, darkened cinema but an unsatisfactory ordinary room with no blackout and sunlight streaming through the window, making the film hard to see. The film also consists of a series of code words that can be put together to create a key idea. However, the people in the room only have half their minds on the film, and one of the people in the room is urging them not to pay any attention to the film and talking to them of important practical matters. Only some of the viewers understand the code in the film, and for them it is not the only influence, for they have also been half-listening to the person talking. Others don't understand it because of the light conditions, and others don't even look at it because they are too intent on listening to the practical person. Later some of those who understood it follow the instructions of the evil code, but not completely or whole-heartedly. Others have only vaguely heard of the code and just try to react positively to the circumstances, though the code still exerts an influence to some extent.

Middle Way Philosophy 1: The Path of Objectivity

This analogy, like any other, will have limitations, but it is intended to dramatise the way that evil is found in metaphysics even though its application is complex. The code here represents evil and the practical talker represents the Middle Way. Unlike in classic religious accounts of the struggle of good and evil, what is going on here is not a straight contest between two codes or two talkers, but rather a contest between two influences, one of which is rigidly defined even though its application is far from definite, and the other of which is primarily practical whilst rejecting the rigid definition. Our perceptions, understanding, attention, other psychological states and social relationships all complicate the ways in which these two influences are actually applied. However, we would not be justified, just because of this complexity, in rejecting the idea of evil altogether.

Once we accept a concept of evil, a concept of good follows (not the other way round) from any decisive rejection of such evil. Evil must be defined first because evil is rigid and self-defining, whereas good can be rigid only in decisively rejecting the rigidity of evil so as to avoid its influence, and its positive activity is much less definable because it consists in a pragmatic response to conditions.

Having clarified this theory of good and evil, then, why should anyone accept it? As usual, the justification interconnects with almost everything else in this book. However, I will list some major reasons below. More details will be found in section 7, where the whole basis of Middle Way ethics is explained in more depth.

1. The metaphysical model has failed us, because it has only left us with a choice between dogmatically asserted moral absolutism or equally dogmatic relativism. Neither of these provides us with any justification for ethics, meaning that we are unable to provide convincing rational justifications for

The Middle Way as moral good

asserting a moral position beyond convention or individual choice. We need an alternative model.

2. The failure to provide convincing rational justification for metaphysical ethics means that the left hemisphere is not on board when it needs to be, and even if we have moral intuitions in the right hemisphere, they are ineffective in persuading the power-centre in the left to change its approach.

3. The metaphysical model of moral justification has thus failed us in practical terms, because it has not succeeded very well in getting people to do good rather than evil. If we start to see good as consisting in addressing as many conditions as possible, we at least stand the maximum possible chance of making good happen. A moral vision that neglects some key conditions (those of motivation) as a basic part of its operation was never going to be very successful.

4. We already implicitly practice the Middle Way as a practical basis of good whenever we do address conditions – to the extent that we do. It is a new conceptual model, but not a completely new departure in practical terms.

5. At the same time, changing our philosophical view of morality does make a practical difference. Even if much of our moral behaviour is unreflective, we introduce a new influence on our reflective behaviour and on others, and the way we address the underlying conditions of our lives will also slowly come to have an impact on our unreflective behaviour.

6. All the main existing theories of normativity (i.e. utilitarian appeal to hedonism, Kantian appeal to rational consistency, virtue ethics) appear to imply the value of experiential adequacy when taken to their logical conclusion. If we bring about the best consequences, it is because we have addressed conditions, and if we use principles consistently, it

is because we are integrated. See 7.c for details of this argument.

7. We badly need an incremental model of ethics to confront every over-simplifying labelling of a complex person or movement as 'good' or 'evil'. We can call metaphysics evil only because metaphysics, on its own account, is absolute, but all the places where metaphysics actually operates involve a complex mixture. Denying evil does not help to channel this tendency to label 'good' and 'evil' helpfully.

8. Ethics needs to integrate with and make use of the insights offered by psychology and any other helpful sciences, rather than the sciences having to be limited by a therapeutic model only. There is no reason why medical and psychological skills should not contribute to making us 'better' in a moral as well as a health sense, as long as this can be reconciled with issues of responsibility (see 7.b).

9. Breaking down the barriers created by the fact-value distinction is also important for integrating ethics more effectively into science. Science and technology are now crossing into increasingly dangerous territory – for example, genetic engineering or climate change reversal engineering – where balanced moral judgement needs to be applied integrated with scientific judgement about the facts.

Defining the Middle Way as good and metaphysics as evil is not itself a metaphysical move, because of the provisional and incremental model that the Middle Way consists in. Although it is a highly generalised theory, it is nevertheless a theory that we could provisionally accept, try out in practice and see how it works. I do not accept that 'good' and 'evil' are themselves metaphysical terms by definition, because we encounter so much in our experience which we find good or evil to some degree. It is only the abstracted turn and the fact-value distinction that has made this experience seem somehow more suspicious or 'subjective' than other experiences, and deprived us of provisional ways of representing it. Just as the meaning of 'God' can be interpreted metaphysically or in terms of experience (see 3.c), likewise good and evil. What makes a belief about good or evil metaphysical is not the concept itself but the justification we give for it.

Similarly, it is important to distinguish between metaphysics being evil and people who believe in it (or religious or other groups who believe in it) being evil. Whilst metaphysics itself is absolute in its own terms, a given person's belief in it is not and cannot be absolute. It is quite possible to have a nominal metaphysical commitment and yet hardly ever make judgements on the basis of metaphysics. Great Christian saints, for example, can be seen as good despite their belief in the existence of God rather than because of it, but also perhaps good because of the non-metaphysical role that God as a symbol and as an experience plays in their lives.

It can also be argued that evil as metaphysics closely fits many aspects of the archetypal evil we experience, because characters that symbolise evil tend to be heavily dominated by the left brain and obsessively concerned with narrow objectives. The archetype of evil is explored in III.4.c and the links between this archetype and dogmatic states in IV.3.n.

J. The Middle Way as integration

The concept of integration, which will be explored more fully in section 6, means that previously opposed energies in the psyche begin to work together. If you accept the theory of the unconscious, this can be seen in terms of different unconscious energies (or unconscious and conscious energies) harmonising. If, on the other hand, you are not happy to accept a theory that assumes the unconscious, you can think of the concept of integration phenomenologically, only in terms of the increasing consistency and adequacy of energies that we experience at different times. If you would rather use the brain hemisphere model, you can think of integration as the integration of the time-fragmented left hemisphere at different times by the time-unified right hemisphere.

In accordance with the account of desire, meaning and belief that has been emerging so far, integration can be understood as occurring at all three of these levels. Desires are directly-experienced emotional energies, but these desires also express themselves in terms of meanings, and assume a framework of belief in which their objects can be conceptualised. Conflicting desires can also create conflicting meanings, because the signs used to represent conflicting desires may not be mutually meaningful: for example, we might find theological language meaningful in one mood but not another. Conflicting desires also create conflicting beliefs both about the way the universe is represented and about justified goals of action within it, whether these are explicit philosophical beliefs or (more commonly) implicit beliefs about the absolute value of certain actions or the complete absence of such value. For example, a would-be murderer with a strong desire to kill someone also has a belief in the value of killing them – perhaps as a belief in the justification of revenge or just in the absolute importance of his own desires being fulfilled –

The Middle Way as integration

at the same time as a belief in society's disapproval of these desires being enacted and a desire to be accepted by others. He will only be able to address his murderous desires in the long-term if those contradictory desires and beliefs work together, rather than the murderous desires temporarily overcoming the social constraint, or the social constraint temporarily holding the murderous desires in check. To re-channel his murderous desires, his belief in the value of the fulfilment of those desires will need to be questioned in the light of his understanding of social condemnation.

One way to understand the Middle Way, then, is as a method of integration. The key point of linkage here is that opposed energies are best able to maintain their opposition through association with metaphysical beliefs. A metaphysical belief serves the interests of an unintegrated desire by representing a universe where that desire is constantly justified, where the beliefs that support it are unassailable, and where opposing beliefs are wholly rather than partially mistaken.

In this view of the universe, the desire perpetuates itself, and creates a sense of security where it feels it can easily defend itself. It may also perpetuate the divide using meaning, by presenting the opposing view as either cognitively or affectively meaningless (or both). However, the division between this desire and 'opposing' desires is a false one. They are both actually desires of the same individual (or at the social level, of the same society) – an individual that would be best served in the long-term by addressing conditions as fully as possible. Yet an unintegrated desire maladaptively creates and maintains conflict where none need exist.

Let's take an example of a fairly clear lack of integration. I used to know a smoker who regularly decided to give up the habit: she would throw her cigarettes in the bin and vow not to smoke any more. At that point she would genuinely desire not to smoke, would really mean it and believe that she could give

Middle Way Philosophy 1: The Path of Objectivity

up in that way. However, the next day she would often fish the cigarettes back out of the bin, and meaningfully believe that she really couldn't manage it – the nicotine addiction was too strong to break. Here, the practice of the Middle Way over time might help her because it would get her to address more of the conditions and integrate her approach. The metaphysical poles involved are freewill and determinism: on one occasion she would believe that she could give up smoking just by deciding to do so – an absolute freewill – whilst on another occasion she would believe the opposite, that she had no choice. The starting point in addressing this situation would be agnosticism about the absolute beliefs involved: she is not able to give up smoking just by deciding to do so, without addressing all the conditions involved, nor is she helpless in the face of inevitable nicotine addiction. Instead, she could investigate different theories about the best way to give up (nicotine patches, gradually phasing out, hypnotism etc) and try them out in a provisional way. These theories would need to address the question of how to get all her desires together working on the same side. The addicted set of desires might need to be channelled into some other sort of pleasure. Awareness and compassion for herself at the two different times might also be needed, in order to find herself at each time affectively meaningful for the other.

Not all lack of integration is as extreme or obvious as this. Some is just a source of distraction, anxiety, or conflicting emotions on the one hand, or arrogance on the other as we fail to acknowledge our other voices. All such inner conflicts, however, can be understood in terms of metaphysical beliefs, very often about opposing values that we take to be absolute at the times we identify with them. Exactly the same model can be applied at a social level to identify conflicts between people or groups. For every piece of injustice, for example, there is a potential doubting voice in the oppressor: a set of desires, meanings and beliefs that might undermine the justifications given for injustice, which are also suppressed.

The Middle Way as integration

The solution to social and political conflict, then, may be possible at a social or political level, but can also occur at a psychological level. The Middle Way can be applied at either level, beginning with agnosticism about the conflicting metaphysical beliefs within individuals, between individuals or between groups, and proceeding to justifiable provisional beliefs that can then assist with the integration of desire and meaning.

A wide range of potential issues about integration have been raised here, all of which will be tackled much more fully later, initially in section 6 and subsequently in more depth in volumes 2, 3 and 4. The main point to be appreciated for the moment is just generally how the Middle Way supports integration.

K. Dialectic and homeostasis

The Middle Way can be described as a dialectic, in that it posits a way that opposing forces can be reconciled and their apparently opposed views transcended. The classic dialectical structure is that of thesis (an initial claim), antithesis (an opposed claim to the thesis) and synthesis (a unification of the two claims). By itself, this basic dialectical structure just explains how progress occurs and how conflict is resolved. The Middle Way does this through agnosticism about both thesis and antithesis where their claims are opposed *a priori*, but the adoption of provisional and incremental views about the topic (which may include aspects or interpretations of the thesis and antithesis). These provisional and incremental theories can then be considered in relation to experience in order to provide a resolution of the conflict, not as exactly stated in the thesis and antithesis, but at a different level where the assumptions of each have been questioned. In some cases the higher level of thought might involve just coming to terms with our lack of knowledge and resting with agnosticism – as in opposed claims about God's existence, for example. In other cases it might need a process of analysis to bring out which aspects of the thesis and antithesis can be understood in incremental or provisional terms in which they can be reconciled through investigation[92], with merely metaphysical aspects of the thesis and antithesis being left to agnosticism.

Dialectical structure only becomes problematic when it is appropriated in the service of a metaphysical assumption that is assumed to explain the dialectic – in other words, where the synthesis is assumed to be metaphysical in nature rather than non-metaphysical in nature. This has often been the case

---

[92] For examples of the incrementalisation of various metaphysical dualisms, see volume 4, or Ellis (2001) 6.b

Dialectical aspects of the Middle Way

when dialectical approaches have been used by great philosophers of the past. Hegel and Marx in the nineteenth century both used dialectic to metaphysical ends.

Hegel's dialectic is based on an absolute idealism, in which history is believed to inevitably bring about the synthesis of all conflicting beliefs, because all such beliefs are ultimately aspects of one universal mind. Thus his overall philosophy assumes a determinism of history – a definite metaphysical view – and that history's pre-determined outcome will be positive – a metaphysical optimism. Many of the syntheses he identifies along the way are also false syntheses, because they consist in a further metaphysical position rather than a pragmatic solution that overcomes the metaphysical assumptions of thesis and antithesis[93].

Marx's dialectic is also historical and determinist, believing that history will necessarily have a good outcome, as conflicting class groups with conflicting ideologies struggle and bring about a synthesis of their opposing interests. This process culminates in the supreme synthesis, the Communist society. Rather than being idealist, however, Marx's account of the dialectic is materialist, the inevitable process of historical dialectic being claimed to be ascertainable from history. Although Marx claims a scientific basis for his dialectic, then, it is just as dogmatic as Hegel's, with his materialism being just as metaphysical as Hegel's idealism[94].

The dialectic of the Middle Way should not be confused with those of either of these two philosophers, as it avoids their overriding metaphysical assumptions[95], makes no claims about the inevitable course of history, and sees synthesis only in the avoidance of metaphysical assumptions. The type of

---

[93] See Ellis (2001) 4.h for a much fuller discussion of Hegel
[94] Ibid. 4.i for a much fuller discussion of Marx
[95] See IV.4.d for more on these assumptions in relation to realism and idealism

Middle Way Philosophy 1: The Path of Objectivity

dialectic involved in the Middle Way is much closer to the epistemological and moral negative feedback loop discussed in 3.e. Here the thesis consists of a theory, the antithesis the falsification of a theory by experience, and the synthesis of a revised theory. This is the epistemological dialectic offered by Popper, which (provided we do not incorporate his assumption of the fact-value distinction or his rejection of psychology) can also provide a model for Middle Way dialectic.

As discussed in 3.f, the Middle Way dialectic also has no final goals. We do not know what the continued use of the dialectic will lead us to in future, as it is merely a method of investigation. It is progressive only in the point that it is leaving behind and improving on the thesis and antithesis, the limitations of each of which can be seen in the context in which the dialectic is used, rather than according to any wider framework. We experience objectivity moment by moment in a dialectical process, but the further we stand back the harder it is to ascertain whether it is objective progress that has taken place. This implies that we should not stand back too far from the negative feedback process, but rather seek a vantage point which balances our immediate experience of progress with an awareness of the intermediate (but not final) goals that may be suggested by a succession of smaller dialectical changes.

A Middle Way dialectic is also a dynamic one, leading to new resolutions of problems confronted by the human system, and should not be confused with the settled patterns of *homeostasis*. In a homeostatic relationship, two systems enter a stable and mutually dependent pattern of balance and thus form a larger system: for example, the population of rabbits and that of foxes that consume them are mutually dependent, and changes in one will force adaptations in the other. Ecological models of homeostasis are far more complex than this because they involve the interactions of large numbers of species or systems forming a complex system that nevertheless has an overall stability – the 'balance of nature'.

Although such a stable balancing reflects that of the Middle Way in important ways, it needs to be noted that the Middle Way is a *dialectic of judgement*, not a homeostatic pattern in total. The Middle Way consists of a maximally balanced response to conditions that may come out of a position that, in the larger analysis, is extremely unbalanced. The position of human beings in the wider ecology of the planet Earth has a good deal of instability about it, and we are currently seeing accelerating extinctions of other species, habitat destruction, rising CO_2 levels, and a threat of melting ice caps and rising sea levels, all of which threaten the homeostasis of the earth's biosphere. A Middle Way response to that situation is not a leap to an ecologically homeostatic position, but rather one in which we, as perhaps unavoidably unbalanced creatures, attempt to address the conditions of this environment as best we can. In the longer term, the closer we can get to homeostasis, the better, but the Middle Way consists in a realistic attempt to get closer to it through dialectical engagement, rather than an idealised attempt to imitate a 'natural' balance.

Middle Way Philosophy 1: The Path of Objectivity

L. Distinguishing the Middle Way from metaphysics

The boundary between provisional beliefs conducive to the Middle Way on the one hand, and metaphysics on the other, is not always an easy one to detect for a number of reasons. The chief of these is the likelihood of a time-lag before provisional beliefs show their worth in relation to experience. Provisional beliefs about everyday facts ("the bus will arrive at 2.05 pm") are quickly verified sufficiently to produce confidence, or occasionally falsified. However, broader theories that are open to experience (such as Middle Way Philosophy itself) may require a good deal of complex evidence over time to be confirmed or falsified to our satisfaction. During this period, there may only be subtle indications that they are not metaphysics. While we are uncertain how much confidence to place in a provisional theory, it is not irrelevant to talk of having *faith* in it – though that faith is not unconditional. *Faith* here is just a way of talking about belief in a way that focuses more on its emotional impact, but neither faith nor belief are necessarily metaphysical[96].

This problem is compounded by the ways in which metaphysical positions can appropriate the Middle Way. People often seem to hear about Middle Way Philosophy and immediately respond, for example, "Yes, that's Aristotle" or "Yes, that's Hegel" and associate Middle Way Philosophy with positions that actually have substantial metaphysical assumptions attached to them. I have even met Catholics who immediately thought that the Middle Way was compatible with St. Thomas Aquinas! Without understanding all the interconnected aspects of Middle Way Philosophy, it is easy to falsely assimilate it to a metaphysical position. It is difficult to

---

[96] See IV.1.d for a fuller discussion

predict in advance how much practical difference this will make, because it depends on the interaction between these beliefs and the other conditions in people's lives, but whenever there's a metaphysical position assumed there is a good chance that it will affect practical judgements, because people start to identify with the metaphysical position and build up a position they feel is beyond criticism.

Nevertheless, judgements have to be made whether to treat a position as provisional or metaphysical. We cannot and should not suspend judgement for too long, for the suspension of judgement infringes experiential adequacy. Just as a rigid view stops us creating provisional theories, so does suspension of judgement from the other side. We have to invest faith in a position for long enough to explore it, even though that faith cannot be unconditional.

One point that may help us make such judgements initially can be adapted from the philosophy of science – that of theoretical fruitfulness. A fruitful theory is one that provides frequent opportunities for testing in experience, by generating hypotheses that can be tested. This is an approach that can be adopted even when the 'testing' is personal and informal. A fruitful theory will be one that is relevant enough to our lives to be tried out often, and also helps to generate further helpful hypotheses which help to explain other aspects of our experience. These hypotheses will be even more informative if they are not otherwise obvious. For example, a provisional acceptance of Middle Way Philosophy might also lead to trying out integrative practices such as meditation, the arts, or critical thinking (all discussed in more detail in volumes 2, 3 and 4 as they relate to the different forms of integration) or any others that might help to develop integration, which may lead to practical results compatible with your understanding of Middle Way Philosophy, at the same time supporting and modifying theoretical awareness through the feedback loop.

Middle Way Philosophy 1: The Path of Objectivity

A further factor when making judgements about a provisional theory is comparison to alternative theories. We cannot manage without some beliefs, so we should not judge which beliefs to accept outside the context of comparison. One mistake often made in metaphysical thinking is the absolute acceptance or rejection of a position only on grounds of (supposed) certainty or lack of certainty about it, without considering whether alternative theories are any better justified. One example of this is the rejection of evolutionary theory on the grounds that it is not completely proven, despite the absence of more informative theories that explain the evidence available to biology. Here I think Middle Way Philosophy has a major advantage, because many other competing theories can be ruled out at the beginning on the basis of their failure to address sceptical argument.

Another factor involved in making such decisions is the need for a wide range of experience to be involved. If we have thought as rigorously as we can, it may be time for other kinds of assessment to take over. Our intuitions may not be more reliable than our intellect, but that does not mean that they are uninformative. The physical nature of our experience makes it likely that there are many unconscious factors involved in judgement. The meanings of the terms involved in our judgements about beliefs, as I argue throughout this book, are not just cognitive, but also relate to our feelings and physical experience. Thus it would be surprising if our immediate responses to beliefs put before us – whether those responses are justified or not – were purely cognitive. Indeed, McGilchrist argues on the basis of a number of scientific observations that our judgements take place unconsciously in the right hemisphere before the left hemisphere can rationalise them consciously[97]. So, our wider experiences may be more informative than we think. For example, we may sense a certain emotional rigidity in people who support metaphysical

---

[97] McGilchrist (2009) p.184

Distinguishing the Middle Way from metaphysics

positions, which we only half-consciously register from their physical stance or tone. This kind of evidence may be especially crucial when it comes to values. Although values tend to come wrapped up with facts (see 1.i) and thus judgements about them are not entirely distinguishable from those about related facts, we may still feel relatively more uncertainty about them. Once we have ruled out obvious metaphysical assumptions, such relative and ultimately unreliable faculties as intuition and feelings may still have a role, as they always have in the practical implicit Middle Way that many people have discovered for themselves.

When we decide to try out a provisional theory in relation to experience, though, how do we reach a conclusion? If our immediate judgement seems to be incrementally confirmed, it seems that we will then not need a distinct discontinuous judgement as to the correctness and genuine provisionality of a theory. We will just come to rely on it more and more. The challenge will then be, not to have faith in it, but to let go of it if we finally discover metaphysics at the bottom after many years of investment in it. This was my personal experience after years of commitment to the Buddhist tradition, for a long time in real doubt as to whether traditional Buddhism was provisional or metaphysical. Resigning from the Western Buddhist Order on concluding that traditional Buddhism was more metaphysical than provisional was one of the most difficult and painful decisions of my life.

In that event, the important discovery was that traditional Buddhism, as a value as well as a set of factual claims, was falsified *for me*. A term of years had passed sufficient for me to make an informed judgement on a theory that I had explored in relation to a wide range of experiences. What that term of years should be in any given case when we have provisionally accepted a theory is impossible to state in advance. Nevertheless it should be finite, and perhaps the important point is to maintain awareness of the question. If we stop asking ourselves whether a theory is justified – if, in other words, we have started to ignore sceptical questions – then the theory is no longer provisional for us[98].

In the context of science, falsification is a somewhat more precise matter, because there are often groups of people involved in researching a theory who have to decide whether or not to continue investing time and resources in it, when it ceases to be fruitful in offering much further opportunity for informative testing. However, even here, as both Kuhn and Lakatos have demonstrated[99], there is a period of difficulty when it is very unclear whether or not scientists would be justified in abandoning an old paradigm. If this is the case in science, we should expect it to be even more difficult in personal commitments.

It would be good to give some more decisive answers on how to distinguish the Middle Way from metaphysics. It would be better still to be able to give immediate strong reasons which placed the justification of Middle Way Philosophy beyond all doubt. However, to do this would simultaneously undermine the central insight in Middle Way Philosophy that all justified judgements have to be provisional. Provisional judgements are hard, tricky, and sometimes painful. There's no way round that. However, that doesn't change the central arguments I have offered here: that provisional theories address conditions in a way that metaphysical theories cannot, and that not just recognisable theories of science, but even the most personal value judgements need to fall under the category of provisional theories in order to be justifiable.

---

[98] See Ellis (2001) 6.c for more discussion of this area
[99] Kuhn (1996) and Lakatos (1974)

4. Aspects of objectivity

I have been using the term 'objectivity' in its incremental sense and applying it to the Middle Way approach in contrast to dualism or a metaphysical approach. I am surprised at how much consternation this use of the term 'objectivity' often seems to provoke, given its close relationship to our experience, common usage, and even some philosophical usage of the term. The point has been reached when a more thorough explanation of this use of the term is needed.

In this chapter I will be putting forward an account of objectivity based on the Middle Way, together with the case for adopting this view of objectivity.

My arguments against the fact-value distinction also raise the issue of the relationship between objectivity of facts and values, and how this is to be understood without the fact-value distinction. Here I shall be clarifying the relationship between factual, moral, and also aesthetic types of objectivity. Finally, I will also consider the relationship between objectivity and adaptation to one's environment, so that ideas about evolution can contribute to, but not unhelpfully dominate, understanding of objectivity as the addressing of conditions.

Middle Way Philosophy 1: The Path of Objectivity

A. The incremental nature of objectivity

There are two main existing concepts of objectivity in common use – an absolute form and an incremental form. The incremental form is commonly used when we say things like "Try to look at this more objectively". Here we are accepting objectivity as the property or activity of a person, assuming both that they have a degree of objectivity and that this degree can be increased. On the other hand, the absolute use is often assumed when we talk about science having "An objective view of the world" – even if we then go on to deny that it does.

The absolute version of objectivity is a God's-eye view, a perfect understanding of all conditions in relation to each other. Given all the sceptical arguments in 1.a it is clear that no human being, or indeed any finite being whatsoever, could ever be objective in this sense. It is relevant to the life of finite beings only in terms of archetypal meaning, not in terms of justifiable claims or arguments. Yet for some reason most philosophers continue to use 'objective' in this sense, and some immediately misunderstand the title of my thesis 'A Theory of Moral Objectivity' to necessarily involve claims about a God's eye view.

However, the incremental version of objectivity is not unknown to philosophy, and I am not the first to put it forward. Arguably it is implicitly present in Hume, and it has been argued for explicitly by Thomas Nagel in *The View from Nowhere,* where he calls objectivity "a method of understanding"[100]. Absolute objectivity would be a view from nowhere, and as we always have a view from somewhere, only incremental objectivity is relevant to assessing this view.

Nagel described objectivity in terms of moving beyond the limitations of our individual standpoint, but in practice our

---
[100] Nagel (1986) p.4

The incremental nature of objectivity

understanding of conditions is limited, not by having an individual standpoint (which is just a given condition) but by a lack of experiential adequacy (see 2.a). Our limited capacity to accept new viewpoints, or even find them meaningful, depends not on having an individual standpoint but on limited identifications. An extension of our meaning identifications might help us to imagine positions beyond our individual standpoint more easily, but this is only one aspect of increasing our objectivity. We become more objective by bringing more unified energy to bear on our whole investigation (through the integration of desire), by gaining understanding of other points of view and other motivations (whether those of others or of ourselves at different times), by using provisional theories, and by examining our experience as openly as possible in assessing those theories.

One common argument against the philosophical currency of incremental objectivity is that it is necessarily dependent on absolute objectivity. It is argued that without a concept of absolute objectivity, incremental objectivity cannot be justified. I have already given the basis for a response to this in several places. It assumes that justification must be absolute (and therefore metaphysical) in nature, meaning that we either accept an unconditional faith in such justification on the basis of dogma, or reject it altogether. In 3.f I also argued that we do not need final goals to pursue the Middle Way, though we may need long-term goals within experience. Incremental objectivity does not need a teleological justification from an absolute final goal, given that justification must occur within experience and final goals do not lie within our experience. Far from incremental objectivity needing justification from absolute objectivity, the opposite is the case. To be relevant to our experience, claims about absolute objectivity would need to be justified in incremental terms – which they cannot be.

Another possible approach to understanding the necessity of reframing objectivity in incremental terms is in terms of brain hemispheres. Absolute objectivity is objectivity as seen entirely in the terms of the left hemisphere, but the left hemisphere both tends to assume certainty[101] and to use sequential philosophical reasoning to undermine it[102]. The right hemisphere, on the other hand, works in a world of uncertainty[103], expecting new experiences to constantly alter our responses. It is clear that the right hemisphere's version of objectivity is an incremental one, but also that the right hemisphere is the only one that provides a basis for judgement that is not self-referential and implicitly circular in its justification. The left hemisphere's representation of the world can be more or less objective in the right hemisphere's incremental sense, but the right hemisphere is simply discounted from all possible objectivity in the absolute left hemisphere sense. So it is the right hemisphere sense of objectivity that provides the basis of union between the hemispheres in a shared understanding of objectivity. The philosophical insistence on absolute objectivity as the only acceptable definition is a sign of unhelpful left hemisphere dominance.

The flip side of objectivity, traditionally, is subjectivity. The use of 'subjectivity', if anything, is even more various and confusing that that of objectivity, as it can be used, not only as an opposite to absolute objectivity, but as a term describing individual experience and its privacy. Thus what I call 'objectivity' in some usages is necessarily 'subjective'. This usage unhelpfully conflates individual experience with a lack of objectivity, and easily promotes the assumption that individual experience is opposed to objectivity – rather than, on the contrary, being a condition for it as I would argue. No experience at all can happen unless it is individual experience, and to call all this experience 'subjective' regardless of its degree of adequacy is a bit like calling everyone 'blind',

---

[101] McGilchrist (2009) pp.80-83
[102] Ibid. p.141
[103] Ibid. p.80

regardless of our degree of sightedness, because we all lack inbuilt X-ray vision.

It is for this reason that I try to avoid using the term 'subjectivity' altogether in Middle Way Philosophy. To try to use it as an opposite to incremental objectivity would be a recipe for confusion. Equivalents like 'lack of objectivity' will just have to do for this purpose.

Why have we got stuck into this habit of seeing the glass of objectivity as permanently half-empty? My guess is because it serves the purposes of metaphysical entrenchment to do so: but this is no more than a guess, and I would not want to turn it into a conspiracy theory. What needs to be appreciated here is that my terminological revisionism (as some see it) is neither especially perverse, nor is it deliberately intended to be confusing. Rather it is an unavoidable part of the content of the message of Middle Way Philosophy, and has the practical intention of helping people to reframe the concepts in a way that they will need to do to fully understand and practice it.

Middle Way Philosophy 1: The Path of Objectivity

B. The dispositional nature of objectivity

For objectivity to be *dispositional* means that it is people who are (incrementally) objective, rather than propositions. To talk of a person being objective is to talk about their dispositions: that is, the pattern of how they tend to behave in certain kinds of circumstances. A rubber band has a disposition to be stretchy, which we only experience in the circumstances when it is stretched, and a courageous person has a disposition to behave in a courageous way, by taking risks in order to create benefits. Objectivity is similarly a disposition of persons, which is displayed when they make judgements that address conditions more effectively than those without so much objectivity.

One theoretical problem with all dispositional qualities is that we might never experience them, because the conditions in which the disposition is revealed may never occur. Obviously a dispositional quality that is rarely evident is unlikely to be of much relevance to us (although this also depends on the power of the disposition – one that saved the world every hundred years would still be quite important to us!). However, objectivity is such a broad quality, and also one that is used every time a judgement is made, that this is unlikely to be a practical problem with dispositional objectivity. In any case, it could be argued that in some sense all qualities are dispositional: even a quality as basic as mass is only evident in some circumstances and not others. So there is no justification for rejecting dispositional qualities for anything other than practical concerns about the frequency of evidence of a given particular dispositional quality, unless one rejects the idea of qualities altogether.

Dispositional objectivity equates conceptually to the idea of virtue, as discussed in both virtue ethics and virtue epistemology, except that it is not merely an analysis of virtues

The dispositional nature of objectivity

recognised conventionally by our society. Nor is it based on a metaphysical belief like Aristotle's notion of form. Since objectivity is determined by experiential adequacy, not by convention, it would be possible for dispositional objectivity to completely defy convention. For example, in a society where the convention is for virtuous women to be highly submissive, a relatively objective woman might have the confidence to try out provisional ideas that defied this view of women, despite social disapproval. However, in many cases there will be a substantial overlap between conventional virtues and the virtues of objectivity.

Dispositional objectivity being a kind of virtue does not reduce Middle Way Philosophy to a virtue ethics or virtue epistemology, if what that means is that all judgements can only be made about the justification of our general dispositions over a period of time rather than our specific judgements at one time. I cannot say that because Henry is a relatively objective man, therefore all judgements made by Henry are equally objective as a matter of definition. If Henry is relatively objective it will only be because of the experiential adequacy of his judgements at different specific times put together. I can thus judge any specific judgement on the grounds of the experiential adequacy with which it is made, as well as judging the character of the person who made them by putting together these different judgements. We are not limited to either diachronic or synchronic judgements, but either can inform the other.

The point that this account of objectivity is the objectivity *of a person* (whether at one time or over time) makes a big difference in other respects, because that objectivity can be understood in relation to our whole experience. We may be more objective, for example, because of the strength of our imagination, or our compassion, or our awareness of our bodies. None of these aspects of objectivity would even figure in an abstract, bloodless, left hemisphere dominated 'view

Middle Way Philosophy 1: The Path of Objectivity

from nowhere'. In such an absolute disembodied position, assuming it was even possible without massive contradictions, we might imagine having an abstract knowledge of all objects and events, but we wouldn't know what it felt like to be a finite being amongst them, and thus would have a less than perfect awareness after all – contradicting the idea of an absolute position again. This is perhaps why angels are sometimes said to envy men and women their flesh and blood.

C. Scientific or factual objectivity

I will now turn to consider some different facets or aspects of objectivity – scientific, moral, compassionate, and aesthetic. These are not different *types* of objectivity derived in different ways (see 1.i), but different aspects of the same objectivity encountered in different contexts. That is to say that there is a conventional distinction between these different types of objectivity, which we can continue to use provided we recognise that this does not indicate different types of justification.

The incrementality of scientific objectivity is probably already recognised by most scientists, who have to make probabilistic judgements based on the weight and quality of evidence in relation to a theory, and then meet public incomprehension of the limited evidential support for some theories that have been prematurely popularised. However, the idea that scientific objectivity is dispositional will probably require much more defending.

The traditional emphasis in Western science has been on the propositional objectivity of a theory rather than the dispositional objectivity of scientists. However, as I have already argued, the idea that propositions can represent reality does not stand up to sceptical argument (see 1.a). Moreover, the meaning of the words out of which a scientific theory is created is not purely representational: some ambiguities and differences in interpretation are unavoidable. The words of the scientific papers only secondarily convey the effects of a scientific investigation conducted with a degree of experiential adequacy. Experiential adequacy determines the success of the investigation in addressing conditions, some of which involves not just judgements about experiments and observations – including the nature and scale of testing, how to interpret the results, and how to judge the relationship of observations to theory – but also how to manage the emotional responses of all involved and how to communicate the theory and the evidence.

If we ask what makes the theory of relativity and quantum physics more objective than Newtonian physics, the answer is not that the modern theories are known to precisely represent reality in a way that Newtonian physics does not, for the historical succession of scientific paradigms has made us aware of the sceptical questions that still give uncertainty even to the latest theories that have gained acceptance. However, the scientists who pioneered these theories have been able to address conditions in a way that the Newtonian scientists have not, by identifying the gaps in Newtonian theory, having the courage to put forward and develop an alternative, and finding evidence that fulfils the predictions of the new theory. In all these respects, and possibly others, their experiential adequacy was slightly better than their predecessors', and it is this experiential adequacy that allows them to be measured against their predecessors despite having a different theoretical paradigm.

Of course, having better experiential adequacy is rather like having a better mesh of net to catch fish in, so there is still a measure of luck in the fish that we actually catch. A scientist with a new theory may have a measure of luck in being able to find evidence for it, when another, whose experiential adequacy is just as good, fails to get the evidence she needs and is thus not taken seriously enough to support further investigation. It might be that the further investigation would, after all, have found the evidence she needed. This is an instance of where issues of presentation and emotion also become relevant to the objectivity of approach of a scientist who seeks support for further investigation. Generally, though, the experiential adequacy of the work done by scientists is the best available measure of their objectivity, because we cannot take account of the unknown factors of luck that determine their success beyond this. Objectivity does not necessarily lead to success in gaining positive results, but it will mean that a greater adequacy has been brought to bear on the investigation that leads to those results.

The objectivity of scientific research does not depend solely on the dispositional objectivity of individual scientists, though obviously these contribute. The experiential adequacy of the whole method used is also a product of the socially agreed methods used by groups of scientists and by traditions of scientific practice. This socially agreed adequacy is also dispositional, but the dispositions are those of a group of people acting together. The success of this social level of investigation depends on its degree of integration (see 6.f on social integration), including the coherence of the approach taken by each member of a group, but also the extent to which they collectively recognise the possibility of error (see 5.c & d).

Philosophers of science have long been questing for an account of the objectivity of science, but have failed to find one. To avoid either naive realism or a scientific relativism in which Aristotle's science is as good as Einstein's, we need to consider the history of successful practice in science without these extremes of metaphysical assumption. The two great figures who have tried to do this, however, Lakatos and Kuhn, both failed to reach an account of the objectivity of scientific theory. Both, however, came close to an account of objectivity in the skills of scientists, limited only from drawing fuller conclusions by their assumption that an account of objectivity could not be psychological, because they believed that this would be irredeemably 'subjective'. Kuhn described these skills and attitudes of scientists as 'puzzle-solving ability':

Taken as a group or in groups, practitioners of the developed sciences are, I have argued, fundamentally puzzle-solvers. Though the values that they deploy at times of theory-choice derive from other aspects of their work as well, the demonstrated ability to set up and to solve puzzles presented by nature is, in case of value conflict, the dominant criterion for most members of a scientific group. Like any other value, puzzle-solving ability proves equivocal in application. Two men who share it may nevertheless differ in the judgements they draw from its use. But the behaviour of a community which makes it pre-eminent will be very different from that of one which does not. [104]

Without such a detailed survey of scientific success here, I can only point to the implicit support offered by the conclusions of Lakatos and Kuhn to the thesis that scientific objectivity consists in the qualities of scientists and their communities. The response to a puzzle depends most basically on the recognition that existing answers are inadequate, and on a continued provisionality in handling possible alternative answers. The need to be able to keep working within a given paradigm, maintaining a justified confidence in it so long as it is fruitful, needs to be balanced with the critical skills involved in deciding whether to move to a different paradigm. The successful scientist has to follow the Middle Way in yielding neither to a dogmatic relativism that would lead her to drop a successful paradigm too soon, nor to a dogmatic attachment to the current paradigm that stops her from treating it critically. The same kind of balancing of judgement also applies to smaller decisions where a particular line of enquiry needs to be continued or dropped within a particular paradigm[105].

One particular scientific issue which illustrates the role of dispositional objectivity in science especially well is that of publication bias. Scientists have an obvious interest in being able to highlight positive discoveries, and are thus very likely to give these maximum publication exposure, whilst negative results often remain unpublished[106]. Given that negative

---

[104] Kuhn (1996) p.205
[105] See Ellis (2001) 2.b for a more detailed discussion
[106] Goldacre (2008) pp.212-16

results may in the long run provide more useful information to guide future theorisation and research than positive ones, this tendency is very unhelpful to the objectivity of science. In 1998 a review found that in the entire medical research taking place in China, no negative findings had been published[107]. One could conclude from this with reasonable justification that medical research in China is less objective than in other countries where at least some negative results are published, not because the theories considered by Chinese medical researchers are necessarily further away from reality, but because the conditions for finding out incrementally how close they may be to reality are not present. Of course this defect in the objectivity of scientific tradition in China may in some cases be compensated by individual objectivity, but the conditions make this less likely.

In parallel to scientific objectivity where the organised social pursuit of knowledge takes place, there is also an individual factual objectivity. This is the degree of objectivity with which a given individual pursues what they perceive to be facts about the universe. Exactly the same criteria apply, apart from a different relationship to the social aspect of scientific objectivity. The individual may still be dependent on the objectivity of organised science to support individual objectivity. In the modern world, the vast majority of our factual beliefs reach us through the education system and the media and are thus social in origin, but we nevertheless need objectivity in assessing the reliability of these sources. Instead of scientific theories investigated directly, the individual may well have implicit theories such as "The BBC is a good unbiased source of political information."

We may be made aware by examples of public ignorance (e.g. the majority of Americans rejecting Darwinism and anthropogenic global warming) that a relatively objective

---

[107] Vickers et al (1998)

science is not sufficient to ensure a population that is objective to the same degree, and the objectivity of science is ultimately dependent on that of the wider population that supports it. I would suggest that individual factual objectivity has been relatively neglected, that factual investigation has been left too much to specialists, and that the influence of the paradigm of knowledge (as opposed to mere 'opinion') rather than justified provisional belief has contributed to this.

D. Moral objectivity

To those used to the fact-value distinction, the idea that moral objectivity may be identical to factual objectivity will come as a surprise. Yet if experiential adequacy enables us to gain the best possible *understanding* of conditions through the refinement of theories that fail to address conditions sufficiently, exactly the same process can be used to explain how we develop the best possible *values* to respond to our conditions. One way of understanding this is adaptive, as will be explored in 4.g. If our ways of behaving and the values that drive us help us to address conditions in our environment, our way of life will be optimised.

However, there is a danger that this will look superficially like a reductive explanation of moral objectivity. Our account needs to do as much justice to the experiences that people throughout the ages have associated with metaphysical beliefs about the good, as it does to scientific accounts that reduce moral objectivity to benefits that are more easily observable from the outside. People have long identified moral objectivity with the ultimate good that they see in God, with laws of nature, or with essential laws in harmony with the underlying structure of the universe. All of these have been very unhelpful when taken metaphysically, but all also represent an experience of trying to get to grips with unknown conditions, with something bigger than us, or at least bigger than our current beliefs and identifications. This yearning for the beyond may have been intellectually articulated in a number of ways, but in relation to our physical, emotional, and intuitional experience it suggests it should be fulfilled by an open attitude to conditions.

The moral aspects of objectivity involve more emphasis on integrating our desires, so as to prevent interference in experiential adequacy by psychic conflict. This integration of desires is also interdependent with that of meaning and belief. The integration of moral meaning involves sympathy and imagination, which will be discussed in the next chapter. However, moral beliefs (both implicit and explicit) are also crucial in directing our judgements about how to act. For moral objectivity, moral beliefs need to be formed with as great an experiential adequacy as possible.

Incrementally objective moral judgements will not be infallible. We can be confronted with moral dilemmas and make the wrong choice because of our ignorance of conditions. Although there may be notionally a right choice – that is, the best available choice – that can be made in any given set of circumstances, we do not have any way of knowing this right choice, so it is not relevant to making our decision. In practice from am embodied perspective, recognising the plurality of moral choice is often helpful: there is not one 'right' judgement for us, beside which all others will be wrong, but perhaps several with complex degrees of comparative adequacy in different respects. It is the various criteria that we can find in our experience (principles, consequences, intuitions, virtues) that are relevant to a decision, and where there is a conflict between the criteria available to our experience, we need to try to discern which of them is the most adequate. But we may not, in fact, be able to discern a difference in some cases.

This discernment of moral adequacy can be most easily handled initially through the avoidance of metaphysical assumptions. If we assume that only one set of absolute criteria provides the correct way to resolve all moral decisions, then we are approaching the decision through metaphysics rather than experience. If we can discern real moral dilemmas between different kinds of values or different criteria which all seem as though they might be morally objective, then we are beginning to address the issue through experience. It is simply not perceiving moral conflict, which forms a basic part of our experience, that detracts most from moral objectivity. If you don't perceive a real moral conflict about abortion, for example, but think it is *obvious* either that abortion is murder or that a foetus has no moral importance because it's merely part of the mother's body, then you need to work harder to understand the moral experience of those on the other side of the divide. The work of Jonathan Haidt in recognising the psychological basis of different kinds of social and political values is helpful here[108], and will be discussed in IV.4.h.

Middle Way Philosophy can contribute to moral discussion, not by offering definite solutions to moral dilemmas, but by pointing out dogmatic assumptions. Very often just the recognition of another point of view will make the best decision clearer. Middle Way Philosophy can also attempt to assess the likely degree of dogmatism behind a particular approach, so that, again, a decision can be made based on maximum experiential adequacy and the avoidance of dogmatic approaches that interfere with it.

This general approach to ethics raises lots of further questions which will be tackled in section 7. This will include discussion of the main different types of moral theory and the ways that they can be used dogmatically or provisionally.

---

[108] Haidt (2012)

E. Compassion

In Middle Way Philosophy, compassion can be seen as an aspect of objectivity which overlaps both with factual and moral aspects. Compassion (or love, of a non-possessive sort – *agape* or *metta*) is the ability to identify with ourselves or others beyond our own immediate interests. However, in 1.j it was argued that given that we do not experience a self but an ego, and our ego-identifications are not necessarily focused on ourselves as individuals, "selfishness" and "selflessness" are not relevant to our moral integration. Instead, I want to argue that compassion consists in the *extension of identifications* from our current limited identifications to both our own at other times, and those of others that we do not already identify with. When this extension of identifications occurs our feelings are channelled with greater experiential adequacy. We feel more with both ourselves and others when our feelings are bigger.

Nobody is ever without the basis of compassion, because we are never without desires that identify with certain objects or persons (usually including ourselves). Our problem is not that we lack the energies to put into compassion, but that those energies are channelled only through limited identification. In some cases we may only be concerned with our own short-term fulfilments, according to unexamined beliefs about what will bring us fulfilment (e.g. drinking too much alcohol). In some other cases (more likely, on average, for women) our limited identification may not just be with ourselves but with other people whom we identify with intensely, such as children, lovers, or heroes. Compassion, then, effectively means extending our identifications both towards our own changing desires and long-term interests, and towards others with whom we do not yet identify.

Compassion

Compassion is a form of objectivity, in which the integration of our desires is linked to a similar extension of meanings and beliefs in relation to people. One major barrier to my compassion towards more distant people is that they are not very meaningful to me – they may just be fodder for statistics, or at the most names and photos. To extend my compassion, the extension of meaning is important – for example, through reading in-depth journalism or travel writing about foreign countries, through forms of distant communication using mail, the internet, or phone, or by recalling distant people to one's imagination. The Christian practice of praying for others, and the Buddhist practice of loving-kindness meditation may both help with this by getting the imagination to work on the meaningfulness of others. If I think about an elderly relative's suffering in a hospital bed, or imagine my tyrannical boss playing frisbee with his children on the beach, the range of experience summoned up for me when their name is mentioned is that much richer, and compassion for them becomes that much easier. At the same time, my view of them has become more objective.

The examining of our beliefs about people also has a role in compassion. A prejudice is a metaphysical view about a person's nature, which attaches a negative (or unrealistically positive) value to them that is resistant to being changed by experience. To overcome, say, racial prejudice, deliberate reflection or argument about that person to test one's views for coherence should soon reveal such prejudices, because the idea that someone is 'bad' because of their race is entirely inconsistent with all of the ways they will appear 'good' in other respects that can be experienced. If rational reflection cannot change our prejudices, sometimes experience itself can. Kathryn Schulz tells the moving story of a C.P. Ellis, a member of the Ku Klux Klan, who gradually extends his identification towards a black woman campaigner for racial justice, when he is obliged to actually experience her and get to know her by working with her on a committee for the racial integration of schools[109].

Compassion, then, comes from fallibility – recognising the limitations of my own views, imaginings and identifications, as well as increasingly recognising and accepting those of others. It works outwardly from wherever we start. In comparison to this, the traditional 'top down' view of compassion or love which is often communicated in Christianity and Buddhism is a non-starter. If I am just told that I *ought* to love everybody in the world because God does, or that is what enlightened people do, even if I identify strongly with that idea, the most that is likely to happen practically is a vague *wish* to love everybody. Since we are situated beings with limited identifications, not actually capable of loving everybody, our love will not in practice progress any further than our objectivity. We need to be able to experience others without interfering prejudices or contrary impulses if we are to love them to any meaningful degree.

Some are likely to find compassion easier to develop than others, because of varying levels of empathy as a starting condition. Empathy should not be confused with compassion (even though the boundary is vague) because (at least in the sense I am going to stipulate here) empathy is a result of past conditions, whereas compassion involves development towards objectivity from our starting point. Just as some people are born blind, which makes it harder for them to engage with conditions through vision, so others are born with lower levels of empathy than others, which makes it harder for them to imagine the perspective of others and thus to extend their identifications in that way. Autistic people are particularly limited in this way, but this does not mean that they cannot extend identifications or develop a degree of compassion. This creates a likely asymmetry in their integration, but may be

---

[109] Schulz (2010) pp.273-9

compensated for in other areas of integration. For example, to some extent we can compensate for difficulties in easily imagining others' perspectives by developing our cognitive understanding of them, and extending our identifications by that means instead. Baron-Cohen presents evidence of autistics (as opposed to psychopaths or other empathy-deficient types) being highly moral in their social interactions, substituting rule-governance to compensate for their lack of intuitive understanding of others[110]. I would argue that such autistics are (perhaps slowly and painfully) extending their compassion by the means available to them, despite their disabilities.

The topic of compassion is sometimes tackled in an over-narrow way by confusing it with empathy. Empathy is a psychologically observable quality dependent on functions in the right hemisphere of the brain[111], but this does not justify the effective reduction of ethics to empathy and the exclusion of the left hemisphere from moral relevance[112], or even excluding the left hemisphere from compassion. The right hemisphere has a crucial role in integrating the motives of the left and making them effective through empathy as well as other kinds of contextual objectivity. However, without the left hemisphere's identification there would be no drive towards compassionate activity. Empathy without directed energy is impotent, even though narrowly directed energy without much empathy may fail to address conditions in important ways because of a lack of compassionate objectivity. There is also no essential discontinuity between a 'selfish' desire for one's own interests and an empathically directed concern for others (or for oneself at other times), just a different degree of integration and contextualisation of the same energies:

---

[110] Baron-Cohen (2011)
[111] McGilchrist (2009) p.57
[112] As McGilchrist does in (2009) p.86. Baron-Cohen (2011) also characterises a lack of empathy as 'evil'.

empathy is necessary for their greater integration, but far from sufficient.

Compassion is an important and immediate aspect of objectivity in everyday life, but its field of application is small, whatever our fantasies about loving everyone. Other aspects of objectivity, whether factual or moral, focused more on integration of belief, often have a larger scope and potential. One can see this in the example of a highly loving mother, whose endowment of empathy has been extended by compassion, and who makes a huge difference to her family and immediate community because of this. However, such love can also sometimes be combined with parochial values and a lack of identification with wider spiritual, intellectual, or practical enterprises that may address conditions far more profoundly. The mother's objectivity could also be applied to these things as far as her capacities allow, but she is not accustomed to doing so. If the dam bursts, the loving mother and her family and entire community may be swept away: it takes the expertise and heroism of the hydraulic engineer to stop it bursting.

F. Aesthetic objectivity

Aesthetic objectivity is perhaps the most immediately available to experience of the different aspects of objectivity. By aesthetic objectivity I mean the capacity to experience beauty.

To give an idea of aesthetic objectivity in experience, compare two scenarios. In scenario one you are walking through a garden in the sunshine. You are relaxed, alert, and contented. You are suddenly struck by the beauty of a flower, and spend several minutes just looking at it with gathering enjoyment. In scenario two you are again walking through a garden in the sunshine, and the flower is still there, in a very similar physical condition to how it was before. However, you are feeling anxious, harassed and preoccupied. This time you walk straight past the flower. Even if you had stopped and looked at it, you would not have taken in what was beautiful about it.

There are two metaphysical extremes of explanation for the difference in your apprehension of beauty between these two scenarios. One just puts beauty down to 'subjectivity', saying that you appreciated beauty on one day and not the other, showing that beauty is not 'really there'. The other extreme would be to say that the beauty was 'really there' all the time, but in the second scenario – perhaps due to your sinful or imperfect human nature – you failed to experience it.

Both of these explanations are metaphysical because they involve big assumptions about a beauty that does or does not 'really exist', beyond our experience of beauty. A Middle Way approach, however, would avoid both these sets of limiting assumption and suggest that in the first scenario you had more objectivity than in the second. In the first case your experience was more capable of appreciating beauty, perhaps because it was available to your experience, whereas in the second it was not.

Your experience of beauty does not necessarily relate to the object, in the sense that you could conceivably have had this experience of beauty (or lack of it) with any possible object. A dead frog, a pile of drunkard's vomit, or a piece of corrugated iron fence may not seem like obvious objects for an experience of beauty, but if you were to deliberately look for beauty in these things, in the right mood, you would probably find them. The strongest demonstration of this is to be found in forms of meditation which involve the aesthetic concentration on a simple object, such as one's experience of the breath. If one can find experience of the breath beautiful, it is relatively easy to transfer that experience to other objects.

In practice, of course, we tend to find some things more beautiful than others: flowers, strong contrasts, healthy young women with clear complexions, and colourful sunsets are more likely to seem beautiful to us because we have an egoistic identification of some kind to start with. They draw our attention and attract us, for a complex range of possible reasons which I will not spend time going into here[113]. Whatever our starting point, however, I argue that it is our experiential adequacy that enables us to develop our sense of the beauty of the object from that point.

On the other hand, it is not the case that any experience is as beautiful as any other experience, because our experiential adequacy enables some experiences to be more beautiful than others. It is thus not just a 'subjective' sentiment attached to an experience that makes it beautiful, as relativists would have us believe.

In terms of the brain, it is the right hemisphere that maintains awareness of all immediate sensual experience[114],

---

[113] See Ellis (2011b) chapter 11 for a fuller discussion
[114] McGilchrist (2009) p.38

experiences sensual objects as a whole[115], and makes fine discriminations in what it perceives[116]. The right hemisphere is thus the aesthetic hemisphere, yet it is the left hemisphere that creates conscious, rational judgments. The conscious belief that an object is beautiful, or that it is more or less beautiful than another, for instance, must be arrived at by the left hemisphere. However, as in all types of objectivity, it is when the various judgements of the left hemisphere are most effectively integrated by the right hemisphere that greater objectivity can result through experiential adequacy. Due to the left hemisphere's will and judgement I may look more closely, or apply a structure of reasoning (for example, awareness of a musical structure such as key modulations) in a way that helps me to more adequately appreciate beauty, using the abilities that the right hemisphere offers. As a result of closer examination using the right hemisphere my left hemisphere judgement may change to become more adequate. The left hemisphere's role will not be any the less even if it is the right hemisphere that unconsciously reaches judgement in a given case, as it is the left hemisphere that drives the direction of both attention and judgement over the longer term.

Another important part of the case, however, is to show that aesthetic objectivity is a different aspect of what is conceptually the same objectivity as factual and moral objectivity. We can experience examples which appear to show a stronger distinction between the three types of objectivity. For example, the Nazis often seemed to demonstrate both factual and aesthetic objectivity without moral objectivity, experimenting on Jewish prisoners in the interests of science, and playing string quartets in the midst of the death camps. However, I would suggest that these show an asymmetry of objectivity rather than an absolute distinction.

---

[115] Ibid. p.46-9
[116] Ibid p.52

Middle Way Philosophy 1: The Path of Objectivity

Generally speaking, and assuming no specific disabilities, the experiential adequacy that enables us to investigate facts more effectively or to develop more adequate values also allows us to appreciate beauty to roughly the same degree. However, we might apply that experiential adequacy far more effectively in one sphere than in another, because metaphysical beliefs intervene to block our experiential adequacy in some areas, and also lead us to habitually exercise one kind of objectivity more than another. There may be strong pressure from groups to maintain metaphysical beliefs that do this. In the Nazi context the interposing metaphysical belief was a strong distinction between those who were or were not thought worthy to be treated as persons and given human rights. This was a specific blockage in the way that these educated, intelligent Nazi officers could develop and display their objectivity rather than a distinction between types of objectivity. As historical sources also record, the same blockage caused Nazis to develop very odd theories on the subject of race, and also regard the beauty of Jewish women as somehow illusory or deceitful[117]. Their aesthetic and factual types of awareness were also affected within the sphere where their objectivity was constrained by metaphysical pressure.

More on the topic of asymmetrical integration can be found in II.5.d, III.7.b and IV.6.b. For the moment, however, the main point is that aesthetic integration *contributes to* overall integration, and thus that, while our aesthetic objectivity may run ahead of or lag behind other aspects of objectivity, a lack of aesthetic objectivity remains a handicap to our total objectivity in the end. Brilliant scientists or saints may be very objective in certain ways, but if they cannot appreciate beauty where it occurs in their experience, they are less objective than they might be, and their engagement with the world will

---

[117] Bradley (2011) seems to sympathise with this Nazi view.

be less intense for it. Similarly, the cultivation of aesthetic objectivity to the exclusion of factual or moral objectivity will limit us. The brilliant artist who beats up his wife in drunken rages may get away with it, and we may not necessarily be able to discern any immediate effect on his art, but his total engagement with conditions will nevertheless be more limited for it.

G. Objectivity, adaptivity and evolution

As a further approach to understanding the nature of objectivity in Middle Way Philosophy, it may be helpful to introduce the concept of adaptivity. It needs to be stressed that this is just a model of explanation that may prove helpful to some readers, rather than a conceptually essential point. It must also not be mistaken for a reductive explanation. The Middle Way cannot be understood solely in terms of evolutionary adaptation, because it addresses conditions in general – not just those of survival and reproduction. However, to consider the Middle Way in terms of such adaptation may nevertheless be illuminating.

According to the general theory of evolution (which is broadly supported by a wide range of biological evidence, even if differences remain on the details of the evolutionary process), biological organisms (or at least, those with sexual reproduction) adapt to their environments by a process of genetic mutation followed by natural selection. A particular organism develops characteristics that are slightly but randomly different from those of its parents, and those characteristics that are well adapted to the environment and make an essential difference to the organism's survival will be passed on, whilst those that impede the organism's survival will not.

The resemblance between this process and the negative feedback loop described in 3.e was noted by both Dewey and Popper. For Popper, the focus here was only on scientific theories, which he saw as being exposed to the conditions of the universe through testing just as new organisms are tested by their exposure to their environment. Inadequate theories, like ill-adapted organisms, will die out, but those that survive the test will become established[118]. Dewey, as I have already discussed, also applied this feedback loop to moral drives.

Nassim Nicholas Taleb alternatively focuses on the point of *optionality* that emerges just after that of frustration[119]. At that point we could adopt any of a number of possible alternative beliefs to the one that has just proved inadequate, and we have not yet entrenched ourselves in a new belief. An organism with more possible new ways of developing or behaving is in a better position to select the one most appropriate to the context. According to Taleb, having more options also helps us to develop *antifragility*, that is, an adaption to a wide range of possible circumstances, including those that are currently unforeseen. The more we are subjected to minor frustrations or stresses that oblige us to open up our options, then, the more antifragile we are likely to become. These concepts of optionality, adaptivity and antifragility will be explored in more detail in IV.2.b-d.

However, it is not theories that are primarily tested in the evolutionary analogy that I am making here, because theories do not exist independent of their interpretation and application. The testing of a theory requires a range of judgements by scientists in relation to what they experience (see 4.c), meaning that the testing is a testing of the objectivity of the scientists in relation to the theory, even though their eventual judgement is about the theory. It is the theory *in the minds of the scientists* that develops in response to new options and then passes or fails the test of conditions. It may then undergo further tests in the minds of others who consider the findings of the scientists. If the theory prevails, however, one could say that it is adapted to its conditions – conditions of survival in the minds of the scientists given the range of experiences scientists are having in relation to it.

---

[118] Popper (1994)
[119] Taleb (2012)

Middle Way Philosophy 1: The Path of Objectivity

We can perhaps see the comparison more strongly in relation to individual factual objectivity and moral objectivity. If we do not have the practical knowledge required for us to survive in a certain environment (e.g. what plants are edible and which poisonous), we will perish. Similarly, if we do not have values that enable us to address conditions in that environment, we will also perish. So, for example, when the Easter Islanders became obsessed with the value of erecting enormous statues that had to be transported using logs, and they cut down the last trees on their island in order to get the logs, the effects on their long-term survival were devastating[120]. Finding a clear survival value associated with aesthetic objectivity is trickier, but perhaps aesthetic objectivity supports a general appreciation of our environment and an attention to it that is beneficial.

So, the concept of objectivity generally can be understood in terms of an adaptivity that, at a basic level, helps us to survive. Beyond this basic level, however, objectivity may also help us to thrive, either as individuals or as societies. This doesn't just mean to be healthy and reproduce ourselves, but also to be happy, fulfil our potential, and develop our skills and technologies. This helps us to compete with other individuals or other societies. However, it should also be stressed that the success of such objectivity is not inevitable and also depends on luck: an organism that is well-adapted to quite a wide range of conditions may nevertheless be wiped out by events that still fall outside its range (such as a falling asteroid, an ice age or an extreme drought).

But if objectivity is generally adaptive, this leaves a central question about the adaptive effects of metaphysics. If objectivity as I have defined it so far has adaptive value, then metaphysics must have a maladaptive effect because it interferes with our addressing of conditions. But if that is the

---

[120] Diamond (2006) ch.2

case, how did metaphysical belief ever evolve, and why has it been tolerated for so long?

One hypothesis I can offer in relation to this (and it is no more than a hypothesis) is that metaphysics has had an adaptive value during earlier stages of the development of human beings. While we still thought of ourselves primarily in relation to groups rather than as individuals, loyalty to the group was the prime requirement for survival. Individual thinking was much more likely to result in death than in a greater chance of survival. Metaphysics, not being subject to challenge from experience, provides a strong sense of group identity by giving the group the impression that it has special, 'true' beliefs that are different from those of every other group. Some metaphysically-justified beliefs (such as Jewish dietary laws revealed by Yahweh) seem to have no evident function other than simply uniting the group with a sense that it is special, and excluding outsiders.

However, in the last 2500 years or so, we have seen the gradual development of an individual perspective in certain places and times. These were particularly ancient India at the time of the Buddha, ancient Greece, and Western civilisation since the enlightenment. In these contexts, individual critical perspectives have emerged, and enabled some judgements to be made on the basis of experience rather than merely in obedience to the group. As a result, objectivity has grown, and so has the effectiveness with which we address conditions, and the competitive advantage of groups with this individual perspective over other groups.

A more complex development of this hypothesis is alternatively suggested by my reading of McGilchrist, who sees the left hemisphere dominance associated with metaphysics to be dangerously increasing. I would suggest that metaphysics has functioned as a support for the introduction of greater left-hemisphere dominance, even though it was the overall contribution made by the periods of left-hemisphere dominance, with a new consolidation of representations, that contributed to objectivity rather than the metaphysics. Given that metaphysics gives apparently impregnable support to the left hemisphere, its use may have helped the left hemisphere to establish a dominance that has proved adaptive in other ways. The explicit development of representations helps us to adapt to our environment as long as that environment remains reasonably stable and predictable, and metaphysics has helped the left hemisphere to maintain the dominance that enabled this development of representations to take place. So, for example, the Protestant Reformation was accompanied by a strong attachment to particular metaphysical claims, such as the literal revelatory truth of the Bible and the value of internal individual experience over external form. However, the greater left hemisphere dominance that commitment to these metaphysical claims supported also enabled other, generally helpful and adaptive, developments by the left hemisphere such as greater stress on individual judgement, critical thinking, capitalism, and greater separation between church and state.

On this hypothesis, one can think of the development of Western civilisation rather like that of a retreating sea (somewhat like Matthew Arnold's "Sea of Faith" in his poem *Dover Beach*, in fact). In general the sea of metaphysics is on the retreat, but it retreats through a series of advances, each of which goes a little less far than the one before. Each of those waves represents a new assertion of the left hemisphere over the right as it advances, but an overall integration as it recedes and the particular metaphysics that it represents is undermined by scepticism. Standing on the beach, we are not in a good position to appreciate immediately that the tide is going out, for with each new wave we fear instead that it is coming in: yet each new wave of metaphysics is slightly less group-dependent than the last and takes for granted more

Objectivity, adaptivity and evolution

integration both of individuals and society. Thus, as McGilchrist charts, there has been a Graeco-Roman wave, a Reformation wave, an Enlightenment wave, and a modern wave, each representing a renewed left hemisphere dominance[121]: to which I would add that there are also new types of metaphysics attending and powering each wave: Stoicism, Protestantism, Enlightenment Philosophy, and modern relativism. With each "melancholy, long, withdrawing roar" as Arnold puts it, we are confronted more with our immediate experience and the mediating function of our right hemisphere, as well as becoming just a little more free.

So, I agree with McGilchrist about the waves, but with Arnold about the direction of the tide. It is not periods of advancing left hemisphere domination we need to fear, for these consist in the left hemisphere successfully addressing conditions in new and complex ways, which will then just need to be more fully integrated. It is the periods of *static* left hemisphere dominance we need to fear, where human beings remain locked into fixed ideas and rigid relationships, and they are least able to respond to new conditions with either hemisphere, as was evidently the case in the Middle Ages. What we have today, in addition to a wide range of techniques involving both left and right hemispheres, is a better developed capacity for sceptical argument that can prevent any one brand of metaphysics from digging itself in for a long occupation of human society.

Helpful as I believe this hypothesis could be to explain how the Middle Way can be seen as adaptive in the context of Western history, not too much store can be set on it. It is a sketch of a way that the matter could be understood, but generally a side issue from the argument that objectivity is dependent on the Middle Way. It should not be hardened into a theory of history, for theories of history make claims about the future course of

---

[121] McGilchrist (2009) chapters 8-12

all conditions, in addition to the human response to them. Whilst I think we have reason to believe that the general human response to conditions is becoming more adequate, we do not know what these conditions are going to throw at us even in the next five minutes, and nor can we predict whether this trend in adequacy will continue or reverse in the longer term.

5. Justification

In this section I want to argue for a concept of *justification* to replace that of knowledge. Knowledge is traditionally defined as justified true belief, but (if we are to accept the sceptical arguments explained in 1.a) we do not have access to truth. Truth is thus irrelevant to us except as a regulative idea, *Truth on the Edge* as I have called it in my book of that name[122]. Our beliefs therefore need to be freed from reliance on appeals of truth, and justified in terms that avoid truth-conditionality.

Without reference to criteria of truth, how exactly can we justify a belief that we provisionally entertain? To explore this I will be using the epistemological concepts of foundationalism and coherentism and suggesting how they can be combined to create a Middle Way theory of justification.

---

[122] Ellis (2011c)

A. Rejection of positive foundationalism

With the concept of justification, we enter back completely in the assumptions of the left hemisphere of the brain. It may often be the case that the right hemisphere makes implicit, unconscious judgements, but the reasoned, explicit ones that we are conscious of are made in the left hemisphere. It is through these explicit judgements that we maintain whatever degree of control we may have over our response to conditions. Even if they do not determine our actions at a given time, they must contribute in the longer term or we would be impotent to shape ourselves or the world. Unless we accept the metaphysical dogma of determinism, which we have no grounds to do if we rely on experience (see IV.4.c), we must work on the assumption that our judgements do make some difference and thus that we should try to make them as objective as possible.

But how should we do this? This is where we need a theory of justification. The terms *foundationalism* and *coherentism* are used in epistemology to refer to two contrasting kinds of justification[123]. A foundationalist theory is one that derives justification of a particular claim from its relationship to a foundational claim that is assumed to be true. The analogy is of a house of beliefs being built on foundations of certainty. Thus Descartes' philosophy is a classic example of a foundationalist philosophy, because it builds up further justified claims from the cogito, the allegedly proven claim that 'I exist'. In contrast, a coherentist theory is one that derives justification for a claim from its coherence with a set of other claims that are already accepted, even if all these claims taken together have no ultimate foundation. These two theories contradict each other because a foundationalist would accept a claim derived from a foundation of certainty even if it contradicted every other claim he otherwise believed, whereas a

---
[123] See, e.g. Everitt & Fisher (1995) chs. 5-8

coherentist would accept a claim that was consistent with her other beliefs regardless of whether it had a foundation.

These two theories at the outset also seem to be the only two possible ones, because coherentism is the only possible alternative when foundationalism is rejected (assuming we want some kind of justification). The direct opposite of foundationalism is just the absence of any justification due to the lack of foundational support. However, in practice, when there is no foundation our experience relies on a coherency of justification. For example, if a random disconnected experience popped up – say a mini flying saucer hovering over my soup – I would rely on the incoherence of this experience to conclude that I was not justified in believing in it. All evidence that arrives to us via the senses seems to rely on coherence, unless we have some foundational reason for believing that the senses must be correct.

The third theory also often mentioned by analytic epistemologists, reliabilism, can immediately dismissed because it is externalist or "non-inferential"[124] – that is, it ignores the question of whether we are aware of our justification, and claims that we are justified if we derive our belief from a reliable source, whether or not we are aware that it is a reliable source. In its abstracted reliance on an absolute standpoint beyond experience this theory has ruled itself out of all relevance to justification in relation to our experience, apart from the fact that the idea of a reliable source otherwise looks suspiciously like another sort of foundation.

My rejection of positive foundationalism will probably come as no surprise to anyone who has read thus far. By *positive* foundationalism I mean a theory of justification that assumes that any claim deduced from a positive metaphysical claim that it is assumed must be true. Positive foundational claims can

---

[124] Everitt & Fisher (1995) p.63 ff

be identified with positive metaphysical claims because they have no further justification – they are taken to be either self-evident *a priori* (see 1.f) or revealed from an infallible source such as God (see 1.g). Positive foundationalism, in effect, is positive metaphysics and positive dogma. Although another possible form of positive foundationalism is empiricist, this would require us to accept the evident justification of our senses without regard for the assumptions with which it had been interpreted or for its coherence with our other beliefs (see 2.e on empiricism).

However, a rejection of positive foundationalism does not necessarily imply a rejection of foundationalism altogether. Given the mutual exclusivity of foundationalism and coherentism, a total rejection of foundationalism would seem to require that we could not adopt any criteria other than those of coherence when judging justification. This, as we will see in the next chapter on coherentism, would be an unsatisfactory commitment to make.

B. Coherentism

Coherentism is a theory of justification that claims that judgements are justified by their coherence with other beliefs we already hold. It does not oblige us to enquire how those previous beliefs were in turn justified (which would lead to the infinite regress problem), but only to consider the coherence of new beliefs in the present time. So, if our sense were to throw up a completely incoherent experience (say, a bear writing a philosophy book), or if *a priori* reasoning were to lead me to a conclusion that contradicts other such reasoning (say, that 2+2=5), then I could justifiably reject these claims.

Coherentism has adopted a range of different accounts of what exactly is meant by 'coherent'. At root it must mean logically non-contradictory, but it can also incorporate requirements for probabilistic or explanatory consistency. A bear writing a philosophy book is not contradictory, but it would be highly improbable within my existing framework of beliefs, because previous experience suggests that philosophy books are only written by humans and that bears show no signs of literacy. The things I consider probable within my framework would, to be consistent, make a bear writing a philosophy book extremely improbable. The hypothesis of a bear writing it would also not be explanatorily consistent, as it would not explain the features of the philosophy book in ways that the hypothesis of a human doing so would. Coherentism would generally require, then, that my beliefs be free not only of contradiction but also of extreme improbability and unfruitful explanation.

Coherentism incorporates all new evidence from the senses so long as that evidence is coherent. As a theory of justification, it is concerned with how we adopt experience into belief rather than with the belief itself. Clearly some aspects of belief will be rejected as incoherent following coherentism (e.g.

hallucinations, mistaken calculations, conspiracy theories), whilst most will be accepted (e.g. everyday experiences within the realm of reasonable probability, for which feasible explanations exist). I might accept that there is a tiger running down an English street (coherent explanation – it has escaped from a wildlife park) but not a dragon (too improbable on the basis of known animals).

Nevertheless, coherentism does not seem to stand up to scepticism any better than positive foundationalism does. A set of entirely logically consistent, consistently probable, and mutually explanatory beliefs could perfectly well all be wrong – an extended construction of deluded fantasy. Anton's Syndrome, where a person who has become blind denies their blindness and describes a perfectly coherent (but from our point of view, false) visual world all around them, is a complete example of this[125]. For this reason we cannot accept coherentism by itself as a sufficient basis for justification.

However, we do also need our beliefs to be coherent. For all that I don't take mathematical claims to be absolute, they are generally correct within the sphere we experience. We would not be justified in believing that 2+2=5 even if God apparently said so. There may also be places where bears write philosophy books, bus conductors suddenly turn into giant parrots, and the leader of the Conservative Party is an aardvark, but not in the world I think I inhabit. Coherence seems to be necessary for our beliefs to be justified, even though it is not sufficient.

Another difficulty with coherentism is its apparent dependence on convention. Beliefs that are taken to be coherent are those accepted by most of the people around us, because the vast majority of what we take to be our knowledge is indirectly justified by the experience of others. Our ideas of what is

---

[125] Schulz (2010) pp. 67-8

probable or of what is explanatory depend largely on reported experience. Even our ideas about what is logically consistent often depend on what others take to be logically consistent, or on what constitutes acceptable premises for reasoning, rather than what we have worked out for ourselves. For example, the tradition of the negative implications of Pyrrhonian scepticism has been conventionally accepted since the Renaissance rediscovery of scepticism, even though there is no contradiction between Pyrrhonism and provisional belief. Even where the reasoning is unquestionable, any reasoning is only as good as its premises, and those of coherentism will unavoidably be conventional.

In schools of thought that rely on coherentism, the absence of a foundational justification is taken to be a reason to rely on convention instead – as in the relativist approach to ethics, where the lack of a universal ethics leaves us with a localised social or cultural ethics. However, the application of analysis to conventional beliefs can still reveal them to be contradictory. For example, it is quite common to make claims like "It's just my opinion, but abortion is absolutely wrong", or "Everyone has their own personal God", which attempt to combine absolute assumptions with conventional ones. Convention can be incoherent just because it does not incorporate awareness of its own limits.

So, we do not need to reject coherentism as necessary on the grounds that it can be used to support conventionalist assumptions, but rather keep up an awareness of the conventionalist assumptions that might be smuggled into coherentist reasoning. Those conventionalist assumptions will undermine coherentism because they do not incorporate awareness of their own limits, but coherentism could still work without them by considering all issues of coherence critically rather than merely in acceptance of convention.

Middle Way Philosophy 1: The Path of Objectivity

If we accept coherence as necessary, we do not have to accept coherentism as a complete explanation of justification, because we do not accept that coherence is sufficient for justification. To identify the other necessary conditions for justification, then, we must go back and reconsider foundationalism.

C. Agnostic foundationalism

So, let us look at foundationalism again. Positive foundationalism, as I argued above, is based on an appeal to metaphysics. If coherentism was accepted because it was judged the only alternative, then this would also be metaphysics – a negative metaphysical position. However, the use of foundationalism as a theory of *justification*, rather than knowledge, does not necessarily have to involve metaphysical assumptions. The distinction between using a foundation for justification and using a foundation metaphysically is that a foundation used for justification would be used provisionally.

If we use a foundation *in order to provide sole justification*, we cannot avoid metaphysical assumptions just because of the very epistemological strategy we are using. If the justification was valid only because of its relationship to the foundation, one would be relying wholly on the foundation even if one notionally called the justification provisional. This would be the case whether the justification was positive (i.e. we relied on a foundational claim that made positive claims) or negative (i.e. we relied on a foundational claim that contradicted positive claims). For example, if my foundation was that I can provisionally rely on my senses, the fact that I would have no other source of justified belief to question my senses would contradict the alleged provisionality. Similarly if my foundation was that I can provisionally not rely on my senses.

So, the alternative strategy is twofold:
1. The foundation we use cannot provide sole or sufficient justification for beliefs, but merely necessary justification
2. The foundation we use must not make definite positive or negative claims, as these would contradict the provisionality of the justification

Middle Way Philosophy 1: The Path of Objectivity

My conclusion is that we do need foundational justification, but the foundation must be agnostic in its content. That is, it must consist only in a recognition that we may be wrong in our assertion of justified claims. It is this very provisionality that provides an essential element of justification for claims acceptable in Middle Way Philosophy. As recognised in the previous chapter, we also need our claims to be coherent, so that coherence provides another necessary but not sufficient element of justification.

In my previous writings I have called this kind of foundationalism *negative foundationalism*. However, I now consider that this term carries too much of a danger of confusion with foundations that make a definite negative claim. I am thus now revising this term to *agnostic foundationalism.*

As previously explained (see 1.c), provisionality is a psychological state in which a belief is held, not a feature of the content of a provisional belief itself. Thus, to summarise my conclusions about justification here: *a justified claim is one that is both coherent with all other claims already accepted, and is also held in a provisional way with awareness of the possibility of that claim being wrong*. This definition clearly differentiates Middle Way Philosophy from forms of negative metaphysics that, having denied an epistemological foundation, rely only on coherence. As sceptical arguments such as the dream argument make clear, we need to constantly make practical allowances for the fact that our coherent world-view may be based on false assumptions.

Although all issues of justification are inevitably left hemisphere based, this account of justification also has the advantage of taking into account the right hemisphere. For where the left hemisphere assumes certainty (whether foundational or coherent), the right assumes uncertainty, so where the left assumes justification, the right merely notes a lack of it and remains on the alert for discrepancies. Agnostic foundationalism offers an account of justification that takes into account the existence of the right hemisphere merely by noting the limitations of what the left hemisphere can do by itself.

D. Agnostic foundationalism in relation to falsifiability

In Popper's account of justifiable scientific theory, one of the key ways that scientific theories are distinguished from metaphysical theories is in terms of their falsifiability. However, as we have seen (see 3.I), there are sceptical problems with this requirement. No observation can be identified with certainty as a falsification of a theory.

Nevertheless I have suggested that falsification is a criterion that can be used imprecisely by individuals uncertain about their commitment to a provisional theory. Rather than either abandoning a promising theory or making an unconditional commitment to it, they should determine their own criteria for falsification in their own time scale. In this way an approximate attempt at provisional belief is made that is open to later refinement, and a theory capable of such treatment can still be differentiated from an obviously metaphysical belief that requires either absolute commitment or nothing.

I can now clarify this point with reference to agnostic foundationalism as one of the two necessary criteria for justification. Agnostic foundationalism requires a theory to be held in a provisional way, a requirement that can only be described psychologically rather than in terms of the content of the theory or its justification. I now want to suggest that agnostic foundationalism is equivalent to falsifiability applied in the way I have just summarised.

Agnostic foundationalism consists of an awareness that the theory one is provisionally committed to could be wrong. To be practically effective, this recognition needs to go beyond a merely abstract labelling of a belief as fallible. The Buddhist tradition provides plenty of cautionary examples of the ineffectiveness of the mere abstract labelling of beliefs as

Agnostic foundationalism and falsifiability

fallible, where beliefs that are said to be 'ultimately empty', like the belief in enlightenment, are still nevertheless often practically treated as absolute metaphysical beliefs[126]. In order to make the labelling effective we need to ensure that a belief we take as provisional is in some way falsifiable for our purposes.

The terms of the falsification must suit the nature of the belief and of the person concerned and their context. For example, a provisional belief that your cat likes fish is fairly well falsified by you placing dish of fish in front of the cat and the cat just walking off – however, perhaps you might try once more to make sure the cat is hungry at the time. A provisional belief that meditation could be helpful to you might require a few months of practice, after which if you have not experienced any helpful developments, you may decide to drop it. A provisional belief that the Middle Way is good may require several years of exploration to falsify, as you understand more deeply what is meant and try out implications of this broader belief. If you dismissed such a complex theory too soon, it might be because you got an auxiliary hypothesis wrong, or you simply didn't understand the theory well enough. Nevertheless, though these possibilities always continue, there is a point where you have to judge them improbable and, if you can find a better alternative theory, move on to that.

Those conditioned into the fact-value distinction may still be wondering here how a value claim can be falsified. I would suggest three possible ways, which may lead to the same destination:
1. Value claims are always associated with factual claims, so you can falsify the associated factual claims
2. Value claims can be tested (imprecisely) against our experience of values, by considering whether they are implied by values we have already accepted through experience. If

---

[126] See Ellis (2011a) ch.6

they are not, they may be falsified for that reason. See 7.c below for ways that existing values found in experience can imply the value of the Middle Way.
3. Values are desires, so they can be tested in terms of whether those desires are wholly or partly fulfilled. So, for example, if you value happiness more than other possible values, you could test this value by acting so as to prioritise happiness for a given period of time and seeing whether you experienced more happiness as resulting for yourself or others. If you did not, the approach of valuing happiness would be falsified for you. Such an approach assumes that we should not value 'moral' ends exclusive of means, and that a pursuit of happiness should produce happiness: if it does not, the pursuit of happiness will not be best adapted to conditions according to its own standard – that of self-fulfilment. The desire concerned would be better fulfilled by being integrated with other desires which will help it to gain fulfilment in the longer term. See II.2 for a fuller discussion of the background assumptions made here.

Neither facts nor values are easy to falsify. Falsification is a complex matter, full of incremental judgements, ambiguity and imprecision. This is the nature of human experience in relation to judgements. If you want precision, then go back to metaphysics, but observe where that takes you. However, an imprecise and individually-judged falsification is far better than none at all, and it gives a specific bite to agnostic foundationalism that it might not otherwise have. The imprecision of the process does not prevent us from distinguishing provisional beliefs that are capable of going through that process from metaphysical beliefs that are not: indeed it is precisely *because* provisional beliefs are imprecise that we can falsify them, so it would be unrealistic to expect a precise falsification given this point.

The justification of our beliefs, as of our values, should not be thought of in terms like that of a mathematician deriving a precise proof. Instead, a better analogy would be with a sculptor. Seeing what our experience is roughly shaped like, and driven by a desire to shape it in a particular way, we chip away at our experience like a stone block to produce a gradually more refined set of beliefs – first crudely and then with gradually more precise tools. We need to adapt both to the structure of the stone as we encounter it and to our vision of what the sculpture will look like, but allow each to interact with the other in the way we create.

6. Integration

Middle Way Philosophy posits a basic connection between philosophy and psychology, in which metaphysical beliefs can only be held dogmatically, and only non-metaphysical beliefs can be held provisionally. Philosophy by itself is only able to establish this argument negatively using sceptical argument, but psychological theory can explain the way that objectivity can be developed through provisionality more positively, using the concept of integration. This psychological theory is compatible with account of self discussed philosophically in 1.j, but its ultimate justification is pragmatic.

The concept of integration has already been introduced (especially in 3.j), but it is now explored more thoroughly. The concepts of ego and psyche as they are used here have a broadly Jungian inspiration, but the psychology developed here is specific to Middle Way Philosophy and should not be assumed to follow Jungian models uncritically. The concept of integration can alternatively be understood in terms of left and right brain hemisphere relationships.

A. Ego-identification

I have already argued in 1.j that we have no grounds for accepting the metaphysical idea of the self, i.e. a fixed and essential basis for my identity. If we can really accept this point, then the analytic philosophers' search for 'continuity' of identity also becomes irrelevant. What we primarily experience is not a self in its full essential glory, nor in its stretched-out version as continuity, but the *desire* to continue to exist – a desire that we may or may not be wishfully projecting onto our mental events when we conventionally identify them as 'me'. This desire is what I refer to as the ego. I am an ego.

The ego consists only of identifications: I feel certain things to be me or mine (e.g. *my* talents, *my* child, *my* achievements). Often the boundary between 'me' and 'mine' is vague: is my big toe 'me' or 'mine'? I want my thing to continue, am upset if it is destroyed, and want it to be fulfilled in various ways. The things I identify with could be my mind, my body, my children, my house, my ambitions, my party, my country or any of a range of other possible things I might identify with.

The relationship between these identifications and my individual body is contingent. We do normally identify with our bodies, but there are some states where we can become alienated from our bodies, as in the cases of people who become alienated from their leg and want it to be amputated. We do not necessarily identify with our bodies more than with other things: for example, a sincere patriot who is willing to die for his country presumably identifies with his country (or with a principle that leads him to fight for it) more than with his body. For some people personal ambitions are in practice more important than bodies, shown by the way they are prepared to fulfil them at the expense of their health. For other people children or a wider family is far more important than any individual ambition, and many parents are far more concerned with their children's welfare than with their own.

Middle Way Philosophy 1: The Path of Objectivity

In this sense, "I" am a far more diffused thing than identification of me with my mental events or my body would suggest. "I" might be fulfilled by the election of an American president many thousands of miles away in a place I have never visited. "I" might also identify with fictional heroes, and in some cases be more concerned with the fate of Harry Potter or Frodo Baggins than with the person I am supposed to be. I may deeply identify with the remote past or the remote future. In some cases I may also be grateful rather than distressed if someone removes an organ from my body or changes my brain states using chemicals.

The case for seeing "I" in this way does not only relate to the failure of metaphysical accounts of the self or its adequacy to the range of my experience. It is also practically very helpful for us to see ourselves in this way, because it enables incremental judgements to be made about ourselves. This is both more adequate to our experience and provides a psychological understanding of the nature of objectivity. If I say "I'm not feeling quite myself today" for example, this makes no sense in relation to essentialist theories of the self – the self is still there, permanently, as much today as yesterday. If I reduce my statement to a material description of brain and body states that are not functioning normally, I also remove the justification from the implied judgement in the idea of "not being quite myself". However, if "I" am an ego we can understand such a statement both psychologically and morally, in terms of integration. I am "not quite myself" because what "I" am varies with my identification, even though the process of identification itself continues. Our identifications may have a good deal of stability that enables us to identify ourselves with what we are most of the time, yet we are still only contingently that apparently stable self.

What makes egos capable of being the objects of incremental judgement is that they are variable, and we can judge their integration in inverse ratio to that variability: the less they vary, the more integrated we are. In some cases (e.g. small children), egoistic wishes can vary from moment to moment with little binding awareness, whilst with others a fair continuity of intention and attention is maintained. However, even for adults used to a fairly disciplined life and habits of concentration, close attention to our desires (for example, in meditation) shows their variability. We get distracted from our main task, especially when this is a subtle one, by other desires that are out of harmony with it, causing fantasies, flights of hatred, anxiety, or doubt. Over a longer period of time, we start intentions that are not fulfilled – for example, books that we buy but fail to read, or friends we fail to keep in touch with.

Nevertheless, the ego only takes into account the wishes of the moment. It can disassociate itself from past and future desires rather than taking responsibility for them ("I was only a teenager"; "Who knows what will have happened by then?"). As in the example of the smoker discussed in 3.j, it can disassociate itself from quite recent acts when desires have changed ("I said that when I was drunk – you shouldn't have taken me seriously"). We do not have to think of the ego as essentially or metaphysically split up into a potentially infinite number of momentary desires: this is just (to some extent) our experience. It is also our experience that these egoistic desires can be integrated by any factor that increases our awareness: maturity, passion, training, health, education, or stimulus. We are not essentially divided beings (pace St Paul[127]), nor are we essentially united beings who only need a revelation to make us eternally integrated: but we can become more integrated within experience.

The ego's contingent lack of integration is reflected not only in desires that change from moment to moment, but also in

---

[127] See Romans 7:14 ff

meanings and beliefs that do likewise. A student stares hopelessly at a maths book, trying fruitlessly to give sense to an explanation that she understood yesterday when the maths teacher explained it, but now means nothing. The revolutionary for whom political rhetoric was supremely meaningful yesterday, wakes up in disillusionment with memories of blood that seem to drain the allure from those words. The politician who strongly defended a position in the past that he has now had to compromise, struggles to explain his motivations to the press.

In relation to the physical structure of the brain, the lack of integration of the ego can be seen as due to the fact that the left hemisphere is responsible for explicit language and conscious will, but that same left hemisphere has no grasp of relationships through time[128]. What we want, then, is experienced in a time vacuum, and awareness of the changing nature of what we want only develops due to connectivity with the right hemisphere. The left hemisphere's insularity has the advantage of enabling it to focus intently on the task in hand, without any concern for what might happen next or doubt about the value of the task. However, it has the marked disadvantage of fragmenting our identifications over time. Our failed relationships, half-read (or half-written) books, extravagant ambitions, and limited attention spans are all obvious indications of this point in everyday life. Although the connection with the right hemisphere gives us the *potential* to then gain awareness of our changing identifications, left hemisphere dominance may still then *inhibit* that awareness to allow greater undistracted focus on current goals.

Another theory that helps to explain our degree of egoistic disintegration is that of the unconscious. This posits that a large section of our minds is not in conscious awareness at any one time, being buried or repressed by the conscious

---

[128] McGilchrist (2009) p.76-7 & 111-112

Ego-identification

mind because it is rejected as incompatible with conscious desires. The unconscious mind nevertheless continues to affect our experience and behaviour in indirect ways, such as affecting our body language, physical state (from excess sweating to false pregnancy), and speech patterns (for example stammering, slips of the tongue). It is most directly expressed in dreams, where the unconscious dominates our experience, and unconscious wishes in conflict with conscious ones can be symbolically expressed[129].

All of this general theory of the unconscious seems helpful and plausible to me. However, there are philosophers who reject the theory of the unconscious on the grounds that we cannot directly observe its causal role (only its alleged effects), and thus cannot justifiably support this view of the causation of, say, dreams, more than any other theory explaining their cause[130]. However, other theories of dreams do not help to also explain egoistic disintegration. Popper objected to all psychoanalytic theory of the unconscious on the grounds that it was unfalsifiable, which by his standards it is[131]. However, there is no better theory available to provide a unified explanation of all the phenomena I have mentioned, so one of the key criteria of judgement against a theory that I mentioned in 3.I, having a feasible alternative theory, is absent.

However, I do not want to enter with too much detail into the debate about the unconscious, because it is not essential to support the theory of the unconscious to support the integration theory I am proposing. The unconscious merely helps to explain the *mechanism* of egoistic disintegration, but the signs of such disintegration are obvious in our experience regardless of the mechanism that is producing them. Rather than worrying about the unconscious, we only have to observe the varieties of desires (and secondarily of meanings and

---
[129] See Jung (1982)
[130] E.g. MacIntyre (1958)
[131] Popper (1963)

beliefs) that we experience over time. Such a diachronic approach gives us a very different view from the synchronic approach that has dominated Western philosophy.

One of the features of a justifiable new theory mentioned by Lakatos and Kuhn is also that it should be able to explain the successes of an old theory[132]. How can we explain the success of the Cartesian self, that puts all the emphasis on explaining identity on self-consciousness, in terms of the ego-theory? Self-consciousness can be seen as a remarkably effective adaptation of the ego, because the egoistic impulse is always to get us to believe that this moment's want is forever and this moment's beliefs are the eternal truth. If we become aware of ourselves at a particular time whilst *wanting* to believe that the evidence of self-consciousness is eternally true, this can support the very interpretation that Descartes gave that awareness. We take the ego's bait, we think we *are* absolute and eternal because we can reflect on our own existence – and carry on doing so.

Thus we become blind to our own changeability, dismissing desires as mere passion, but not taking into account the ways that even our beliefs are affected by those desires. If we think dualistically – assuming that the only alternative to this model is not existing at all – and in terms of the abstracted turn, which leads us to ignore the concrete processes that accompany our abstracted cognitive function, then we have even more motive to cling on to self-consciousness as truly us.

Descartes' metaphysical views about the self, like other metaphysical views, contribute to detracting from our experiential adequacy by reinforcing conflict models. For more on this process please see 6.c below. However, before discussing conflict models I must examine the wider context in which the ego works.

---

[132] Lakatos (1974)

B. The psyche

If the ego consists only in desires (with associated meanings and beliefs) that may only be momentary, but can integrate those momentary desires, what does it integrate *into*? From the point of view of the ego at one point, desires at another point may be completely denied, so we cannot say that the ego integrates with itself. The term *psyche*, then, is used to refer to the whole set of potential desires, meanings and beliefs that could be integrated into the ego, as well as those currently identified with by the ego.

Here we come to a crucial point in the critique of most Western thought that I am offering here. If we think of the self as fixed, and accept the ego's account as the last word on itself, then incremental progress becomes inconceivable. In one sense we do experience ourselves as egos with limited identifications, meanings and beliefs that we defend, but in another we experience ourselves as psyches with much wider identifications, meanings and beliefs, without that defensiveness. However, to see ourselves as psyches we have to take a diachronic rather than synchronic view of ourselves, seeing ourselves over time rather than at a given time.

A diachronic view is not merely speculative. If we look back at our past experience we can see many changes of egoistic identification and (certainly in childhood) a development of our experiential adequacy in the process. From the perspective of a past self, we can now see that our potential identifications were much wider than we thought at the time. Our general experience is one of changing and integrating identifications, so it is a provisional theory that we can support from experience that identifications exist beyond the ego, as our experience is diachronic as well as synchronic.

Middle Way Philosophy 1: The Path of Objectivity

However, our experience does not tell us about the bounds of our potential identifications, and thus it seems that the psyche has very vague outer boundaries. It is as if we can look up out of the narrow entrance of a cave to get glimpses of a vast sky outside, but we cannot see the horizons of this outer world, and do not know what objects exist or do not exist in it. Potentially, it seems, the psyche contains all possible identifications, all possible meanings, and all possible beliefs. However, it is the identifications, meanings and beliefs that we have experienced as other, without identifying with them, which are of most immediate practical relevance in the psyche. Identifications that we have deliberately rejected and fought against, but which nevertheless have a strong conditioning effect on us, loom in the foreground of the psyche beyond the ego – rejected religion from childhood, old enemies, neglected friends or relatives, or widespread habits we did not take up. For example, personally I have never smoked a single cigarette nor ridden a motorcycle, but I regularly dream about smoking or about riding motorcycles. In a wider sense, I do know what it is like to smoke a cigarette or ride a motorcycle, and to identify with those activities.

Another experience we have that shows the wider psyche in operation is that of *alienation*. If I act in accordance with a narrow conception of my duty, against what I experience as my inclination, we can describe those unfulfilled inclinations as alienated energies. For example, I might be revising for an exam when I feel much more like listening to music. Such energies are likely to recur and distract me from my duty. There seems a strong case here for claiming that I have these alienated feelings at the same time as the dutiful ones, that even at one time my identifications are plural. Viewed strictly from the point of view of the ego these alienated energies cannot be acknowledged to exist, so they must suddenly spring mysteriously into existence at the time when I switch from duty to distraction, and then disappear just as mysteriously when I return to duty. This is hardly a convincing

The psyche

picture. We have to posit a psyche in order to explain how I can have both at the same time.

In terms of the structure of the brain, the psyche can be identified with the contextualising capacities of the right hemisphere, which can comprehend relationships over space and time in a way that the left hemisphere cannot. The right hemisphere does also offer us a wider version of ourselves: as individuals like others and as beings that exist over time[133]. It is undoubtedly the right hemisphere that provides us with our integrating *capacity* to see the wilful synchronous selves of the left hemisphere as part of a greater whole. Yet at the same time, the right hemisphere does not maintain an objectified identity that can be understood in explicit conscious terms. The increasingly unified ego continues to be represented in the left hemisphere, drawing on its connections with the right, rather than in the right hemisphere. So, whilst the right hemisphere represents the capacity for expansion, it does not provide a representation of what a more unified ego would be like. For this reason we cannot justify any particular beliefs about what the psyche contains or does not contain, nor how it starts or finishes in time.

The relationship of the psyche to the individual with which it is mainly associated is also ambiguous. 'My' psyche may theoretically contain representations of others that I may come to identify with in future, that I have not even heard of now: for example, twenty-five years ago I had not even heard of the woman who is now my wife, yet because she was an object of potential future identification for me it could be said that she was present in my psyche at that time. Similarly, many of the beliefs I have expressed in this book were not at that time consciously available to me – I might just about have heard of the Middle Way as a concept in Buddhism, but no more than that. Because these beliefs were potential ones then, though,

---

[133] McGilchrist (2009) pp.87-9

they were in a sense part of my psyche. In terms of left-hemisphere representations, then, we can describe the psyche as infinite. All the beliefs, meanings and desires experienced by sentient beings in past, present and future are potentially part of my psyche.

However, as they loom incrementally closer to my present experience, they become more specific. In practice, the more immediate psyche (the one I dream about, for example) tends to make use of desires, meanings and beliefs that are at least close enough to present experience to be identifiable in a reconfigured form.

It is this type of reflection about the potentially infinite collectivity of the psyche that gave rise to Jung's concept of the collective unconscious, but it is worth distinguishing Jung's concept from my account of the psyche here[134]. The collective unconscious was put forward by Jung to explain the shared meaning that we find in archetypes, that he thought were genetically inherited and thus a universal aspect of the human psyche. However, it is not necessary to raise possible controversy by insisting on a genetic rather than environmental origin for archetypes, nor to insist on their absolute universality. I will be discussing archetypes in more detail in III.4, but suffice to say for now that I take them to represent different functions in the relationship between ego and psyche rather than more specific genetic inheritances. Archetypes also represent the expressions of desire in terms of meaning rather than desires themselves. For example, the Jungian archetype of the Shadow represents the aspects of what I do not identify with that I am afraid of and project as 'evil': dark lords, villains, personal enemies etc. I may share this archetype with others, but how far I do so depends on how much of my desires are channelled into the form of meaning taken by this archetype. So, whilst I may share certain

---

[134] Jung (1968)

meanings with others I do not necessarily hate my version of the Dark Lord to the same extent as they hate theirs. Our energies remain individual.

Identification with others, then, is a function of desire that, though it may be contingently affected by meaning, operates independently of the collective unconscious as Jung envisaged it. If my ego-identifications can be with others (more than myself, on some occasions) and these ego-identifications are drawn from the wider pool of the psyche, it seems possible that all others are part of my psyche – at least, in an attenuated sense. However, the self of apperception continues to operate in making the others in my psyche subject to the limitations of my representations of them. I imagine Dr Jekyll, my charming neighbour, not Mr Hyde, his alter ego, because I have never experienced Mr Hyde. My identifications remain merely mine in terms of how I represent them, but they can get progressively closer to others in terms of how many people I identify with, how much my representations have overcome limiting delusions (e.g. by finding out about Mr Hyde), and how strong my identifications with them are. The psyche is not collective in the sense of pooled consciousness, but can evidently be so in the sense of pooled identifications.

C. Conflict models and integration models

In more fully explaining the relationship of the ego-psyche theory to the concept of experiential adequacy, it will be helpful to consider the models of conflicting identifications set up by the ego, and how these change in the process of integration.

The unintegrated ego works primarily through a conflict model in the beliefs it promotes about other identifications. This means that the ego sees itself as opposed to other identifications, which it needs to deny and squeeze out in order to dominate the individual at that moment and become the basis of action. The beliefs that suit the ego best for this purpose are metaphysical beliefs, because these are apparently impregnable and not amenable to compromise. Alternative desires must be labelled as *other* and expelled.

Let's take the example again of the imposition of duty. Supposing I have a piece of urgent but uninteresting work to do one evening. I reflect that I must do this work in order to fulfil social expectations and to maintain my competitive position at work, which will be to my own long-term advantage. However, I feel like relaxing and am very disinclined to do the work. In order to force me to do the work in these circumstances, the unintegrated ego has to effectively expel the contrary inclination. To do this it has to present the value of doing the work as absolute. The possible threat to my position at work if I don't do it becomes envisaged as a threat to my self. Anxiety is triggered and I force myself to get on with it.

This same conflict model can be readily found at a political level. Take the example of the debate between Irish nationalists in the Irish Dáil (provisional parliament) in 1921, after Arthur Griffith and Michael Collins had returned from

Conflict models and integration models

London with a negotiated compromise treaty with Britain, which created the Irish Free State, a dominion with substantial self-government but within the British Empire, and maintained the recently created partition from Northern Ireland, rather than the Republic of the whole island all the nationalists had hoped for. Eamon de Valera spoke as follows:

I am against this Treaty.... I wanted, and the Cabinet wanted, to get a document we could stand by.... That document makes British authority our masters in Ireland.... If the representatives of the Republic should ask the people of Ireland to do that which is inconsistent with the Republic, I say they are subverting the Republic. It would be a surrender.... to sign our names to the most ignoble document that could be signed.[135]

De Valera's language here is full of metaphysical absolutes which deny the possibility of compromise. Firstly, that British authority to any degree in Ireland is absolutely wrong, second, that the Republic has to take an inflexible definite form, which cannot be compromised without a threat to Ireland's essential identity. His rhetoric at the end becomes hyperbolic, turning a compromise into a surrender and a negotiated treaty into "the most ignoble document that could be signed". De Valera's attitude here defined the anti-treaty movement that created the Irish Civil War, with massive further bloodshed between 1922 and 23.

In contrast, both these situations could be approached not with a conflict model but with an integration model. An integration model recognises the provisionality and incrementality of the concepts with which the ego identifies. It does not ask the ego to give up these identifications, which would involve negative metaphysics, asserting the opposite of the concepts identified with by the ego. Instead it tries to bring the opposed energies together by understanding them in terms that enable them to be re-channelled and to address conditions together.

---

[135] Quoted by Bardon (2008) p.469

Middle Way Philosophy 1: The Path of Objectivity

The integration model can be symbolised by the two mules, a classic set of pictures used by pacifist campaigners. Here the two mules just have to reframe the way they are thinking about the situation in order to both get what they want.

To apply the integration model to the 'imposition of duty' example requires me to recognise that the way my anxiety is framing the requirements is much more absolute than is necessary. Perhaps if I relax a little and then do part of the work that evening and the rest the following evening, my position at work will not be affected to nearly the extent my absolute conceptions are demanding. Of course, a realistic appraisal of the work situation might indicate that my job really is on the line, in which case an imposition of duty might still be appropriate – but very often it is not necessary.

In the De Valera example, Griffith and Collins had already done the compromising, and what De Valera probably needed to do was accept the compromise treaty, rather than imposing absolute concepts on it. The irony in De Valera's case is that after sacrificing many lives fruitlessly for it, he later managed to turn Ireland into a fully independent republic peacefully through political means. The partition with Northern Ireland remains, however, and is a monument to the metaphysical dependence of another absolute thinker, James I of England, who sought to ethnically cleanse the native Irish from Ulster in the seventeenth century and replace them with English and Scottish Protestants.

To criticise rigid thinking with the benefit of hindsight is nothing new, but the role that metaphysics plays in the conflict model is less widely appreciated. It is also too common to blame the ego for its pride, when the ego is equally essential to a more integrated model. There is nothing wrong with the normal human state of wanting things, but when the energies of want are maintained in an unintegrated form by unnecessary rigidities of belief, it is not humans and not egos that can be described as the basis of evil, but metaphysics.

D. Integration in relation to objectivity

I have established in the previous chapter that integration helps us to avoid a destructive conflict model that stops us from addressing conditions by polarising our responses, but perhaps more needs to be said here about how integration can be claimed to be equivalent to objectivity and experiential adequacy. Experiential adequacy is not merely reduced by the imposition of dualistic metaphysical beliefs, but also intruded upon in other ways by the unintegrated ego.

As argued in 2.a, the adequacy of experience is based on how far I can select features of my experience for attention that do not merely reinforce pre-conceptions, but enable me to engage with new conditions. The unintegrated ego, however, limits that adequacy by focusing only on conditions that relate to the desires that have been selected for current attention, neglecting or dismissing the remainder. One way that my objectivity is limited by the unintegrated ego, then, is perceptual: I do not actually experience or notice the points that are not relevant to the goals I currently identify with. The teacher, intent on getting across certain crucial points to conclude his topic, does not notice some subtle signs of alienated feelings amongst his students. The mother, intent on the welfare of her children for many years, fails to notice the creeping signs of her own emotional alienation and withdrawal as her non-maternal energies get no outlet. A politician, intent on making plans for what he believes is a principled and necessary pre-emptive invasion of another country, receives a 900-page report from his subordinates offering detailed plans for reconstruction and political settlement of the country after the invasion, and throws it in the bin[136].

---

[136] The country, as you may have guessed, is Iraq in 2003. The politician to whom this happened was Donald Rumsfeld. See http://www.bbc.co.uk/news/mobile/world-middle-east-11135500, where

The adequacy of experience is also affected by what we choose to signify about that experience, and the way in which we signify it, which can then also feed back into our perceptions. Our descriptions are affected by the unintegrated ego because they make our descriptions selective, biased and emotive. We had an example in the previous chapter where De Valera described the 1921 Anglo-Irish Treaty as "the most ignoble document that could be signed". If he had made the effort to use more neutral language in this context, he might have helped himself and others to focus on the positive aspects of the treaty as well as the negative.

The objectivity that is affected by the unintegrated ego in this way can be seen in factual, moral or aesthetic terms, as described in section 4. The factual objectivity aspect should be obvious from the examples just given above: the alienated feelings amongst the students or the positive aspects of the Anglo-Irish Treaty for Irish nationalists are factual aspects of the situation which were not being recognised. In these examples, too, moral objectivity is limited because the values of the participants are too narrowly focused in line with their perception of the situation. The teacher could teach better if he could maintain awareness of the value of the students' emotions at the same time as the value of his subject. Similarly, De Valera would have made a moral advance if he had borne in mind the value of maintaining harmony and avoiding immediate conflict at the same time as the value of the freedom from oppression that would be given to the people of Ireland by a republic. Aesthetic awareness is clearly influenced by our over-intentness on one goal at the expense of others, for we simply do not experience beauty unless we are open to it. If De Valera had stopped to look intently at a

John Simpson writes "Mr Rumsfeld was sent a careful, conscientious 900-page report by the state department containing detailed plans for the post-invasion period. He reportedly dumped it, unopened, straight into his waste-paper basket".

Middle Way Philosophy 1: The Path of Objectivity

flower on his way to that Daíl meeting, might he have been in a less narrowed state of mind and averted a war? Of course, this is speculation about a hypothetical event, but not improbable.

However, it is important not to confuse this avoidance of narrowed intentions, narrowed perceptions or narrowed descriptions with an endless suspension of judgement. Objectivity in addressing conditions does not result merely from suspension of judgement, but from maximising the adequacy of the experience on which a decision is based. The adequacy of the experience will include perceptions of urgency or of practical requirements in time. De Valera could very likely have stopped a moment to look at a flower and had a different meeting, but he could not have stopped so long that he didn't turn up to the meeting at all, where his presence was central. Nor am I suggesting that disposal experts who are busy defusing a time-bomb for public safety should stop in the middle to look at their wider surroundings, or consider different provisional theories about the bomb. Sometimes intentness on a goal is practically important, but at other times it interferes with experiential adequacy. Lack of intentness on a goal, and the inability to temporarily suppress conflicting feelings, may also be a factor in other situations that stops people addressing conditions (e.g. a day-dreaming student). In this example, perceptions are narrowed, not on the task in hand, but on other matters not relevant to the task in hand.

My overall argument here, then, is that integration is equivalent to objectivity. In other words, the same factors that interfere with our experiential adequacy are those that interfere with integration. Both objectivity and integration, in turn, need to be interpreted with a balanced regard for the practical situation.

E. Integration in relation to justification

In section 5 I explained the way in which both coherence and an awareness of the possibility of being wrong are necessary aspects of justification without metaphysics. These points, too, can be related to the model of integration.

Firstly, we need to note the requirement in all egoistic identification for justification through synchronic coherence. Coherence is a tool of the ego because it constructs a model of the world in which the conditions for action are clear and goals can be reached. If, on the contrary, we are confused about the conditions surrounding us, we feel unable to act. This coherence enables us to get to grips with all conditions relating to our desires, but in our focus on these desires we are liable to neglect those that we do not see as relevant in the short-term. It is in this way that conditions that do actually influence us can be neglected by unintegrated egoism – for example, by the pursuit of economic growth in the nineteenth and twentieth centuries neglecting environmental conditions. From the standpoint of the unintegrated ego, coherence is a sufficient condition for justification.

The unintegrated ego can also adopt positive foundationalism, but this operates differently. It is not a mechanism for addressing conditions so much as one for avoiding the recognition of challenging alternative identifications. If you had asked a nineteenth-century mill owner about environmental conditions, and perhaps explained to him recent scientific findings about anthropogenic global warming, his response might well involve an appeal to God. God looks after the world as a whole and will save us from climate change, he might say. However, in his business dealings he would not have brought God's will into play, unless to enjoin basic honesty. He would be aware that successful business dealings require a comprehensive understanding of the conditions around – the market, the labour force, the supply of goods, the competition. This sort of awareness is needed to fulfil the goal of making money through business. Thus, although both foundations and coherence might be appealed to at different times to provide types of justification, they are not likely to be in the same contexts.

To move forward from the degree of unintegrated egoism represented by our nineteenth-century mill owner, then, we need to shift from a positive (or negative) use of foundationalism to an agnostic one that merely takes an awareness of the possibility of error to be a given for all judgements, as argued in 5.c. If both coherence and agnostic foundationalism are taken to be necessary but not sufficient for justification, we are able to harness the basic egoism of the pursuit of ends in recognition of coherent conditions, and mitigate it by a practical (not just theoretical) awareness of error and a requirement for the personal falsifiability of theories.

The use of agnostic foundationalism opens the door not only to other factual theories, but also to other values and perceptions, enabling the continuing integration of our identifications. The justification offered, then, by the addition of this requirement to that of coherentism, is that of optimal response to our circumstances. We do not have an optimal response to our circumstances, and are not improving experiential adequacy as much as we might, if we merely seek our goals based on current ego-identifications without an effort at diachronic awareness and a review of our assumptions in the light of challenges.

F. Group integration

I have already mentioned in discussing integration that it does not apply only at the level of the individual, but also at the social level. This is an important point in providing the basis of a Middle Way political philosophy and showing that the Middle Way is just as relevant to problems understood at a social level as those understood at an individual level. In relating these two levels I am drawing on a tradition of macrocosm-microcosm comparisons in western thought that goes back to Plato, who thought that the structure of the ideal state should mirror the ideal structure in the soul of human beings[137]. I think he was correct on this point of comparison, just because the same psychological conditions operating in an individual can be observed at a social level, rather than through any metaphysical beliefs about hermetic parallels. Acknowledging this, however, does not indicate support for Plato's totalitarian account of what the ideal structure should be both for the individual psyche and the state[138].

Whilst at the individual level, integration consists in the ego expanding its identifications (and thus also its meanings and beliefs) to create greater consistency of identifications over time, at the social level, integration can consist of increasing synchronous consistency between individuals, increasing diachronous consistency in the view dominating a group, or synchronous consistency between groups relating to form larger groups. To add to the complexity of social integration, the integration of each individual in the group also plays a part. For example, a group in harmonious agreement but consisting of individuals that are highly unintegrated will have its general level of integration greatly reduced by this. Since group loyalty is a major factor in maintaining metaphysical commitments

---

[137] Plato (1987) § 235
[138] See Ellis (2001) 3.d

that interfere with individual integration, this scenario is a common one.

This type of example also makes clear the importance of agnostic foundationalism in group integration. For an individual, diachronous integration can only be achieved to the extent that he or she is able to come to terms with the possibility of error at one time compared to another, so the factors of consistency and agnostic foundationalism over time are mutually dependent. For groups, though, a superficial harmony is all too common, based on the imposition of some type of power, linked to an ideology with metaphysical assumptions to entrench that power. Think of the superficial harmony created in religious or political groups by everyone subscribing to heavily idealised, unfalsifiable claims, without which one could not be a member of the group. For experience to be effectively applied as a basis of judgement in the group rather than metaphysics, an awareness of the limitations of that metaphysics and the possibility of other views needs to be present. It needs to be possible to raise ideas that challenge the group-view, and for leaders to listen to such ideas and address them. It is much easier for individuals to have the confidence to challenge a group in this way if they are themselves more integrated, and can see the advantages of a critical perspective in their own lives.

It may be a surprise to find diachronous consistency in the view dominating a group to be a possible way of judging the integration of that group. However, groups are no less prone than individuals to the illusion that an absolute belief answers all the questions and will never change. Just like individuals, they are forced to change with conditions nevertheless, but then tend to deny their change of belief. Even the Roman Catholic Church, that bastion of eternal dogma, has during its history changed its position on the celibacy of priests[139], the

---

[139] The First and Second Lateran Councils (1123 & 1139) explicitly forbade

acceptability of early abortion[140], and the infallibility of the pope's judgements *ex cathedra*[141] – all points that are conveniently forgotten given the absolutism with which judgements on these points are made now. It is by the group's changes of view coupled with denial and with a lack of provisionality towards the status of those views that a lack of integration can be detected.

Groups also exist at different levels, from a partnership of two people to the group of the whole human race – with many points in between including teams, companies, churches, organisations, classes, nations and international groupings. Such groupings fit into each other in a pyramid structure, and the larger and more complex the group, with the greater number of sub-groups, the more complex the question of its integration becomes. Nevertheless it is important for us to consider the integration of such groups, because it is their integration that determines the experiential adequacy of their decisions, and thus their justifiability.

Groups are subject to desires, meanings and beliefs just as individuals are, but because the medium of discussion within a social group is that of beliefs, belief tends to be much more to the fore as the means by which we can detect integration or a lack of integration in a group. We tend to use beliefs about the group's goals to detect how far a group has consistent desires, but of course implicit beliefs could still conflict with explicit ones. Shared meanings also tend to be an important condition for cohesion in the group: these are reinforced by jargon,

---

priests to marry, even though this had previous been tolerated in some circumstances. This ruling subsequently came to be interpreted to mean that men who were already married could not be ordained as priests.
[140] Until the 1917 Code of Canon Law, the Catholic Church made distinctions between the degree of sinfulness of early and late abortions, influenced by the Aristotelian and Thomist belief that ensoulment of the foetus takes place during the course of pregnancy, not at conception as the modern doctrine insists.
[141] Promulgated at the First Vatican Council in 1870

Middle Way Philosophy 1: The Path of Objectivity

shared stories and rituals. However, misunderstanding or varying interpretation of shared meanings can also cause rifts. The disputes in the Christian churches over the exact relationship between the persons of the Trinity[142] or the significance of the eucharist[143] provide well-known examples of this. Although at one level these rifts were based on differences in belief, at another these beliefs may shape differences in the experienced significance of potent religious symbols for different groups of believers.

Group integration also forms the basis of political integration, which determines the degree of justification of decisions made by governments, or by other leaders of groups. The political decision is justified to the extent that it is integrated. Political integration depends not just on the integration of the members of the government with each other, but their integration with the people they are ruling, the integration within the group of people they are ruling, and the integration of each of the individuals in the national group.

Volume II.6 will look in detail at the integration of government and its implications for the politics of the Middle Way. The social level of integration will also be a constantly recurring aspect of the different types of integration discussed in parts 2, 3 and 4.

---

[142] The *filioque* clause, added to the Nicene creed to signify the direct relationship between the Holy Spirit and the Son in the Western (Roman) Church was the catalyst for the schism between eastern and western churches in 1054.

[143] The Catholic belief in transubstantiation, where the body of Christ is believed to be literally present in the bread and wine, contrasts with Protestant beliefs in consubstantiation or in the merely symbolic value of the eucharist.

G. The three types of integration

The three types of integration – of desire, meaning, and belief – have already been introduced and discussed in a number of places. Each of these types of integration is the subject of a whole remaining volume of this series, where it will be discussed in detail. The purpose of this chapter is just to summarise the differences and clarify the relationships between them. It is a highly compressed version of points that will be unpacked later.

The integration of desire refers to the extent to which our desires identified with by the ego are consistent over time. Since one of the features of the ego is its denial of desires at other times, such consistency requires that the desires to be made consistent are accompanied by an awareness of their limitations. Being aware of our inconsistency is the first step towards uniting our desires.

However, desires define a context in which they can be fulfilled in terms of beliefs, and these beliefs are expressed in language or other symbols which must be meaningful in order to express those beliefs. Since beliefs are used by the ego to gain its ends, usually some beliefs need to be integrated in order to enable desires to be integrated. We cannot reflect on either desires or beliefs in order to become aware of their limitations if we do not have meaningful signs. Although it may be possible to integrate desire directly in some cases (such as in meditation), usually we have to work at all three levels in order to remove the barriers created by metaphysical identification to the integration of desires, and thus gain sustainable integration rather than brief temporary integrations (see II.5.a).

The integration of meaning becomes necessary where there is *fragmentation of meaning*: that is, where there is ego-identification with particular signs that are exclusively linked to particular unintegrated desires or beliefs, and integration of desires or beliefs cannot occur because they do not share symbols in which to accomplish it. The extension of meanings may occur both affectively and cognitively – that is, we may not understand another perspective (whether that of another individual, or ourselves at a different time) because we do not relate strongly enough (or we relate negatively) to the language or other symbols it is using, or we may not understand another perspective just because we do not comprehend their language or other symbols. If I made a secret mark in my diary last year, I may be prevented from integrating with that past self by forgetting what I took the secret mark to mean, or I may just not care.

The integration of belief is also made necessary ultimately in order to integrate desires, and can only take place if sufficient integration of meaning is already in place to enable mutual understanding. But understanding an opposing belief is not enough by itself to accept it, and this is where reasoning may have a role in helping to bring about consistency of belief. Beliefs are prevented from integrating by metaphysical beliefs, which block the awareness of possible error. Metaphysical beliefs can, in their turn, block the integration of desire or meaning by preventing alternative language even being used, or alternative feelings even being considered, because of their incompatibility with metaphysical belief. For example, the language of a rejected race may be ruled 'barbarous' and the dominant race may refuse to speak it, or consider the feelings of those who do, because of an absolute belief in their own racial superiority.

Our desires are most basic to our physical experience, but in the long term, as human beings, it is beliefs that we use to help order our groups and our wider societies. It is thus beliefs that must be addressed for long-term change. The relationships between the three levels of integration are

The three types of integration

contingent, but our experience of their interrelationship, I would argue, overwhelmingly tends to show that all three levels need to be addressed for substantial and sustainable integration.

7. Ethics

As I have argued so far, moral objectivity is a central aspect of Middle Way Philosophy. Given that objectivity is a characteristic of people's judgements rather than states of affairs out there, values are not in any way inferior to facts in their capacity for objectivity. This recognition puts us in a position to create a new, more effective kind of ethics in which we avoid the confusion, dogmatism and false neutrality that bedevil contemporary moral debate.

This section puts forward an outline of such an effort, dealing with the most likely issues raised and offering a broad solution to the wider question of how we can know how to live and how to act. These issues include exactly why we 'ought' to become more integrated and objective, to what extent we are responsible for our actions, and how we can reconcile the conflicting guidance of different moral theories.

A. Resolving relativism

Relativism is the belief that any given opinion is as well justified as another. Philosophically it tends to bring together and conflate two assertions: that our judgements are dependent on a certain limited standpoint (which is obviously the case) and that no particular standpoint of judgement is better than another (a completely unconnected, and much more dubious, assumption). In moral relativism, all universal standards for moral judgements are denied, because it is claimed that there are no justifiable criteria with which to choose between the competing claims. Instead, the moral beliefs we may gain from the conditioning of our society or group (cultural relativism) or even those we may decide on for ourselves as individuals (subjectivism) are taken to be as well justified as any others and "true for us".

Traditionally there is a distinction between descriptive types of relativism (which aim to merely describe different moral positions without judgement) and prescriptive moral relativism (which asserts that people should follow the morality of their group). However, since this distinction is based on the fact-value distinction (see 1.i) I do not accept it. Descriptive moral relativists cannot in fact be merely descriptive, as the people holding that view have to be flesh-and-blood people with desires and hence values. Assertions about morality relative to different groups cannot be made in practice without some implied approval or disapproval of the relative state of morality. All relativism is both prescriptive and descriptive to some degree, with the distinction being only a matter of emphasis.

An alternative philosophical version of this approach is perspectivism, where there is believed to be an inaccessible truth and many incompatible perspectives on it created by individual conditions[144]. Nietzsche, the originator of this view,

---

[144] Nietzsche (1967) §481

Middle Way Philosophy 1: The Path of Objectivity

did not believe that all the viewpoints were equally valid. Nietzsche may have grasped the idea that objectivity is based on our experiential adequacy, but nevertheless he did not offer a way of making moral judgements to practically help us move beyond relativism, apart from the aesthetic elitism of his *Übermensch* ethic[145]. Without a convincing alternative, the practical implications of moral perspectivism are very similar to those of moral relativism. The term "perspectivist" may be applied to Middle Way Philosophy provided that the varying objectivity of perspectives is considered compatible with it, and that experience is recognised to offer us resources for incremental objectivity of judgement. Whether all of this is really compatible with what Nietzsche meant by "perspectivism", given the notorious difficulties in interpreting Nietzsche, is a moot enough point for me to avoid going out of my way to call Middle Way Philosophy "perspectivist".

Moral relativism creates widespread practical problems. Where there is a conflict between incompatible cultural or individual wishes, without an accepted universal morality we have no way of resolving it without either the imposition of power by one side or an appeal to the law. At the most local level there may be a dispute between two neighbours about noise levels, or at a bigger level a dispute between two religions over a holy site (think of the Ayodhya mosque, or the Dome of the Rock in Jerusalem). The increasing globalisation of our world through much improved travel, trade, and communications has only been made possible without huge conflicts by a corresponding process of legalisation, together with a certain amount of Western cultural dominance. But both the law and any other, less justified applications of power are a crude and expensive device for resolving disputes compared to morality, which resolves disputes immediately at their source – how much better if we had a generally recognised universal morality! The resources required for such a morality

---

[145] See Ellis (2001) 4.g

Resolving relativism

are philosophical, and it is philosophers who have the responsibility to question the assumptions that stand in the way of a credible universal morality and to develop it – a responsibility that they have failed to fulfil due to ingrained dualistic thinking.

The problem of relativism in Western thought is due to the perceived dualism between absolute and relative. It is thought that either we accept an absolute perspective on metaphysical grounds, or that without those grounds any one opinion is as well justified as any other. This set of assumptions entirely neglects the way in which the objectivity of our judgements depends on experiential adequacy. Once we recognise that the world we perceive is not entirely 'objective' in the God's-eye-view sense, and our individual responses to it are not entirely 'subjective' in absolute opposition to this 'objectivity': in other words that our objectivity is incremental, the grounds for belief in either absolutism or relativism, or the perception that they are the only two options, dissolves.

It is as though we have been confined in a dark prison with no source of illumination inside and windows covered in dirt. It has been assumed that the only way we could find light was to go outside the prison – which we cannot because the doors are eternally locked – but all we have to do to get light inside is to clean the windows. The cleaner we make the windows, the more light we allow inside.

The groundwork for the resolution of relativism has already been laid in the previous chapters 1.i, against the fact-value distinction, and 4.d, on moral objectivity. It has also been argued in 3.i that we should understand the Middle Way as good, rather than either metaphysical dogmas or conventional conditioning. Even if the only argument for this switch in the concept of good was the pragmatic one that we could thereby have an alternative set of philosophical conceptions that enabled us to avoid relativism, there would be a strong case for it.

The resolution of relativism requires us to think of universal theories in ethics as justifiable within experience, rather as theories of science already are. When we adopt a moral theory, we cannot expect certainty about it. However, we will make a significant start on creating a justifiable theory of ethics if it appears from the beginning to meet both our criteria of justification – coherence and agnostic foundationalism. It will be coherent if it is consistent with our factual and aesthetic beliefs and with our moral experience. It will be agnostically founded if it avoids metaphysical assumptions that make it incompatible with experience. Chapters 7.d-j below are concerned with discussing how the main existing theories of moral decision-making relate to these criteria.

However, once we have a provisional theory of how to make moral decisions, generally or in a particular area of experience, it can be further refined in the light of experience just as a scientific theory can. This, in a sense, is a further extension of the criterion of coherence as it continues to be modified through time. We may find that a particular moral strategy leads to unintended moral consequences, that it has a negative effect on our character, or that it involves conflicts of principle, and thus find that we need to modify it. On the other hand our experience may continue to confirm a moral strategy (for the moment) by producing positive outcomes.

The resolution of conflicts with others requires us to seek integration with those others by harmonising our moral perspectives. This is much easier to do if both sides can appeal to experience without fear that their appeal will be undermined by metaphysics. A degree of compassion (see 4.e) helps to create the objectivity required for a recognition of others' perspectives, which then become the basis of learning from each other and of joint investigation of conditions.

Established mediation techniques tend to focus on getting each side to recognise the experience of the other, after which integration becomes possible as opposed to mere compromise. By making another's desires, meanings and beliefs part of my own, I make my own experience more objective, rather than alienating my identifications to achieve compromise that merely avoids conflict.

Such resolution of moral issues also has two other conditions. Firstly, both sides must take responsibility for resolving it. The question of responsibility is discussed in the next chapter. Secondly, both sides need to feel that they ought to resolve the issue. The whole question of what we mean by 'ought' and how we justify normativity or 'oughtness' is discussed in 7.c.

The most basic challenge to relativism, however, is simply that its most basic claim, that one view is as good as another, is defeated by the recognition of objectivity and integration as I have explained them above. A more objective and more integrated view is better than one that is less objective and less integrated, just as a clean window allows us to see more than a dirty window. A more objective view will lead us to widen our own perspectives and integrate them with those of others wherever we can. Such incrementally objective views are focused in judgements, which is the point where we can best compare them.

This response to relativism also contains the basis of a response to anarchism. If others lack objectivity, and the situation is practically urgent enough to require the use of power, we have to appeal directly to our more objective view to justify any such use. This is an issue of political philosophy that will be tackled II.6.

B. Responsibility

The question of responsibility has been much influenced in Western thought by the metaphysical dualism between freewill and determinism. According to this dualism, responsibility depends on our capacity to make free choices unaffected by determinants such as those created by brain or body states, or by prior genetic or environmental conditioning that would lead us to act inevitably in a certain way. We are only acknowledged to be responsible for the moral complexion of our decisions if we made them freely in this way.

If we did not do so, then determinism is assumed to be the only possible alternative. According to determinism, our actions are judged to be inevitable regardless of whether or not we experience making choices, because physical causes can be attributed to all our actions, and our choice-making thus appears to be illusory. If determinism is correct, it appears that we have no responsibility at all: we are puppets of fate and thus cannot be justifiably praised or blamed.

A fuller discussion of the freewill-determinism dualism will be made in IV.4.c, including a refutation of the idea that compatibilism, a form of determinism that claims that determinism is compatible with freewill, offers any solution to the dualism. However, the broad lines of the argument against this dualism are that both freewill and determinism are metaphysical positions incompatible with an account of choice and responsibility that is based on experience. Instead of accepting either position we need to be rigorously agnostic about the metaphysical dualism, and try to explain experiences that relate to it only in terms of incremental qualities.

Determinism takes a set of phenomena that we experience, namely conditioning, and extrapolates it to a totality – to 'laws of nature' that are claimed to operate universally, even beyond our experience. Just the very basis of this move is, when you start to consider it, incredibly arrogant. The sphere of conditions experienced by human intelligence draws on a miniscule section of space and a miniscule section of time in the history of the universe, with our beliefs about other places and times all being indirect, and yet we claim to know 'laws of nature' about the whole universe! Though it may be that certain scientific 'laws' (which I would prefer to call well-supported theories) are without exception in our experience, this is hardly a wide sample of the universe as a whole. Our knowledge of the brain, a notionally complete physical explanation of the workings of which is relied upon in the deterministic claim that freewill is illusory, is hardly much better than our knowledge of the other side of the universe. Yet this is the basis on which determinists attempt to tell us that our experience of responsibility is illusory!

Instead, we experience physical limitations, and within that a degree of conditioning, which is sometimes extremely strong and difficult to break. Abused children, for example, tend to suffer massive negative conditioning for the rest of their lives, and have a much increased statistical probability of becoming abusers themselves. Nevertheless, there are also many stories of people who have overcome extremely severe negative conditioning. It is even difficult to draw a precise line between physical incapacity and conditioning, because things that we might not once have thought possible have been well attested as occurring. Human beings cannot fly – and yet now they have aeroplanes. Blind people cannot see, except that sometimes astonishing cures or adaptations have occurred. For example, there are blind people who can ride a bicycle through heavy traffic using echo-location techniques[146]. The line between what we can't do and what we might possibly do (and are thus to some extent responsible for not doing) is an

---

[146] See http://www.worldaccessfortheblind.org/

Middle Way Philosophy 1: The Path of Objectivity

unavoidably vague one. If we take sceptical arguments about our limited knowledge seriously we should not try to make this line prematurely clear through unnecessary metaphysical assumption.

The other type of metaphysical assumption, however, freewill, is no more accurate in conveying our experience of our degree of responsibility for our lives. According to freewill theory, we are totally responsible for all actions that we take within our physical capabilities. Even if we did not consciously make a choice about all our actions, if it can be judged that we might have done so, or that we might have put ourselves in a condition to do so, we are still responsible for that situation. So, if I lost my job due to my employer closing down, then I became depressed due to unemployment, became a heavy drinker, and then killed someone through drink-driving, I must be judged just as responsible for my actions as if I was in full employment and robust mental health. The 'freewill' that the depressed drink-driver had all the way along the line is, like all metaphysical beliefs, a possible interpretation of our experience, but one that is, on the whole, imposed by a group wanting to enforce its codes of conduct rather than derived from the observations of individuals charting their experience of responsibility.

One way in which philosophy has charted the divergence between conventional beliefs about responsibility based on metaphysical freewill and our experience of responsibility as individuals is in the phenomenon of moral luck[147]. For example, a drunk driver who knocked over and killed a child gets more conventional moral blame than one who was just as drunk but lucky enough not to hit a child. If the freewill belief was even used consistently to provide a basis for responsibility, we would treat these two cases as morally alike. However, instead, we recognise a degree of vagueness and

---

[147] See Nagel (1979). Also discussed in IV.3.h.

ambiguity in our understanding of responsibility. We do not know whether the 'lucky' drunk driver was 'luckier' because of relatively greater awareness and caution, or really because of events beyond his control, or even whether the 'unlucky' one really intended to hit the child: we have to make our judgements on the basis of limited, ambiguous evidence of how far responsibility goes.

The solution that helps us to understand responsibility, then, once we have got our heads out of the closing dualistic vice, is to refuse both freewill and determinism, not only in philosophical theory but in the social attitudes that depend on those philosophical theories, and instead to think *incrementally* about conditioning. The solution in one respect is straightforward – I am responsible inversely to the extent to which I am conditioned. Since no scientific description of conditioning ever reaches absolute status, it can never reach deterministic status either. We never lose our responsibility. On the other hand, our responsibility is never total either.

'Taking responsibility' should always be 'taking a degree of responsibility', and 'holding someone responsible' likewise should always be 'holding someone to a degree of responsibility'. This means always working against the tendency of our current egoistic identifications to hold someone totally responsible through anger, or to let ourselves off the hook by exaggerating the degree of conditioning we are subject to. The government official whom we want to blame for losing our paperwork was not entirely to blame, because he was under stress and working in a system that was under stress. To some small extent, I am responsible for accidentally dropping my mother's cut-glass vase, however little I consciously wanted to do it.

In another respect, however, to stop with that formula for incremental responsibility would not address important aspects of our experience. When we take responsibility for our actions, we are not only responding to a degree of conditioning, but shaping experience for ourselves by planning and acting on our plans. In the process we both act on our environment and act on ourselves so as to change the impact of the conditioning we are subject to. Our capacity to effectively change these conditions depends, not just on the conditions themselves, but on our degree of integration, which allows us to act with a degree of adequacy in relation to them.

Our active degree of responsibility, then, depends on our degree of integration as well as our degree of conditioning. Given our experience of making choices and acting on the world we perceive, integration is not just a matter of the conditioning we receive from the past or from encroaching physical conditions, but also a matter of how we respond to it. It is our ability to gradually influence conditions by small changes both to the conditions and to our response to them that corresponds to our experience of 'freewill'.

Our work at increasing integration and at modifying conditions has to be gradual, because of a tendency for big or sudden efforts of will to be counter-productive. This can be accounted for in terms of the operation of the ego at a particular point. If the ego gains a powerful identification with a particular effort at one point, counter-impulses will have to be suppressed, making it very likely that they will re-emerge at a later point and undermine the effort by introducing doubts or mental weariness. If, on the other hand, we can make a moderate effort at one time and link it to further moderate effort at other times, we begin to build up a new helpful conditioning in the direction of the outcome we want, and reactions, although they will probably still occur, will be easier to cope with. Take the example of someone who suddenly resolves to give up smoking: the wilful effort merely suppresses the addiction without addressing its conditions over time. For more on the nature of effective gradual effort to produce integration, see II.2.b.

Overall, then, it does make sense to talk about 'responsibility', and it is both possible and very important to place responsibility in a framework of experience rather than of metaphysical abstraction. It is only by cultivating responsibility in the sense of increasing integration that we are able to develop our ability to make justifiable moral decisions and put them into effective operation.

C. Normativity

Normativity is the quality of 'oughtness' that somehow makes sense of moral terminology. It would be easy to create an explanation of moral action based on psychology, experience, and common sense, which would nevertheless leave the question of 'ought' unanswered. It is a valid question that relates to questions that are likely to come up in experience: why *ought* we to follow Middle Way Philosophy, to develop objectivity and integration?

Any such 'oughtness' cannot descend from on high as a metaphysical benediction, but must arise in our experience. So the best answers I can give to the question of 'oughtness' are ones that analyse ways that people already commonly feel it, and show how these ways imply the normativity of experiential adequacy. Once we have acknowledged the normativity of experiential adequacy, that of all the other aspects of Middle Way Philosophy will follow.

Normativity as it is often remarked in experience can be identified in three forms. Firstly, we can feel that we 'ought' to do something because it is rationally consistent, in accordance with a 'duty' that we have imposed on ourselves as a matter of principle (the Kantian type of 'ought'). Secondly, we can feel that we 'ought' to do something because we desire it, or at least part of us desires it – perhaps for long-term benefit that we can see as desirable (The hedonist or utilitarian type of 'ought'). Thirdly, we can feel that we 'ought' to do something out of social convention, to fit in with the expectations that we know other people will have in our society (The conventional type of 'ought'). Sometimes these people are those that we have other reasons for respecting beyond the mere power of social conformity. I want to argue that all three of these types of normativity in experience imply the normativity of

Normativity

experiential adequacy (and thus of Middle Way Philosophy) when analysed further.

Firstly, the Kantian type of 'ought'. The appeal in the Kantian type of analysis is to consistency. We may feel it is wrong to break a promise, for example, as Kant did, because we would not want to live in a world where everyone broke promises (as Kant alleges, we could not even make sense of the idea of a promise in such a world)[148].

I find it odd that Kant's categorical imperative (his appeal to consistent reasoning as the basis of the principles that we should follow) is applied by him only synchronically in terms of the consistency of our implied principles in an ideal world at the moment, rather than diachronically to test the consistency of our reasons over time. Surely if we ought to be consistent at one time, we ought to be consistent over time too? Furthermore, it seems that we frequently feel this – for example, being ashamed at our lapses from our own stated principles.

Whether synchronic or diachronic, though, consistency of principle requires experiential adequacy to maintain. We will not be able keep our promises, for example, if we do not integrate our wishes sufficiently, so that we still want to keep the promise enough when the time comes to make sacrifices in order to keep it. We also need to address conditions enough to ensure that we are not derailed from our principles in other ways, for example that we don't forget our promise due to getting drunk at the wrong time.

If we feel a moral duty to be consistent, is this really compatible with a failure to address the conditions that allow us to be so? Surely a Kantian impulse should be addressed in whatever way fulfils our duty most effectively? I would thus

---

[148] Kant (1995) §422

conclude that the normativity of the Kantian type of 'ought' also implies the normativity of maximising our experiential adequacy through objectivity.

A Kantian might here object that I am turning a Kantian deontological 'ought' into an empirical matter of the kind that Kant thought were morally neutral. However, this would be to misunderstand the kind of justification for Middle Way Philosophy that I put forward in section 5. There it was argued that coherentist forms of justification (whether understood as logical non-contradiction or as probabilistic or explanatory consistency) fell foul of sceptical arguments by themselves, and thus needed to be combined with agnostic foundationalism for justification. Kant's reasoning, though based on a synthetic understanding of the conditions for experience rather than merely logical non-contradiction, never gets beyond the limitations of coherentism because no transcendental deduction can be proved to be the only possible one[149]. Even if we ignore the many other issues attending Kant's ethics, his appeal to consistency of reasoning in moral principles alone implies the impossibility of proving the non-existence of alternative (and possibly equally consistent) moral principles forming the conditions for other kinds of moral experience. Kant's approach is thus inconsistent in its own terms if it cannot be fully universalised, and the only way to fully universalise it is to take account of the possibility of the moral principles being wrong (agnostic foundationalism)[150]. Universalisable principles can only become genuinely universalisable in their moral force when they are combined with recognition of their actual lack of moral universality.

Let us turn, then, to the second type of 'ought' – the hedonistic or utilitarian type. Here, it is a desire that we feel we ought to

---

[149] As shown in Körner (1967)
[150] See Ellis (2001) 3.g for a fuller discussion of these issues surrounding Kant

fulfil. This may be as basic as feeling that a repressed desire 'ought' to get its expression, such as feeling that we 'ought' to relax after too much devotion to work. In other cases, the desire is a long-term one to do with our sustainable welfare – such as a desire to give up smoking for the benefit of health. In this sort of case, it is obvious, based on the arguments I have already made about integration, that integrating our desires addresses this kind of normative experience more effectively than merely trying to impose a higher level desire onto an immediate one.

However, in utilitarian arguments the desire that we fulfil can become a good deal more remote than this. We feel, in a much more rationalised way, that a greater long-term happiness should outweigh a lesser that conflicts with it: so, for example, people living in the way of a new road, or a hydroelectric dam, which will benefit lots of people, will have to be displaced. However, if it is true that we ought to bring about the greatest good of the greatest number and we feel this as a normative pressure, then surely we should make judgements about consequences that do so as objectively as possible so as to make sure as far as we can that our actions *do* have the intended consequences. To do this, of course, we need to make our judgements with maximal experiential adequacy.

Middle Way Philosophy here goes far beyond utilitarianism, by offering not just an abstract calculation as the basis of moral prescription, but also a moral motive that utilitarianism lacks. Utilitarianism professes itself indifferent to our moral motives, as long as we act so as to bring about the best consequences. Middle Way Philosophy should bring about the best consequences because it takes into account limitations in knowledge when considering consequences as well as our coherent beliefs about the outcomes of our actions, so Middle Way Philosophy should thus better fulfil the moral normativity of utilitarians, if they had one in the first place.

Middle Way Philosophy 1: The Path of Objectivity

Thirdly, the 'ought' of social convention is probably, in practice, by far the most widespread 'ought' that we feel. For example, we don't want our relatives and neighbours to know our shameful secrets. If we consider the claim that we ought to do what our society tells us, though, the question immediately arises of what we mean by 'our society'. We may belong to many different groups, from immediate family to nations, ethnic groups and religions. This 'ought' is not going to help us to differentiate a moral action where any of these different social groupings are in conflict, or even when individuals within a group disagree. We can only follow the normativity of a group to the extent that that group is integrated so as to make the "ought" clear, and only follow a general social normativity to the extent that the different groups we belong to are integrated. This thus implies that social normativity implies the normativity of group integration, but group integration, in turn, implies the normativity of experiential adequacy to provide grounds for groups to integrate.

It thus seems that whatever the moral normativity we feel as being the basis for our moral duty, that duty will be fulfilled better if we try to bring about experiential adequacy. In other words, all forms of moral normativity[151] imply the Middle Way.

---

[151] See Ellis (2001) 7.b for a similar account of aesthetic and scientific normativities.

D. Dispositional objectivity and virtue

In 4.b it was argued that objectivity is a dispositional quality: that is, a quality displayed by human beings in circumstances that call upon it. Morally positive dispositional qualities are commonly called virtues, and morally negative dispositional qualities are commonly called vices. So far I have also identified objectivity with integration, in a way that should make clear my theory of virtue: that virtue is integration. It would thus be helpful to explore here the relationship between Middle Way Philosophy and virtue ethics, the theory that virtues are our basis for moral judgement.

Virtue ethics gives priority to diachronic qualities – that is, to moral qualities displayed regularly over time. According to the stronger versions of virtue ethics[152], these diachronic qualities should take precedence over any synchronic considerations in judging the worth of an action. So, it is claimed, for example, that if a virtuous person commits a murder, we should nevertheless consider that murder as good so long as it remains part of a pattern of behaviour that, taken as a whole, is virtuous, for the virtues of these agents are constitutive of good moral motives. We have no other way of judging what is good other than what virtuous people do, so an isolated piece of apparent vice in the behaviour of a virtuous person should be considered virtue. There are obvious problems with this, because it restricts us from applying other criteria of judgement that may form an important part of our experience. If a wise and compassionate person suddenly starts acting foolishly and cruelly, we need to be able to apply our experience of the moral negativity of their foolishness and cruelty to the judgement rather than deny on principle that it is cruel and foolish. We cannot accept in advance any claim that their apparent foolishness and cruelty necessarily has a good

---

[152] E.g. Michael Slote's 'agent-based' virtue ethics: see Slote (1997)

justification beyond our initial recognition, without any evidence for it, but rather just have to weigh up what we understand of the person's qualities together with the reasons for their actions.

On the other hand, if we were to make moral judgements from a purely synchronic perspective, based only on our estimation of the worth of a particular action ('Act ethics'), this would amount to treating the self as fixed and our perspective as incapable of integration. If we just treated murder as murder without taking into account the character of the person who did the murder, and the possible reasons they might have for doing the murder consistent with that character, we are neglecting an important aspect of conditions. For example, the murder might have been motivated by a desire to save several other lives.

We thus need to resolve the division between virtue ethics and act ethics using the Middle Way. This will require the integration of the diachronic and synchronic perspectives. Thus whatever moral positions we identify with at the moment, we need to consider them in relation to the degree of integration with which we are judging them, and reduce the credibility that we attribute to them proportionately. The vicious are not in such a good position to judge the virtuous. This needs to be done in relation to our own judgements, but also those of others. The credibility of moral judgements made by others depends not only on synchronic moral considerations, but on their character as we understand it. Also, when we compare moral judgements made by different people, the credibility of their characters based on integration needs to be taken into account.

Traditional virtue ethics is based either on analysis of conventionally accepted virtues or on metaphysical justification (such as Aristotle's appeal to the notion of form). To base virtue on integration, however, avoids the epistemological problems of either of these approaches, and justifies our understanding of what is virtuous progressively according to its adequacy to experience.

Thinking of virtue as based on integration also deals with the philosophical problem of the 'unity of the virtues', which is created by the fact that different virtues can conflict. For example, courage and kindness are both traditionally seen as virtues (in Western culture at least, and also elsewhere), but being courageous (for example, in challenging someone's views) may also be seen as unkind, or conversely kindness as cowardly. Aristotle offered 'the mean' as the basis for mediation between conflicting virtues, whereby the mean between the excess and the deficiency of a quality of character is seen as the level that is compatible with all other virtues[153]. However, it is unclear what the justification of this mean might be if it is not either conventional or metaphysical.

We can see this problem from a different perspective if we consider it in the light of integration, for then a virtue such as courage can be seen as a moral characteristic we identify with at one time, kindness at another. These different virtue-identifications can be gradually unified in relation to experience through testing of their adequacy. For example, we learn through experience in what kinds of situations courage or kindness is more appropriate. As Aristotle recognised, our judgements on this depend on the cultivation of practical judgement as well as factual understanding of conditions. What I am suggesting we should add to Aristotle's account here is a psychological understanding of the process of objectivity, which he only described in conventional-analytic terms. This psychological understanding will be developed in detail in volumes 2, 3 and 4.

---

[153] Aristotle (1976) pp.100-8

The balance between virtue and other moral concerns affecting our judgement is also an immediate question in relation to our moral judgements. How far should we prioritise investing in our future characters, and how far present concerns? This is an obvious issue as regards meditation, which can have a very positive effect on the development of our characters, working directly on our experiential adequacy, but obviously takes time during which we are not working directly on the world or interacting with it in other ways. Our investment in experiential adequacy is likely to make our actions more effective in the longer-term because conditions will be better addressed, but at the expense of shorter-term priorities. Obviously a balance will need to be struck, and the nature of this balance cannot be specified in advance, as it depends on all the conditions surrounding an individual judgement. However, the arguments in 7.f ,g, h & i, which are all concerned with the specificity of moral judgements, should be applicable to this problem alongside many others.

E. Virtues and practices

If objectivity is to be seen in terms of virtue, it becomes possible to incorporate many of the strengths of virtue ethics into Middle Way Philosophy. One of the most fascinating and fruitful accounts of virtue to be produced in recent years is found in Alasdair MacIntyre's book *After Virtue*. MacIntyre relates virtues closely to the practical context in which we develop our habitual desires, meanings and beliefs through his concept of goods in a practice.

MacIntyre defines a 'practice' as

Any coherent and complex form of socially established co-operative human activity through which goods internal to that form of activity are realised in the course of trying to achieve those standards of excellence which are appropriate to, and partially definitive of, that form of activity, with the result that human powers to achieve excellence, and human conceptions of the ends and good involved, are systematically extended.[154]

His starting point for explaining how virtue is developed is our activity in such a 'practice'. For example, in football (which MacIntyre mentions as an example), skills are developed such as running, kicking accuracy, awareness of others, heading skills etc, which are recognised as 'good' in the context of football. This context is one of the shared social recognition of certain 'goods'. The practice of football enables these 'goods' to be systematically extended, as does any other practice, such as farming, sociology, web design or playing the harp.

This provides a strong account of how virtue is developed in practical terms, and also shows its inter-dependent relationship with skills and justified beliefs. Conventionally we

---
[154] MacIntyre (1985) p.187

may not feel that football skills have anything to do with morality, but the success of football training in providing young men with a sense of purpose and discipline gives an immediate contrary indication. Still, MacIntyre does not provide any way of linking this practical insight into virtue with a universal theory of ethics that could help us justify football training in a larger context. After all, football training is not necessarily always the best thing to do. If we are busy doing football training when we should be farming, maybe our children will starve as a consequence. MacIntyre appeals to life-narratives and moral traditions, both of which provide further, and perhaps bigger, contexts in which to make moral judgements about a given practice[155]. However, in the end, he has no response to relativism. He cannot show us how to justify one moral tradition over another, but merely leaves us with an account of competing moral traditions[156].

To show how goods in a practice can help us with moral objectivity that can be more broadly justified, I think we need to look at the psychological effects of developing goods in a practice within the individual experience. A youth who learns football skills learns to address conditions in specific new ways: by understanding more about his own body and the actions of others, by being able to move faster and more flexibly and thus act more effectively himself, and by being able to shoot to a target. More broadly, his intense, goal driven activity within football matches provides a temporary integration of desires that might otherwise be in conflict. The larger goals of winning matches, even beyond the time he is actually playing, require him to limit distractions or conflicting activities, and also limit beliefs that might conflict with the ones associated with his football priorities (for example, the belief that over-eating can make you happy).

---

[155] Ibid chapter 15
[156] See Ellis (2001) 4.b.iv

Virtues and practices

All of these 'goods' have an integrating effect that might not have occurred if the youth had not taken up football and accepted its socially-agreed virtues. Such an integrating effect will of course subsequently affect his approach and his effectiveness in other contexts and other activities. This does not mean, of course, that the same integrating effect might not also have been achieved by farming, sociology, web design, or harp-playing. To resolve questions about prioritisation between practices we would have to look at the youth's personal situation, his mental and physical capacities, his social responsibilities and economic context, and his existing patterns of preference and psychological habits. It is only in the light of these other conditions that we could conclude that football training was good, and should be given priority over farming or playing the harp, even though other opportunities to develop virtues and skills are obviously always lost as we adopt one avenue of specialisation in a practice.

So, what makes 'practices' good is the extent to which they address conditions, and in order to weigh one practice against another we have to weigh up the conditions in which those practices may occur and how much scope they have for developing integration. If we do this, not only are practices potentially unified rather than in moral conflict with one another, but a universal account can be developed of the role of practices in moral practice for all. Rather than having to appeal to moral traditions as the highest basis of judgement, traditions just provide further contexts for practices. For example, the practice of football is only judged good in the context of the tradition of football and the rules developed and accepted by football clubs and football associations. If you wanted to develop a different game that you felt addressed conditions better, you might have to use this previous tradition as a point of departure. Similarly, in developing moral habits and judgements, specifically moral traditions (e.g. Hindu, Thomist, or Utilitarian tradition) provide a starting point where we can address the conditions of our background and society

Middle Way Philosophy 1: The Path of Objectivity

and begin to develop goods in a wider practice. However, it is the extent to which those traditions help us to address conditions (and thus the extent to which they are disabled from doing so by metaphysics) that provides a wider basis of judgement between and beyond them.

Large sections of volumes 2, 3 and 4 will be devoted to fuller exploration of specific practices that might be particularly helpful in the development of integration of desire, meaning or belief. However, in principle (as MacIntyre makes clear) any practice can be helpful in this respect, depending on the precise conditions involved. Every practice will also involve desires, meanings and beliefs that need to be shared to appreciate the goods within that practice, and that will be developed by those following the practice. The issue will only be that of which practice it is most important to focus on in one's present circumstances

Just as integration of the individual can be understood as developed by practices, similarly one can understand practices engaged in by groups at a broader social level. For example, going back to the practice of football, one can talk about the virtues of individual football players, but also the virtues of football teams. One team may have stronger attacking skills, working together effectively to score goals, whilst another may work together better in defence but not so well in attack. These group virtues can again only be judged in the wider social context of the practice of football, but their value needs to be judged in terms of the integration of the group promoted, which again helps the groups to address conditions more effectively.

F. Deontological ethics and agnostic foundationalism

Our moral judgements are not only concerned with the diachronic building up of integration to increase our objectivity, but also with our judgements at any one moment. To judge with maximal objectivity we need to be able to take into account as wide a range of conditions as possible (including the internal conditions of our own future virtue). However, how do we decide what will do this? This is where it will be helpful to discuss both the deontological and consequentialist approaches to moral decision-making traditional in Western thought, to see how far either of these approaches to moral judgement succeeds in helping us to address conditions. Deontology will be discussed in this chapter and the next, consequentialism in the following two chapters.

Deontological ethics are ethics that appeal to principle as the basis of moral judgement. At their most rigid, deontological ethics are commandments or rules, and when less rigid, they take the form of guiding principles or rules of thumb. Regardless of the rigidity of the principle, deontological ethics offers a justification for the principle itself as an expression of normativity, regardless of the consequences of following it.

Classic sources of deontological ethics are metaphysical ones which yield absolute justification to the principle. For example, revelation from God and Natural Law each offer universal and absolute grounds for principles gained from claimed experiences. We can be sure that these experiences do not support the universal claims they are supposed to support, simply because the experiences are finite and the scope of the moral rules that derive from them infinite (see 1.g). This derivation of moral principles from an absolute source of knowledge can also be described as positive foundationalism (see 5.a).

Middle Way Philosophy 1: The Path of Objectivity

Middle Way Philosophy can obviously not accept such metaphysical bases for ethics, but nor can it accept moral coherentism, the opposed view that rejects any universal principles and takes morality to be justified only relativistically, by groups or individual choice[157]. Moral coherentism must ignore the possibility of a coherent principle nevertheless being wrong due to conditions beyond the sphere of coherence. The solution, then, for moral principles (as already argued in section 5 for theories in general) is for agnostic foundationalism to be combined with coherentism to provide justification for provisional moral principles.

The rational consistency of principles, as Kant recognised, is a key way of assessing their objectivity. The only mistake that Kant made here is to assume that objective and universal principles must also be absolute, and that absoluteness offers the only way to find objective principles. An objective principle is one that leads us to address conditions better than we have been so far, not an absolute one derived from the Categorical Imperative. A universal principle is one that applies to all conditions as far as we are aware so far, and has universal scope and applicability. Provisional moral principles need to be universal in this sense if they are to avoid being merely relative, but their universality does not need to imply absoluteness.

With these limitations in mind, Kant's Categorical Imperative can be immensely helpful to us as a test for the universal coherence of moral principles, which needs to be supplemented only by the agnostic foundationalism that is needed to make those principles provisional. Kant offered three kinds of tests for the consistency of moral principles: non-contradiction in the law of nature, non-contradiction in the will[158], and treating others as ends in themselves[159].

---

[157] See Ellis (2001) 4.a.i

Deontological ethics and agnostic foundationalism

The first of these I will ignore because it involves the derivation of metaphysical claims from a priori reasoning, of a kind I rejected in 1.f. Kant writes of principles that cannot even be conceived as universal without contradiction, but there is no reason why such principles, even if they are believed to exist, should be morally normative, as like, mathematical principles, they only tell us about an assumed *a priori* model in a given set of meanings that may be internally consistent, but has no necessary relationship to experience. My conception of a promise or of a lie, and thus whether it can be universalised without contradiction, may be different at different times depending on the experiential and cultural context, but Kant's formulation of non-contradiction in the law of nature allows no incrementality, but only a metaphysical assertion of the acceptability or rejection of the principle as a whole in an assumed background where it makes sense in the way Kant intended. I do not intend to enter into any further discussion of this point here, since my main purpose is not to criticise Kant's ethics. Rather, I want to focus on the ideas of non-contradiction in the will and of treating others as ends in themselves to explore how they can provide useful tools in Middle Way Ethics.

Non-contradiction in the will suggests that, for a moral principle to be justified, I must be able to wish to apply it universally without contradiction. For example, it would not be a justifiable moral principle for me to say that polluting the atmosphere is acceptable for myself, if I am not prepared to accept others also doing so. If I think it's a justified principle that others shouldn't waste their talents, I also should not waste my own. Principles are justified through being universalisable, as long as I do not make any exceptions, for myself or for others.

---

[158] Kant (1995) § 424
[159] Ibid § 429

If we were to try to adopt this criterion for justifiable principles, it seems that it would also apply in other ways that Kant does not consider. Not only should I not make an exception of myself, but I should also not make an exception of others I identify with (such as my children) or make an exception of myself or others at one given time as opposed to another time. For example, a past self who was drunk, or a self twenty years ago is not exempt from the moral principle. We can apply Kant's approach beyond the assumption of the absolute self which accompanied it in his time.

This point suggests the usefulness of non-contradiction in the will as an indicator of integration. If my will at different times holds consistent beliefs, this is a good indication that it is integrated, and the rational reflection that I ought to hold and practise consistent moral beliefs is one way of encouraging integration. It is not enough by itself, as applied naively it might just lead to the repression and alienation of contrary "immoral" feelings. However, if we combine the attempt to practise principles that avoid contradiction in the will with integrative practices (of the kind discussed in II.4, III.6 and IV.5) then non-contradiction in the will can offer us a useful moral challenge.

However, if we are to avoid interpreting non-contradiction in the will absolutely we will also need to take into account the limitations that accompany any deontological approach to ethics. A verbal principle is subject to linguistic scepticism and does not have an absolute representational relationship to reality. Rather it is the *function* of any such principle in relation to our experience that offers us objectivity by prompting us to address conditions that we would not otherwise have addressed. No deontological command can help us more than functionally, assuming it avoids the unhelpfulness of metaphysical justification.

Deontological ethics and agnostic foundationalism

So, to return to the example of pollution, the value of reflection about the consistency of my attitudes to pollution caused by myself and by others is a prompt to objectivity. However, it need not stop me weighing up the importance of pollution against other values (7.h). I may consider that the amount of pollution my actions will cause is justified by the way, for example, pollution-causing actions may help me to fulfil other moral values (for example, when travelling to see friends or broadening my cultural understanding). It is the awareness of the issue and an expectation of consistency that make the principle of non-contradiction in the will a useful one, rather than an impotent absolute *a priori* moral command that I am then likely, in practice, to ignore because it conflicts too much with my other wishes.

It is only when interpreted in this way that non-contradiction in the will is freed from the criticism I just made of non-contradiction in the law of nature as a criterion: that is, of absolutising a certain context of meaning and being non-incremental. The meaning of a principle developed at one time, in one state of the ego with its associated belief, may vary from another, so a universalisable principle can only be universalisable to the extent that those meanings overlap. The principle will also only be applicable to a certain extent in the new situation at another time. Nevertheless, if we bear both these limitations in mind, it can be a useful objectivity-check.

Such distinctions become clearer if we apply them over a longer period of time. So, to return to the pollution example, the meaning of a principle like "pollution is acceptable" in the context of nineteenth-century industry is clearly different to that of a modern individual considering transport options. Without understanding of the long-term global effects of air pollution, a nineteenth century mill owner is not in a position to assess the universalisability of principles regarding pollution in the same way. We can make justifiable moral judgements about the justification of a mill-owner continuing to pollute the atmosphere only to the extent that the background information and cultural limitations overlap. This does not mean that we should not make them at all, or that we should merely assume total determination of past moral choices: rather that the way universal moral principles apply to such past circumstances must be tempered by a process of imaginative recognition of the full circumstances.

Kant's third kind of test for principles, that of treating persons as ends in themselves, can be treated as a specific application of the second. We should not treat others as means to an end, it is argued, because we cannot universalise a principle expressing this, as we would not wish ourselves to be treated as means to an end by others.

In interpreting this approach we will need to break down Kant's assumptions about 'self' in the terms I argued in 1.j. An egoistic identification at one time may very well be quite happy to treat the identification at another as a means to an end, so the consistent identification of 'self' that Kant relies upon is not as dependable as he seems to assume. For example, I might be quite happy to tell an embarrassing story about myself twenty years ago, abusing "my" reputation as a means to the end of gaining amusement and social credit as an entertainer, in a way I would not be happy to do for my current self, or even for a child or partner with whom I have a strong identification. One may not even identify with one's own body or one's own social reputation at present, as the self-sacrificing may identify much more with an abstract ideal to which they sacrifice themselves as a means to an end. To be useful to us, then, this approach has to be seen as a principle of not treating anyone we do not identify with as a means to an end.

Another barrier is the lack of incrementality in Kant's conception of means and ends. We may all quite frequently treat others as means to an end to some degree, with only a

Deontological ethics and agnostic foundationalism

passing or abstract awareness of the personhood of those we thus "use": for example, in making purchases or any kind of trade, we "use" others to provide goods and services. Sexual activity also involves a strong sexual objectivisation of another's body, surely a classic case of treating another as a means to an end, but whether this is morally problematic depends on the context and the degree of objectivisation. Not all sex is rape[160].

Nevertheless, Kant's way of testing principles here is another useful tool for testing objectivity in our experience. It is likely to ring alarm bells if we are considering a course of action that violates human rights or basic human dignity. For example, in circumstances where the use of torture might seem to be an acceptable means to a practically necessary end, Kant's principle suggests a *prima facie* objection that should make us think very hard indeed about such actions. The press of events and the need for swift decision making in some contexts, plus a fixation on certain goals, can lead people to make hasty judgements which do not take into account all the conditions in such cases: for example in the case of torture, the long-term psychological effects on both victim and perpetrator, the political and social effects of the information that torture is being used, and the unreliability of information gained through torture in any case. To take into account our weaknesses in making objective judgements in stressful circumstances, perhaps we still need big Kantian principles like these.

The type of objectivity that such a principle might help us to observe at a basic level is compassion. Awareness that others are persons like me is basic aspect of conditions that I neglect at my peril. Though Kant's principles only work at an

---

[160] See Ellis (2011b) chapter 3 for discussion of sexual ethics, including objections to the Buddhist idealisation of celibacy, which contradicts a more incremental approach to sexual issues in other contexts in Buddhism.

intellectual level, they might help to set up the conditions in which compassion for others (or for oneself) can develop.

In using such a test of principles I would have to take into account differences in the understanding of 'means' and 'ends' in different contexts. The end of one situation is merely the means in another. I may have to ignore a great many minor and ambiguous cases where this principle does not clearly help us to be more objective. Nevertheless, there are some occasions when it does so, when the cultivation of virtue or the calculation of consequences is not enough to alert us to the kind of objectivity that a life-or-death situation demands of us.

G. Moral authority

The idea that universalisable moral principles can usefully challenge us, however, offers little guidance on the more difficult question involved in moral judgements. How should we judge the debatable cases where these principles may or may not offer the most objective perspective available? Most of us do not have too much trouble refraining from the more obvious kinds of activity prohibited by Kantian principles, such as violence, theft, or the grosser forms of deception. It is where there is debate between deontological and consequentialist approaches (for example, lying to avoid conflict, or an issue like abortion), or where we have to choose between alternative goods (such as which skills to develop) or alternative evils (such as risky surgery), that we have more difficulty knowing how to act. One way of approaching this within a deontological approach is to rely on the guidance of moral authorities, which I will consider here. Another, which I will consider in the next chapter, is through consequentialist calculation.

The extreme of moral authority is an absolute moral authority: revealed holy scripture, God incarnate, God's prophet, the enlightened guru, or the absolute wise man or woman who has penetrated the secrets of the universe. I have already given a case against relying on revelations from such sources (see 1.g). However, that case still leaves further questions about non-absolute moral authorities. How far is it useful to rely to a degree on the advice of others, particularly those that we consider wise?

Where objectivity is concerned, the advice of individuals has many advantages over other sources of moral guidance. Since, as I have argued, *people* are the source of objectivity rather than propositions (see 4.b), we can judge that objectivity most directly in a person, assisted not just by observations but by intuitions that provide us with short-cuts in deciding how far to trust a person.

By 'intuitions' here I do not mean any kind of mysteriously authoritative faculty, but merely unconscious processing, based on experience and in this case depending on our physical relationship to another person (or perhaps to other physical aspects of our environment). Given that meaning is not entirely a matter of cognitive content, there is no reason why communication should be either. When we meet someone face-to-face far more is communicated physically and emotionally than in terms of the discussion of beliefs, and thus we have a quick, though rough and not entirely reliable, guide to a person's objectivity. Even if we have not met a person face-to-face, but corresponded by email or even read their writings, we get a certain sense of them as a person which is more than just a process of conscious deduction.

This advantage is compounded when a person tailors their moral advice to the specific situation of another person. If objectivity is a matter of engaging with conditions, those conditions can be engaged with much more effectively when they are the specific conditions of an individual life. If a moral advisor is aware of specific circumstances then her advice is likely to be far more relevant to those circumstances than any general moral principles could be. The intuitive aspects of a human relationship that might lead someone to turn to a moral advisor are also redoubled when that advisor also responds intuitively in their understanding of a moral situation.

"Advice" is probably too crude a term for what another incrementally more objective person, a "moral advisor" can offer. "Morally challenging or supportive input" or just "friendship" might be a better way to put it. Since an aspect of objectivity is the addressing of psychological conditions, and since those psychological conditions might well mean that directly given "advice" would interfere with the sense of moral responsibility of the "advised", the input might well just be gentle encouragement of a more adequate action or a challenge to consider alternatives beyond those routinely considered. Since the prime moral need is for the objectivity of a person making a decision, the advisor needs to work in whatever way best supports that objectivity. In some cases (as in very urgent matters, or where the person concerned is very inexperienced) direct advice to act in a particular way might be the best way to do this, but in others (perhaps with a more long-term decision or with a more experienced person) moral guidance may amount more to subtle nudges in the direction of greater objectivity.

The roles of parents, mentors, older friends, and teachers (whether educational or spiritual) obviously fit this model. These people have moral authority only in the sense of having greater objectivity than those whom they advise and support. At its best this is a very helpful way of importing specificity to the Middle Way. However, we also need to consider when it is appropriate to rely on such guidance, and what kind of epistemological balancing is needed to avoid moral authority either being exaggerated into revelation or, on the other hand, being diminished by relativism into nothing.

The balancing, I want to argue, is the same as that we would need to make in relation to any theory using the feedback loop (see 3.e), except that it involves personal relationships of trust and elements of intuition rather than just the assessment of evidence considered cognitively. The Middle Way of trust involves the avoidance either of excessive trust or of insufficient trust. Excessive trust undermines trust in the long term because it involves an intuitive response that is too open in relation to the conditions, probably leading to betrayal at some level. Insufficient trust, on the other hand, limits objectivity because it stops us using others as a resource to support our objectivity[161]. Excessive trust relies on positive metaphysics that idealises a person and gives them an absolute status in relation to us, whilst insufficient trust involves a negative metaphysics that refuses to accept the basis for trust offered by experience.

A process of balanced trust, then, needs to be provisional in the same way as a falsifiable theory. We choose to trust someone based on our experience of their degree of objectivity so far. Doing this means that we may well be able to improve the objectivity of our own judgements through their support, but our trust cannot be unconditional. We can justifiably enter into a relationship of trust and accept moral authority only as long as we continue to encounter the Middle Way broadly expressed through that person's attitudes and actions. If that person starts to appeal to absolute sources of authority (or absolute denial of authority), or is found in major practical inconsistencies, these are strong preliminary indications that our trust may have been misplaced.

Moral authorities that strike the Middle Way also need to be known personally in order to strike this balance. The investment of trust, with its many intuitive features, into a relationship that extends far beyond immediate experience is mistaken because we can so easily project trustworthy features onto a person who is largely beyond immediate experience. We can still rationally weigh up the credibility of a source only known remotely, such as the BBC as a source of news, but this credibility nevertheless declines steeply the less we understand of the context in which the source of information was created, and needs to be distinguished from personal trust. I may decide that the BBC offers a credible source of news from places remote from me such as Burma or Libya, but this arises from a general assessment of the group-objectivity of the BBC, not an intuitive response to the reporter as a person.

---

[161] See Ellis (2008) for a fuller account of trust

The projection of trustworthy features to those only vaguely known can be seen in the idealisation of distant leaders: whether communist leaders, Buddhist or Hindu gurus, or saints. When an acceptance of revelation becomes confused with the use of a person as symbol, it becomes fairly clear that neither the trusting relationship with a friend nor a critically weighed assessment of credibility is at stake, but rather the intrusion of excessive trust into an uncritical relationship with a distant figure.

We cannot 'trust' a figure such as Jesus or the Buddha, because in effect by trying to do this we are adopting an *account* of a person mediated by a long tradition of transmission, which is in effect a theory accepted regardless of its relationship with experience, even though we may feel about it as we feel about a relationship with an individual. A remote individual can have a symbolic function for us in supporting integration, or may offer general moral principles that we consider credible. However, they are not in a position either to be the object of trust based on immediate relationship, nor to offer moral guidance based on personal understanding, so some crucial aspects of the trusting relationship are absent even whilst we may be trying to maintain the appearance of it.

To speak today of the 'moral authority' of a figure like Jesus, St Francis, or Washington, say, is thus perhaps to speak of the meaning of these figures for us as symbols which may help with the integration of meaning, or perhaps also to speak of moral principles attributed to these figures that we may have initially considered because of the credibility of their origins. However, moral principles offered by Jesus, such as "Love your neighbour as yourself" have to be interpreted as moral theories in their own right, and considered for their relationship with experience regardless of their origins.

Middle Way Philosophy 1: The Path of Objectivity

The disciples who actually knew Jesus in person, such as Peter, John or Matthew, might have been able to speak of his moral authority in a much more immediate way. For example, when he meets Simon Peter and Andrew and tells them to follow him and become "fishers of men"[162] we might take this as a piece of personal advice directed to those fishermen, who subsequently became his disciples. The objectivity it gained from those specific circumstances, where Jesus knew them as individuals and they knew him, cannot be imported into the church sermon of today in which we are all vaguely understood to be fishermen and to be commanded to evangelise. The objective power of a 2000-year old piece of advice is unavoidably diluted almost to nothing by being turned into a general moral commandment delivered, not by an individual, but by a tradition for whom Jesus is just a legitimating symbol.

Nevertheless, we should not underestimate the power and helpfulness of moral authority when based on experience. The reverse extreme of concluding that there is no moral authority is equally to be avoided. The many young people who have failed to heed the advice of their elders – perhaps because it was imperfect and they detected elements of hypocrisy in them – have made an equal mistake to those who idealise the moral authority of a figure like Jesus or the Buddha. The fact that all figures of moral authority are imperfect in their moral activity is not a reflection that need reduce us to moral relativism, but on the contrary a necessary condition for useful moral friendship.

---

[162] Matthew 4:18-20, Mark 1:16-18

H. Calculating consequences

Beyond the general principles offered by the Kantian approach and the advice of moral authorities, the main way of making precise moral judgements is through calculations of consequences. This is the approach used by utilitarians, who classically act so as to create consequences that maximise the happiness of the greatest number. As a means of addressing conditions, this initially seems to have a lot going for it, for in considering consequences we have to face up to the complexity of the conditions that may interfere with the fulfilment of our wishes, and to the many side-effects that our actions may have. It becomes clear, for example, why I may need to lie to save lives.

However, the consequentialist approach raises two kinds of issues, both of them ways that calculating consequences may actually make it harder to address conditions. The first issue is that of the objectivity of the person making judgements of moral consequences. If people have little understanding of the conditions, them making calculations is likely to lead to worse results, not better, than if they followed general moral principles. To some extent this point applies to everyone, as we are all ignorant of conditions to come degree. The second issue is that of identifying the kinds of consequences that are most morally important. It is not self-evident, from the many philosophical discussions that have taken place about hedonism (the prioritisation of pleasure as moral good) that good consequences are those of pleasure, or that we can easily identify other supremely good consequences apart from pleasure.

A utilitarian response to the first issue, regarding the objectivity of those making utilitarian judgements, is often to make utilitarianism esoteric: that is, to specify that utilitarian justification for an action does not necessarily imply the use of utilitarian judgement[163]. If we are judging only on grounds of consequences, it does not matter how the moral decision was arrived at, but only what consequences it had. A judgement that is the best available by utilitarian standards thus may actually be judged by appeal to principles, or even just by unreflectively following convention or immediate individual wishes.

This is not a helpful solution in the terms of Middle Way Philosophy, as it involves the abstracted turn found in analytic philosophy that I have already criticised in 1.f. When consequentialism is made esoteric in this way, it becomes irrelevant to the question of how we should make moral judgements. Objectivity is a function of judgement, not of a state of abstract justification beyond experience. The utilitarian here is guilty of *ad hoc* argument, which maintains the abstract 'truth' of utilitarianism at the expense of its relevance to experience.

The issue of a lack of objectivity in judgements of consequences is not dealt with just by abstracting the problem. We can see the problem having practical results wherever consequentialist justifications are given for decisions that, with the benefit of hindsight, can be seen as addressing conditions poorly. Utilitarian decision-makers destroy crucial features of the environment, launch disastrous wars, create famines through misguided aid, and appease ruthless dictators. In practice we can see that appealing to consequences does not always in fact lead to better consequences, and this point alone should be sufficient to make us wary of moral decisions that are justified only through consequences.

We can also see the lack of justification for purely utilitarian judgements using the account of justification given in section

---

[163] Railton (1984)

Calculating consequences

5. Consequentialist calculation depends on coherentist assumptions because it assumes that the consistent account of conditions we have developed is the correct one. If we are to also take into account the likelihood of error, we should build agnostic foundationalism into our moral judgements as well as coherentism.

Objectivity in decision-making is cultivated by virtue, as discussed above in 7.d. Thus, in order to make increasingly more objective decisions we need to cultivate increasing degrees of integration both as individuals and as groups. This means that our justification in making consequential decisions is not based solely on the more desirable consequences that a given action is said to bring about compared to another, but also on our ability to address conditions in estimating those consequences, which we can judge best from our degree of integration. The less our integration, the greater the probability of error.

Thus neither virtue nor consequentialist calculation is enough by itself, but rather judgements in specific cases need to be determined by both in conjunction. If my judgement is justified proportional to my integration, the moral choice is justified both by my judgement and the external grounds of the moral choice.

In considering my own judgements, then, the reliance I place on them should depend on my understanding of my own objectivity. If I know my own objectivity to be limited, I will probably do better to rely on moral advisors, moral principles, or provisionally derived rules (see 7.i below). On the other hand, if I know my own judgement to be relatively objective, I am justified in having confidence in it even when there is some opposition. Of course, cognitive bias tends to lead many of us to over-estimate our own objectivity. We will be even better justified to the extent that we manage to take this psychological condition into account.

Middle Way Philosophy 1: The Path of Objectivity

Our estimations of others' degree of objectivity are also relevant here, wherever we attempt to assess the rightness or wrongness of a decision, or to compare different judgements of the same problem. Here the questions of moral authority considered in the previous chapter coincide with those concerning consequentialism. Greater moral authority implies greater weight given to consequentialist reasoning by those with such authority, on the grounds that the consequences are more likely to be correctly understood. Some of the conditions that need to be taken into account may be those of a particular factual area where specialised knowledge is relevant, but the mere possession of such specialised knowledge does not necessarily imply more objective judgements about issues connected with it. For example, doctors and medical researchers will understand the factual background to medical ethics issues better than others, but the priority to be given to their judgement will depend on their degree of integration, not just on their medical expertise.

From this point comes a central principle of Middle Way political philosophy. If the issue is one of using power, then the justification for doing so depends on the degree of integration of the person (or group) wielding power relative to the person (or group) against which power is wielded, rather than just on a consequentialist calculation. For example, a justified punishment needs to wielded by the more objective against the less objective, in addition to being justifiable in other ways. The punishment of a school-child for a misdemeanour will probably be justified, in most cases, by this principle, but the execution of Socrates was not (contrary to Socrates' own estimation of his absolute duty to obey the state[164]). Middle Way political philosophy based on this point is developed in more detail in II.6, III.8, IV.4.h and IV.7.

---

[164] See Plato (1993) 50a-51c

Calculating consequences

Let me turn now to the other issue with consequentialism that I mentioned at the beginning of this chapter: the question of which consequences are to be considered good ones. Two common answers to this in utilitarianism are pleasure (as in the hedonistic utilitarianism of Bentham) and fulfilled preferences (as in Singer's utilitarianism). Both of these give rise to a number of problems.

Pleasure is difficult to define when people may sometimes prefer hardship, duty or even (in the case of masochists) pain. If we count these preferences as in some sense pleasure, then we effectively reduce pleasure to preference. If on the other hand we claim that those who actually prefer hardship, duty or pain in some sense *should* prefer pleasure, on what grounds can we do so? Then even if we were to accept psychological hedonism (the claim that everyone in fact seeks pleasure), the issue would still remain as to whether this hedonism is normative.

These difficulties for hedonism are compounded by the problem known as the *paradox of hedonism,* or the *hedonic treadmill*: that is, the recognition that the best way to ensure pleasure is often not to pursue it. Fulfilling our desires (for example, getting the sexual partner we've been pursuing) is not necessarily as pleasurable as the anticipation. We become bored or surfeited, and our appetites vary with our physical and psychological states. Over-indulgence in pleasures can prevent us from appreciating more of them in future, for example by destroying the liver, or the environment of the once-lovely seaside resort now stacked with concrete hotels. Pleasure is not a simple quantity or a single kind of experience, and not easily predictable as the result of certain kinds of action. Psychologically, our levels of pleasure also tend to normalise a short while after exceptional events that elevate or depress them[165].

---

[165] See IV.3.h

Middle Way Philosophy 1: The Path of Objectivity

The paradox of hedonism is the implication of assuming a metaphysical self who is the same when pleasures are received as when they are anticipated. If, instead, we think of ourselves dynamically, as changing desires with associated meanings and beliefs, it becomes an obvious danger that the pleasures we anticipate will not be fulfilled by the time we get them. 'Pleasure' is not a coherent object for us to value because the conditions affecting it are far more complex than our egoistic projections suggest. The anticipated experience varies from the eventual one because the desires of the self who anticipated are different from the desires of the one who experiences the 'pleasure'. At the same time, our egoistic denial of this change means that we are still trying to impose the pleasures we anticipated on those we eventually have: insisting on finishing that plate of food even though we are not hungry, or pretending to have 'a good time' at a party even when we are not.

So, the alternative offered by utilitarians is the valuing of preferences. According to the preference utilitarianism of Peter Singer[166], the consequences we should value are those of the maximum fulfilment of preferences, with reflective preferences prioritised over unreflective. This has the advantage of allowing a preference for consequences that are not pleasurable, but it still gives priority to a process of reasoning in deciding our moral goals, without specifying anything about how that reasoning should proceed. It doesn't matter how our preferences are arrived at provided that we determine our own preference.

If we consider this diachronically, it seems only a partial advance on hedonistic utilitarianism. Our rationality enables us to weigh up different desires that we are aware of at a specific time, in the light of the beliefs that we hold at that time, and

---

[166] Singer (2002) and elsewhere in Singer's many writings

thus a degree of integration may be achieved at that point between the desires we hold then. However, our preferences may still vary hugely between different times, even if we have reflected on them to a degree. Preference utilitarianism merely aggregates these preferences at different times (or of different people) rather than providing us with a moral justification for integrating them. In the process it may also repress those desires that we do not prefer.

Thus Singer's approach is helpful both in recognising the value of reflective decisions about preferences, and also giving value to preferences without this reflectiveness (as in the case of the preferences of children and animals). However, seeking consequences that maximise the fulfilment of preferences will not necessarily aid the integration of those preferences. For example, in a group that is sharply divided in their preferences between two incompatible options in the proportions of 60% to 40%, the maximum fulfilment of preferences is reached just by doing what the 60% majority want. The integrative solution, however, might well involve dialectical probing of the assumptions behind both the two incompatible arguments and the people's preferences for them. The integrative solution would address the conditions far better than just imposing the majority will, because it will also channel the wishes of the minority.

It could be argued that a preference utilitarian has no reason to reject integrative solutions, and that the partial fulfilment of a greater number of preferences might seem preferable to the complete fulfilment of a smaller number of preferences. However, preference utilitarianism does not give us any particular reason to seek such integrative solutions either. Preference utilitarianism can be made more sophisticated in response to psychological awareness, but would address conditions even better if it avoided the limitations imposed by the utilitarian framework.

Middle Way Philosophy 1: The Path of Objectivity

Both the versions of utilitarianism I have considered here make the mistake of considering good consequences in terms of desires that are selected in a certain way, rather than just in terms of desires. Given that not all our desires are for pleasure, why should those that are for pleasure be singled out as specially valuable? Similarly, given that not all our desires can be selected as preferences, why should those that are not be considered less valuable? My basic thesis here, in contrast, is straightforward: desires are good. There is no difference between desire and value, and we do not have to select between desires in this way to only find some of them valuable whilst rejecting others. When desires conflict, however, they should be integrated, not aggregated. Aggregation can lead either to majority imposition or to the lowest common denominator, but integration, through a dialectical process involving meanings and beliefs as well as desires, considers how desires can best be channelled in the light of the conditions.

This takes us back to the question of what sorts of consequences should be considered good ones when we calculate how to act so as to bring them about. The answer here has to be incremental, avoiding abrupt discontinuity between some kinds of desire-fulfilment and others, but at the same time allowing moral differentiation between desires. All fulfilments of desire are good to some extent, but the better consequences that we can more justifiably prioritise are more integrated ones. More integrated desires may be the ones that we can identify ourselves as based on the consideration of a wider range of conditions, or they may be the desires that moral advisors have helped us to identify as more integrated.

There are occasions when we need to calculate consequences, and when doing so is the best way to face up to the demands of a situation objectively. Let's take a classic utilitarian medical ethics example, that of to whom to give a kidney transplant when there are several people who need it

Calculating consequences

equally urgently, but only one kidney available. In these circumstances, whatever our general principles, they are not likely to provide differentiation in judging between different needy individuals, so deontological approaches are practically useless here. In these circumstances a utilitarian solution is to work out the quality adjusted life years (QALYs) that each candidate is likely to gain from the kidney. However, such calculation takes no account of the degree of objectivity either of those on the medical ethics committee who judge such things, or of those who might receive the kidney. All the patients desire to live, and all the medical staff and the relatives would like all the patients to live, if possible. But how integrated are these wishes?

We cannot pretend that any consequential calculation is a precise one, or that calculations of this kind, where some may live a bit longer and others probably die, are at all easy or to be entered into lightly. Yet in some circumstances it may be necessary for us to make choices like this. It is no solution to the difficulties to throw up our responsibilities and to invoke God or cast lots to make the decision for us, for that may well lead to a worse outcome which we will have failed to prevent. Supposing we have three patients all in need of the kidney: one is a loving mother with three children, another is a twelve-year old boy, and the third is a scientist engaged in important medical research. We might all have opinions about whether youth, care of children, or medical research provide greater benefits to society, or how much weight we should give to vague potentiality like that of the boy. Yet in these cases there would also be other complicating factors: different temperaments, family relationships, or even pressure from the public due to media interest. How could such a judgement be made more objectively?

We can only try to make such decisions as objectively as possible by trusting the most objective people available with the decision. Of course, this requires a prior judgement as to who are the most objective people available, in which, whoever we are, we have to have confidence in our own judgements. Being more objective in such circumstances is not necessarily a matter of not having vested interests. The most objective person available may happen to be the mother of the twelve-year old boy, for example, yet if she has that objectivity we should be obliged to trust her despite this, because her objectivity will enable her to move beyond the distortion of narrow identification with her child. If she does not feel able to do this, and does not, on the other hand, also feel free to choose her own son, she should refuse the task.

Part of the dilemma in such a case will implicitly involve a choice of what should be considered good consequences. Is it better to have consequences that create more future years of human life, or to maximise discovery, or to maximise loving, supportive relationships? We cannot specify this in advance, yet one of these kinds of consequence will address conditions better than the others in every case, and we can only try to find people who can discern which. If we cannot do so, and there is insufficient trust in an objective person or persons to make the best possible decision, then we have to fall back on the traditional committee vote. Yet even then committees can work in ways that either give more priority to addressing conditions through incisive consensual discussion, or more priority to the false equality involved in merely aggregating everyone's opinion whether soundly based or not.

One of the things we would also need to take into account in such a case, much as it may pain our egalitarian instincts, is the relative objectivity of the patients. In circumstances where some have to live and others die, it is better on the whole if those who are more objective live. However, I am not going to suggest how this criterion can be prioritised amongst other desirable consequences: such issues will have to be left to those who can fully assess a given situation.

Of course, not all consequential judgements are as difficult or painful as this one. If we have to decide whether to pretend we liked a kindly-meant present, or to prioritise fair-trade over organic when buying bananas, the judgements are less important, even if the basis for them is no more obvious. Since it would be impractical to consult the wise on all such decisions, we just have to weigh up the consequences giving priority to our own more objective judgements, and identifying the types of consequence that we think are important as far as we are able.

However, it may not always be practicable to spend time weighing up such questions at the times that we have to make such judgements. Some urgent decisions, indeed, require split-second timing. So, this leads us to the question in the next chapter, as to whether practical rules can be provisionally derived from consequential calculation.

I. Provisionally derived rules

Having considered the limitations of general principles in 7.f above, it may seem unnecessary to return to the subject of moral rules. However, it is important to do so in order to complete this conceptual outline of the ways that we can find justifiable grounds for moral judgements. We have considered the role of Kantian moral principles, and I have suggested that they provide a useful test of objectivity, even though we need other methods of determining the exceptions to such principles. We have also considered the role of moral authorities and of consequential calculation, which turn out to be interdependent given that consequential calculation is more justified when it is made by those who are moral authorities. Both of these approaches help to provide specificity to our moral judgements. However, we have not yet fully considered the effects of the practical demands placed on calculations of consequence. The need for prompt moral decision-making may lead us to return to rules once again, but this time ones that are justified by consequential calculation.

There is a tradition of derived rules in utilitarian ethics, known as rule utilitarianism. Here rules provide justified guidance for our moral judgements if following the rule, on the whole, leads to better consequences. Given the practical demands on decision-making (which include not only time constraints, but also those of ignorance or of limited awareness), it may often lead to better consequences if one follows such rules than if one tries to work out a justified response to every moral issue on the spot. For example, given that honesty supports mutual trust in society and dishonesty undermines it, it may be better to follow a rule of honesty to avoid the negative effects that generally follow from dishonesty. This rule utilitarian tradition can be applied to any kind of consequentialist calculation.

Provisionally derived rules

One of the difficulties in this debate has always been how strongly these rules should be adhered to. Strong rule utilitarianism requires an absolute commitment regardless of the circumstances, whereas weak rule utilitarianism allows for the breaking of such rules in circumstances that seem to demand it. Since I have already argued against absolute moral principles, it should be obvious that in the terms of Middle Way Philosophy, all rules whatsoever must be provisional. However, there are good arguments for adopting such provisionally derived rules if they enable us, in practice, to address conditions better than we would otherwise.

Provisionally derived rules also have the advantage over Kantian principles of not necessarily being universal. They may even specify the circumstances in which a general principle can be broken. For example, I may have a general rule never to give bribes or gifts in business transactions, but when trying to do business in a very corrupt developing country find it impossible to make any deals without participating in the customary petty bribery of that culture. One might then weigh up the consequences of participating in such bribery against those of not doing business at all, and conclude that the minimum necessary bribery is justifiable in that particular country. Rather than going over the issues whenever one is subsequently confronted with a situation where a bribe is demanded, a provisional rule will then have been made for operating in that country, to operate prima facie in all cases within it.

One of the difficulties of such rules is that in practice they often become socially sanctioned, and are reinforced by convention when they need to remain under scrutiny. A personal rule, that starts off as a provisional one, suspending honest dealings when in a corrupt environment, can easily come to support the customary approach of a whole group, and thus have a substantial effect in maintaining corruption. The group of all Western business-people who do business in India, for

312

Middle Way Philosophy 1: The Path of Objectivity

example, may develop a reinforcing culture whereby going along with corruption becomes an unquestioned social rule – perhaps one based on metaphysical assumptions such as those of cultural relativism. A strong rule about acquiescence in bribery could easily become indistinguishable from an unreflective 'when in Rome' metaphysical relativism, and this might also affect attitudes in other situations. For this reason, the provisionality of derived rules is vital. Such rules can only remain provisional, in practice, by being frequently reviewed, and by being firmly based on individual judgement rather than social practice, even when the rule itself concerns how far to go along with a specific social practice.

This kind of procedure can also be applied at a group level when considering the making of formal rules by social groups, up to and including the laws made by governments. Laws and other formal social rules can be seen morally as provisionally derived rules, the prime moral justification for which is the consequences of the legislation as considered by those with objectivity. It is our responsibility to obey such laws or other rules, not just when our individual assessment of the consequences coincides with that of the law-makers, but also when we are aware that the laws have been made with greater objectivity than we as individuals are able to bring to bear on a judgement about them. Just as we are practically unable to make constant new judgements and so need provisionally derived rules for ourselves, so do we need them in society given that we as individuals are practically unable to make informed practical judgements on many matters that have been legislated about. For example, if the government has done careful research on the probabilities and effects of vehicle collisions at different speeds, together with an informed and consensual debate on the laws concerning speed limits, we have no justification as individuals for breaking those speed limits on the basis of an appeal to our own limited objectivity on the matter, unless to ensure consequences which outweigh these considerations (for example, saving a life).

Many political questions are raised by this point about law, of which perhaps the most important is that of how we are to judge the integration of governments and their judgements, and thus be able to judge objectively when we are justified in breaking the law. This is an area that will be discussed in much more detail in II.6.

J. Rationality and emotion

In this final chapter of the ethics section, I want to stand back a little from the process of moral judgement as I have outlined it, and consider it in relation to two concepts often used in Western accounts of ethics – those of rationality and emotion. Kant thought that ethics are entirely a matter of rationality[167], Hume that they were entirely a matter of emotion[168]. To overcome the false dichotomy between these two ways of thinking we need to adopt the dialectical approach of questioning these two terms and re-conceiving them in incremental and experiential terms. What do we mean by rationality or by emotion?

Rationality is the ability to use reason, and reason is the drawing of conclusions from assumed premises (when it is deductive) or from a selection of evidence (when it is inductive). Reason, then, can no more be used to solve moral problems without prior assumptions than we can light a fire without fuel. Rejecting purely *a priori* starting points (see 1.f), all our prior assumptions must come from experience in some way. Our rationality, then, is only of use to us in making consistent use of the evidence of experience. Numerous single examples of reasoning fit together to form a web of mutually-dependent coherence in our understanding of the world.

Emotion, on the other hand, is another way of talking about desire. A desire drives my mental states and behaviour in a particular way, which then changes its mode or intensity of expression in response to the way that conditions have impacted on my desire. If I am frustrated in my object of desire by someone's interference, I may feel hatred, or if I lose it

---

[167] Kant (1995)
[168] Hume (1975) & (1978)

otherwise, I may feel sadness. If the fulfilment of my desire seems close, I may get excited, or of it seems far away, I may feel wistful or nostalgic. Extreme emotions, as Sartre suggested[169], are a means for us to try to magic the object of our desires into fulfilment, as when Romantic passion tries to gain possession of an unattainable beloved, or extreme anger tries to smash through the barriers to us getting what we want.

In terms of values, then, emotion provides us with our starting point. It is fruitless to attempt to have emotions that we do not have, but at the same time, given that they are only energy, we do not have to think of our emotions as fixed and can re-channel their energy. Emotions are also a response to our environment as we understand it, and it is this represented understanding that is the starting point for rationality.

There is thus no incompatibility between rationality and emotion, but rather a mutual dependency. Without rationality, we cannot assemble a coherent representation of the world around us in which to act, but would just be responding inconsistently to experiences. Without such consistency, our desires would have little effectiveness when attempting to gain fulfilment. For example, if I didn't implicitly reason that a given nut, like the other examples of its kind, had edible content inside its shell, and that previously successful methods of cracking nuts could be tried again, I would not be able to eat the nut. However, without emotion, my recognition of the way to open the nut would be purely abstract: I would have no drive to actually open it.

"Rationality" and "emotion" have frequently been falsely reified in Western thought in ways that neglect this interdependency. When this happens we can mistake badly-adapted emotional responses for "emotion" and emotional responses motivated by metaphysical abstractions as "rationality". There is no such

---

[169] Sartre (1993)

thing in practice as a desire without a belief or a belief without a desire. We need to start seeing alienated boffins not as "unemotional" but as people with over-abstracted metaphysical beliefs that interfere with their emotional integration. Similarly, an "emotional" person has lots of beliefs which they are reasoning about a good deal: just on the basis of over-narrow assumptions.

It is this false dichotomy between rationality and emotion that, I think, more than anything, is responsible for moral failures in the history of Western thought. It is responsible for the fact-value distinction (see 1.i) which tries to separate the objectivity of science from that of ethics. In the theories of ethics considered in the earlier parts of this section, it is also responsible for the absolutising of moral theory. If we see morality as a product of the passions alone (as though anything could be!), then relativism prevails. On the other hand, if we see morality in the terms of rationality, then moral theory is developed in abstraction from the question of what we are actually motivated to do. For Kant, then, we "ought" not to lie even to save a friend's life, while for utilitarians we "ought" to act so as to bring about the maximum pleasure of an unknown person on the other side of the world. Such abstraction has made ethics impractical, and thus sidelined it from serious influence on much day-to-day thinking. Absolute ethics becomes a preserve for the hypocritical cant of politicians and churchmen, not part of the everyday talk of farmers and stockbrokers.

If we really want ethics to make a difference to the world we live in, then, it is time to adopt a vision of ethics that is no longer dependent on this dichotomy between "reason" and "emotion". Instead we need an account of ethics that helps people to address conditions wherever they are, beginning with their starting point and moving forward. This is not a matter of merely limiting our social expectations, but of changing our framework for thinking about ethics.

In the Middle Way account of ethics, emotion becomes the means by which moral ideals are fulfilled, not by which they are undermined: yet the more integrated that emotion, the better fulfilled those ideals will be. Rationality, on the other hand, is not merely the construction of coherent ideas, but will also require an emotional recognition of the possibility of them being wrong, and an effective integration of energies, for its fulfilment.

Because I want this series of books to ultimately be a tool for practical change, I am not stopping here. The practical implications of the ethics worked out here will be considered in relation to psychology, and increasingly in relation to different practical spheres, in the remaining three volumes of this work. A different approach to the application of the ethics given here, in terms of practical ethics issues, can also be found in Ellis (2011b). Wherever else thought and action lead, this philosophical framework is only the beginning.

Bibliography

Aristotle, trans. J.A.K. Thomson and Hugh Tredennick (1976) *Ethics*: Penguin, London

Ayer, A.J., (1946:2nd Edn) *Language, Truth and Logic*: Penguin, London

Bardon, Jonathan (2008) *A History of Ireland:* Gill & Macmillan, Dublin

Baron-Cohen, Simon (2011) *Zero Degrees of Empathy*: Allen Lane, London

Bernhardt, Dan, Stefan Kresa and Mattias Polborn (2008) "Political Polarisation and the Electoral Effects of Media Bias" *Journal of Public Economics* http://works.bepress.com/cgi/viewcontent.cgi?article=1012&context=polborn

Bradley, Amanda (2011) *Nazi Fashion Wars part 2* http://www.counter-currents.com/2011/02/nazi-fashion-wars-the-evolian-revolt-against-aphroditism-in-the-third-reich-part-2/

Burnyeat, M.F., (1980) "Can the sceptic live his scepticism?" from *Doubt and Dogmatism* ed. Malcolm Schofield, Myles Burnyeat & Jonathan Barnes: Oxford University Press, Oxford

Burton, David (2001) "Is Madhyamaka Buddhism really the Middle Way?" *Western Buddhist Review 3* p.180 http://www.westernbuddhistreview.com/vol3/madhyamaka.html

Chabris, Christopher & Daniel Simons (2010) *The Invisible Gorilla*: Harpercollins

Dawkins, Richard (1996) *Climbing Mount Improbable*: Viking

Dawkins, Richard (2007) *The God Delusion* Black Swan

Descartes, Rene, trans. John Veitch (1912) "Meditations" from *A Discourse on Method, Meditations and Principles*: J.M. Dent, London

Dewey, John (1896) "The Reflex Arc Concept in Psychology" from *Psychological Review 3.4*:

Bibliography

http://wexler.free.fr/library/files/dewey%20(1896)%20the%20reflex%20arc%20concept%20in%20psychology.pdf

Diamond, Jared (2006) *Collapse: How societies choose to fail or survive*: Penguin, London

Ellis, Robert M, (2001) *A Theory of Moral Objectivity* (Originally Ph.D, thesis "A Buddhist theory of moral objectivity", Lancaster University 2001): published Lulu, Raleigh 2011 and also online at http://www.moralobjectivity.net/thesis_index.html

Ellis, Robert M. (2008) *The Way of Trust*: Talk delivered to members of the Western Buddhist Order at Padmaloka in Feb 2008, see http://discussion.fwbo.org/wp-content/upeksacitta-the-way-of-trust-full-text.pdf

Ellis, Robert M. (2011a) *The Trouble with Buddhism*: Lulu, Raleigh. Also online at http://www.moralobjectivity.net/Trouble_with_Buddhism.html

Ellis, Robert M. (2011b) *A New Buddhist Ethics*: Lulu, Raleigh. Also online at http://www.moralobjectivity.net/New_Buddhist_Ethics.html

Ellis, Robert M. (2011c) *Truth on the Edge*: Lulu, Raleigh

Everitt, Nicholas, and Alec Fisher (1995) *Modern Epistemology: A New Introduction:* McGraw Hill, New York

Flew, Antony (1984) "The Presumption of Atheism" from *God, Freedom and Immorality, A Critical Analysis:* Pemberton Press

Goldacre, Ben (2008) *Bad Science*: HarperCollins, London

Haidt, Jonathan (2012) *The Righteous Mind: Why Good People are Divided by Politics and Religion*: Penguin, London

Harvey, Peter (1990) *An Introduction to Buddhism*: Cambridge University Press, Cambridge

Hume, David (1975: 3rd Edn) *Enquiries concerning Human Understanding and Concerning the Principles of Morals:* Oxford University Press, Oxford

Hume, David (1978) *A Treatise of Human Nature*: Oxford University Press, Oxford

Middle Way Philosophy 1: The Path of Objectivity

Husserl, Edmund, trans. Dorion Cairns (1960) *Cartesian Meditations*: Martinus Nijhoff, The Hague

Jung, Karl (1968) "The Concept of the Collective Unconscious" from *The Archetypes and the Collective Unconscious* (p.42 ff): Routledge, London

Jung, Karl, trans. Philip Mairet (1982) "The Analysis of Dreams" from *Dreams:* Routledge, London

Kahneman, Daniel (2011) *Thinking, Fast and Slow*: Penguin, London

Kant, Immanuel, trans. Lewis White Beck (1995) *Foundations of the Metaphysics of Morals*: Prentice-Hall, Upper Saddle River NJ

Körner, S. (1967) "The Impossibility of Transcendental Deductions" from *Monist* 51

Kuhn, Thomas (1996:3rd Edn) *The Structure of Scientific Revolutions*: University of Chicago Press, Chicago

Kuzminski, Adrian (2008) *Pyrrhonism: How the Ancient Greeks reinvented Buddhism*: Lexington Books

Lakatos, Imre (1974) "Falsification and the Methodology of Scientific Research Programmes" from *Criticism and the Growth of Knowledge,* ed. I. Lakatos & A. Musgrave: Cambridge University Press, Cambridge

Lakoff, George (1987) *Women, Fire and Dangerous Things:* University of Chicago Press, Chicago

MacIntyre, Alasdair (1958) *The Unconscious:* Routledge, London

MacIntyre, Alasdair (1985: 2nd Edition) *After Virtue:* Duckworth, London

McGilchrist, Iain (2009) *The Master and his Emissary: The Divided Brain and the Making of the Western World*: Yale University Press, New Haven & London

McGrath, Alister & Joanna Collicutt (2007) *The Dawkins Delusion*: SPCK

Moore, G.E. (1962) "Proof of an External World" from *Philosophical Papers*: Collier Books, New York

Murata, Sachiko & William C. Chittick (1994) *The Vision of Islam*: I.B. Tauris, London

Bibliography

Nagarjuna, trans. Jay. L. Garfield (1995) *The Fundamental Wisdom of the Middle Way: Nagarjuna's Mulamadhayamakakarika*: Oxford University Press, New York

Nagel, Thomas (1979) "Moral Luck" from *Mortal Questions*: Cambridge University Press, Cambridge

Nagel, Thomas (1986) *The View from Nowhere:* Oxford University Press, New York

Nietzsche, Friedrich, trans. Walter Kaufmann (1967) *The Will to Power:* Vintage Books, New York

Nussbaum, Martha (1994) *The Therapy of Desire:* Princeton University Press, Princeton

Ostrom, Thomas M., Sandra L. Carpenter, Constantine Sedikides & Fan Li (1993). "Differential processing of in-group and out-group information.": *Journal of Personality and Social Psychology* 64 (1): pp. 21–34

Plato, trans. Desmond Lee (1987) *The Republic*: Penguin, London

Plato, trans. Hugh Tredennick and Harold Tarant (1993) *Crito* from *The Last Days of Socrates*: Penguin, London

Popper, Karl (1945) *The Open Society and Its Enemies* (2 vols): Routledge, London

Popper, Karl (1957) *The Poverty of Historicism*: Routledge, London

Popper, Karl (1959) *The Logic of Scientific Discovery*: Hutchinson, London

Popper, Karl (1963) *Conjectures and Refutations:* Routledge, London

Popper, Karl (1994) *Knowledge and the Mind-Body Problem*: Routledge, London

Rahula, Walpola (1959) *What the Buddha Taught*: Unwin, London

Railton. Peter (1984) "Alienation, consequentialism, and the demands of morality" from Samuel Scheffler (ed.) *Consequentialism and its Critics*: Oxford University Press, Oxford

Middle Way Philosophy 1: The Path of Objectivity

Russell, Bertrand (1940) *An Inquiry into Meaning and Truth*: Allen & Unwin, London

Sangharakshita (1987, 6th Edn) *A Survey of Buddhism*: Tharpa, London

Sartre, Jean-Paul, trans Philip Mairet (1948) *Existentialism and Humanism*: Methuen, London

Sartre, Jean-Paul (1993) *The Emotions: Outline of a Theory*: Citadel Press, New York

Schulz, Kathryn (2010) *Being Wrong: Adventures in the Margin of Error*: Portobello Books, London

Searle, J. R. (1964) "How to derive 'ought' from 'is'", *Philosophical Review* 73: p. 43-58

Segall, Marshall H, Donald T. Campbell, Melville J. Herskovits (1963) *Cultural Differences in the Perception of Geometric Illusions:* Science, New Series, Vol. 139, No. 3556

Sextus Empiricus, trans. Benson Mates (1996) *The Skeptic Way: Sextus Empiricus's Outlines of Pyrrhonism*: Oxford University Press, New York

Singer, Peter (2002) *Unsanctifying Human Life*: Blackwell, Oxford

Slote, Michael (1997) "Agent-based Virtue Ethics" from *Virtue Ethics* ed. Roger Crisp and Michael Slote: Oxford University Press, Oxford

Taleb, Nassim Nicholas (2012) *Antifragile:* Penguin, London

Vickers, A et al (1998) "Do certain countries produce only positive results? A systematic review of controlled trials" *Controlled Clinical Trials* April 1998 19 (2) pp.159-66

Wittgenstein, Ludwig, trans D.F. Pears & B.F. McGuiness (1961) *Tractatus Logico-Philosophicus*: Routledge, London

Wittgenstein, Ludwig, trans. G.E.M. Anscombe, (1967, 3rd Edn) *Philosophical Investigations*: Blackwell, Oxford

Wittgenstein, Ludwig, trans Denis Paul and G.E.M. Anscombe (1969) *On Certainty*: Blackwell, Oxfor

Brief Glossary

The following brief glossary of key terms is provided as a ready reference, for anyone who needs a reminder during reading of some of my distinctive uses of terminology. Any frequently used terms not in it can reasonably be assumed to follow a standard English dictionary definition.

Aesthetic objectivity The aspect of objectivity (q.v.) applied to judgements of beauty (not a distinct type of objectivity, but a way that objectivity in general can be applied).

Agnosticism The deliberate avoidance of either accepting or rejecting a claim, particularly a metaphysical claim. In Middle Way Philosophy this term is roughly equivalent to *hard agnosticism* used elsewhere. It does not imply either indecisiveness or an expectation of further evidence.

Agnostic foundationalism The requirement that a necessary (but not sufficient) condition for justification is the recognition that one may be wrong, either in positive or negative claims.

Coherentism The requirement that a condition for justification is the logical or explanatory coherence of a new belief with our existing beliefs. In Middle Way Philosophy this is a necessary but not a sufficient condition for justification.

Compassion The aspect of objectivity (q.v.) applied to the extension of identifications with ourselves or others. Objectivity, including compassion, can be developed, whilst empathy (an emotional capacity) may be a result of conditions.

Conditions The way things appear to be as they impact on us from the outside (or inside) world. Many writers use the terms

Middle Way Philosophy 1: The Path of Objectivity

'reality' and 'nature' for this concept, both of which I prefer to avoid because of their metaphysical connotations.

Dialectic A process of uniting or synthesising apparently opposed entities, where both are assumed to address conditions to some degree but to be limited by unnecessary opposed assumptions. In Middle Way Philosophy this is an epistemological process rather than a historical one.

Dispositional objectivity Objectivity (q.v.) seen as the characteristic of a person and their habits.

Dogmatism The psychological expression of metaphysics, where beliefs are held strongly because they are thought to be intrinsically true, regardless of experience.

Dualism The belief (or implicit assumption) that a metaphysical understanding of experience is unavoidable, or even to be welcomed.

Ego Our experience of having wishes and identifications (with both ourselves and others), including our desire to continue existing as a self

Experiential adequacy The extent to which our experience is able to understand conditions without interference from dogmatic assumptions

Factual objectivity The aspect of objectivity (q.v.) applied by an individual to reach a degree of understanding of facts – that is, of how things are as far as we can ascertain.

Falsifiability The potentiality for falsification (q.v.) of a theory in a coherently imaginable scenario.

Falsification The justifiable (but not certain) conclusion that a theory is wrong because of its incompatibility with evidence. In

Glossary

Middle Way Philosophy falsification can be undertaken by individuals, not just by scientists using strict research methods.

Identification The sense of possessiveness towards oneself, a person or an object, making them in some sense "me" or "mine".

Incrementality The conceptualisation of qualities as a matter of degree on a spectrum, rather than as absolutes that are either existent or non-existent.

Incrementalisation The process of re-conceiving absolutes as a spectrum of qualities that are a matter of degree.

Integration The progressive uniting of apparently opposed entities by incrementalising (q.v.) them and adopting the qualities of each to the extent that they address conditions. This is a dialectical process (q.v.).

Justification The finding of adequate (though not certain) reasons to believe or disbelieve a claim. In Middle Way Philosophy this requires both coherentism (q.v.) and agnostic foundationalism (q.v.).

Meaning The relationship between symbols (including language) and experience which impacts on us so as to lead us to associate the symbol with the experience. In Middle Way Philosophy both cognitive elements (representing the supposed world) and affective elements (impacting on us) are necessary parts of meaning.

Metaphysics Positive or negative claims that are asserted without any possible justification (q.v.) from experience, using absolute claims or absolute sources of justification (or their denial), and a lack of any possibility of incrementalisation (q.v.).

Middle Way Philosophy 1: The Path of Objectivity

Middle Way A philosophical and practical approach that avoids both positive and negative metaphysical claims, seeking to address conditions by adopting beliefs that go beyond the assumptions of both sides.

Moral objectivity The aspect of objectivity (q.v.) that is applied to moral judgements as to how to live and act (not a distinct type of objectivity, but a way that objectivity in general can be applied).

Negative metaphysics Claims about the non-existence of a metaphysical (q.v.) entity beyond experience.

Non-dualism A philosophical and practical approach which avoids the assumption of absolute metaphysical entities or their denial.

Objectivity The incremental (q.v.) quality of a person or group of persons that enables them to understand and address conditions (q.v.). In Middle Way Philosophy this term does **not** mean 'a God's eye view of the universe'.

Positive Metaphysics Claims in support of the existence of a metaphysical (q.v.) entity beyond experience.

Pragmatism A philosophical approach that emphasises practical usefulness rather than adherence to an absolute view of how things are. In Middle Way Philosophy this practical usefulness is understood in a long-term sense.

Provisionality The psychological state of holding beliefs flexibly enough to enable them to be changed in the light of new evidence. This also requires the avoidance of metaphysical beliefs because they cannot be held in this way.

Glossary

Psyche The total potential identifications of a given ego, into which current identifications may be integrated.

Representationalism The belief that language has only cognitive meaning gained from its representative relationship with the world (for example through truth-conditions).

Revelatory metaphysics The type of metaphysical claim that appeals to an absolute (usually religious) source for its justification.

Scepticism The belief that no claims (or their denials) can be certain.

Scientific Objectivity The aspect of objectivity (q.v.) which is applied to theoretical judgements about the universe using scientific method (not a distinct type of objectivity, but a way that objectivity in general may be applied). Some of this objectivity may be individual, some the quality of scientists as a group.

Truth on the edge The regulative idea of an ultimate state of affairs, which is meaningful but cannot be the object of justified assertions.

Printed in Great Britain
by Amazon